ST. MARY'S COLLEGE OF MARYLAND

W9-ATE-756

How The Soviet System Works

This book is dedicated to those refugees from Soviet communism who so earnestly aided our labors by working together with us and by supplying from their own life experiences the information that made this work possible.

The Russian Research Center of Harvard University is supported by a grant from the Carnegie Corporation. The Center carries out interdisciplinary study of Russian institutions and behavior.

40901

How The Soviet System Works

Cultural, Psychological, and Social Themes

Raymond A. Bauer, Alex Inkeles, and Clyde Kluckhohn

HARVARD University Press, Cambridge, 1964

© Copyright 1956 by the President and Fellows of Harvard College

Distributed in Great Britain by
Oxford University Press
London

Fourth Printing
Library of Congress Catalog Card Number 56–8549
Printed in the United States of America

Acknowledgments

This final report, like the entire Harvard Project on the Soviet Social System, has been made possible by the devoted work of our collaborators in this undertaking and by the generous help and wise advice supplied by many persons not directly associated with the Project. Our obligations are manifold, both to United States Air Force personnel and to academic colleagues.

Within the Air Force our thanks should first be expressed to Dr. Raymond V. Bowers, formerly Director of the Human Resources Research Institute (HRRI). The initiative and much of the original conception were his, and he continued to give excellent support and assistance, both intellectual and practical. We are equally grateful to Colonel George W. Croker, who was Deputy Commander of the HRRI. His enthusiasm encouraged us, and his patient effectiveness in resolving complicated procedural problems made a smooth operation possible. We have debts to many other members of what was formerly the HRRI staff, especially to Dr. Carroll L. Shartle, onetime Director of Research, and Dr. Frederick W. Williams, an early monitor of the contract. Particularly during the last two years of the Project program, Dr. Herman J. Sander, previously Acting Director of Reseach at HRRI and currently with the Officer Education Research Laboratory, Air Force Personnel and Training Research Center, and Mr. Edmund O. Barker, our Project Officer in that office, have shown us much consideration and have given us strong support in carrying out our mission.

Within Headquarters USAF our particular thanks go to Dr. Charles E. Hutchinson of the Human Factors Division of the Directorate of Research and Development. Dr. Hutchinson has most ably and generously handled a great variety of problems of liaison and communication, and his competence as a professional social scientist has also helped us greatly.

During the field work in Europe we owed much to Mr. William F. Diefenbach, our Business Manager in Munich, who took time from his business responsibilities to aid us with administrative problems. It is also necessary to call attention to the collaboration of the Munich Institute for the Study of the History and Culture of the USSR. Its Scientific Council, made up of leading representatives of the *émigré* community, particularly its Director, Mr. Boris Yakovlev, were of great help in our relations with the refugee community. We wish also to acknowledge the technical collaboration provided our field team by the group from the Bureau of Applied Social Research at Columbia University, particularly its senior staff members, Mr. Lee Wiggins and Mr. Dean Manheimer.

Inevitably, a Project operating on so large a scale as that on the Soviet Social System has created burdens for many persons other than those most immediately responsible for its operation. Many University officers, whose already heavy duties were increased because of problems raised by the Project, were always friendly and considerate. We wish particularly to express our appreciation to former Provost Paul H. Buck, who at various critical points was extremely kind and helpful. At a later stage, Dean McGeorge Bundy extended aid which enabled us to complete some critical work in the last days of the Project. The revision of our report for publication was completed during the summer of 1955, when all three authors were in residence as Fellows of the Center for Advanced Study in the Behavioral Sciences. We express our gratitude to the Director, Dr. Ralph Tyler, and his staff for their aid and support. We also thank Mr. R. W. Pratt, Director of the Office for Government Contracts, and Messrs. R. W. Dempster and M. C. Barstow for their technical guidance and careful handling of our accounts.

So far as our colleagues at the Russian Research Center are concerned, our deepest obligations are, naturally, to those immediately connected with the Project. Professor Fainsod and Mr. Paul Friedrich conducted the pilot phase of this investigation, and our work was made much easier as a result. Professor Fainsod has continued to help us immeasurably, and we owe more to his knowledge and wisdom than can easily be put into words. Dr. George Fischer and Mr. Fred Wyle performed invaluable services in establishing friendly relations with the *émigré* groups in Europe and in generally launching the Project under favorable circumstances. Dr. Ivan London directed interviewing in this country and made other valuable administrative and scientific contributions. Mr. David Gleicher's work on the design of codes and his later supervision of the execution of our coding and processing and many phases of analysis, as well as his own direct contributions to the analysis, were of inestimable value. In the first version of this report, completed in 1954, he contributed the section on the military; we have drawn heavily on this section in our revision.

In preparing this report we have, of course, benefited from the contribution of all of the numerous persons who have conscientiously contributed through interviewing, processing, and analyzing our materials. We regret that we cannot here give full acknowledgment to each. We have sought to discharge our obligation at least in part by citing at various points in this study the author and title of the report on which the presentation rested most heavily. In addition, in the appendix we have given a complete list of the reports delivered by the Project, which indicates the author of each item. Finally, we trust that our senior analysts will gain their appropriate measure of recognition through the association of their names with their independent publications completed and in progress.

We are also greatly in debt to our colleagues at the Russian Research Center who were not formally members of the Project staff. In particular we would like to mention the members of the Senior Seminar which met in 1953: Professors Michael Karpovich, Merle Fainsod, Robert Wolff, Harold Berman, and Alexander Gerschenkron, Dr. Barrington Moore, Jr., and Mr. Marshall Shulman. (It should be emphasized, however, that, while the counsel and information provided by the Senior Seminar were of great significance to the Project, its members must not — either individually or collectively — be held responsible for any statement in this book other than those documented by citation of their published writings.) Unfortunately, one member of the Executive Committee of the Russian Research Center, Professor Talcott Parsons, was in England during the time the Senior Seminar was meeting. However, beginning with the first informal explorations of the Center in the German-Austrian area which he carried out in 1948, he advised and aided the Project in countless ways. During the academic year 1954–55, Professor William Langer, Director, and Mr. Marshall Shulman, Associate Director, of the Russian Research Center facilitated additional analysis of Project data and the revision for publication. Finally, various staff members at the Center not directly connected with the Project kindly provided materials from their personal files for the use of the authors: Irene Hay on religion, Nicholas DeWitt on professional personnel, and Dr. Richard Pipes on nationalism in Central Asia.

Professional colleagues from other universities have likewise been of considerable help. Professor Jiri Nehnevajsa, who was in Cambridge on leave from the University of Colorado, provided substantial assistance at various points, and prepared an extensive memorandum on Soviet strengths and weaknesses which was influential in shaping the drafts of our statement on that problem. We must mention particularly four colleagues outside Harvard who have read and provided valuable comments on this report: Professors Philip E. Mosely, Frederick C. Barghoorn, Walt Rostow, and Max Millikan. Their close reading of our early drafts and their freely and forcefully expressed criticism have led to improvements on almost every page of this report.

We also wish to express our warm thanks to those of our associates at the Russian Research Center who gave us the benefit of their critical judgment on this document. Professors Fainsod and Karpovich and Dr. Moore gave generously of their time and made detailed suggestions on the whole draft. In addition, sections or chapters were read and criticized by Babette Whipple, Mark Field, Richard Pipes, David Gleicher, Leopold Haimson, and Eugenia Hanfmann.

We have drawn upon the published writings of these and other Russian specialists, sometimes without the fullness of acknowledgment which would be customary in a manuscript originally intended for publication. But in a book which owes so much to so many, it seemed to us pedantic to footnote each borrowed idea or phrase, especially since we have blended our own points and ways of expression so intimately with those of our colleagues and with those of specialists from other universities.

We are grateful to Mr. Michael Maccoby, who undertook a critical editorial reading of several chapters. We are also in debt to Mrs. Nancy Deptula who collated our various corrected drafts into a true master copy; to the Project secretary-typists, Miss Lillian Battle and Mrs. Alice Ryniewicz; to our Office Manager, Mrs. Elizabeth Fainsod, who lifted many an administrative burden from the shoulders of the Project directors, thus freeing them for analytic work; and to the Center's Administrative Assistant, Mrs. Helen W. Parsons.

We have dedicated this book to the refugees from the Soviet Union upon whose information this study is based. We are deeply grateful for the honesty and sincerity with which they reported their life stories and offered their opinions. Without this earnest coöperation our work would, of course, have been inconceivable.

We must conclude with the conventional, but by no means unnecessary, phrase: our debts are many and our appreciation great, but final responsibility is ours. No one of the persons mentioned above must be understood as approving this report in general or any specific part of it. In some instances we have stubbornly resisted criticisms that may well have been correct, but of the validity of which we were ourselves not convinced.

Finally, we would like to "acknowledge" our own contributions to this book. At the end of more than five years of fruitful and pleasant collaboration, the only issue of consequence on which we could not agree was the relative importance of the work we had done: each thought the labors of the others had exceeded his own. This is, in a way, a most gratifying form of disagreement and a note on which it might be desirable for all collaborations to end; but it does pose an impasse in considering the order in which the names of the authors should be listed. After many months of irresolution we decided to let alphabetical sequence determine the order of our names on the title page. This listing should not, however, be construed either as reflecting or as not reflecting our relative contributions to the book.

In view of the somewhat special nature of this undertaking, including our many obligations to organizations and individuals, we did not feel that it would be proper for us personally to accept any royalties from this book. Any royalties that may accrue will go to the Russian Research Center to be used in support of future, more technical publications resulting from the Project. We state this explicitly lest there be any misunderstanding on this subject.

Raymond A. Bauer
Alex Inkeles
Clyde Kluckhohn

Contents

Part I INTRODUCTORY

1 The Harvard Project on the Soviet Social System, and Its Data — 3

Part II OPERATING CHARACTERISTICS OF THE SOVIET SYSTEM

2 A Brief Review of the Formal Characteristics of the System — 19

3 Creating and Maintaining Myths — 29

4 Planning and Controlling — 36

5 Problem Solving, the Overcommitment of Resources, and "Storming" — 46

6 Refusal to Allow Independent Concentrations of Power — 53

7 Terror and Forced Labor — 68

8 Informal Adjustive Mechanisms — 74

9 Rigidity – Flexibility — 82

10 Caution at Major Risks in Foreign Affairs — 86

Part III THE INDIVIDUAL IN SOVIET SOCIETY

11 Soviet Policy Toward the Individual — 93

12 Sources of Satisfaction and Dissatisfaction — 96

13 Attitudes Toward the Soviet System — 114

14 Attitudes Toward the West — 123

15 Some Aspects of Russian National Character — 134

16 Political Loyalty of Individuals — 143

Part IV SOCIAL AND PSYCHOLOGICAL
CHARACTERISTICS OF SPECIFIC GROUPS

17 The Ruling Elite   155
18 The Intelligentsia   174
19 The Peasants   181
20 The Workers   186
21 Generational Differences   190
22 Nationality Groups   199

Part V CONCLUSIONS

23 Summary   211
24 Some Evaluations by the Authors   220
25 Some Forecasts by the Authors   236

Appendix REPORTS AND PUBLICATIONS
OF THE HARVARD PROJECT ON THE
SOVIET SOCIAL SYSTEM   252

References   259
Index   267
Russian Research Center Studies   275

Part I

INTRODUCTORY

1

The Harvard Project on the Soviet

Social System, and Its Data

This book represents an attempt to assess the social and psychological strengths and weaknesses of the Soviet system from the perspective of a unique body of data — interviews with hundreds and questionnaires administered to thousands of refugees from the Soviet Union, in Europe and the United States, in 1950 and 1951. These data were products of the Harvard Project on the Soviet Social System, whose purpose was to utilize this particular source of information as a supplement to more ordinary avenues of knowledge of the Soviet system.

The Project was sponsored as part of the basic research program of the United States Air Force and conducted under Air Force research contract No. 33(038)–12909 between the Human Resources Research Institute, Maxwell Air Force Base, Alabama, and the Russian Research Center.[1] As basic research, the work was under the sole technical direction of the Russian Research Center at all times and its findings are the complete responsibility of the Center's staff. The Air Force restricted its role to facilitating this work through funds and logistic support, and has taken no position, either of agreement or disagreement, with regard to any of the conclusions. We must emphasize that, despite our debt to the Air Force and many individuals who are or were connected with it, neither the Air Force nor any of its personnel should be construed as approving of any of the statements contained herein.

In its present form this volume is, with the exception of certain minor changes, substantially the same final report which the

Harvard Project completed in the fall of 1954. The revision consists of stylistic changes designed to improve the presentation and to accommodate the document to the needs and interests of the general reading public, and footnotes required to bring our references to the contemporary Soviet scene up to date.

This book is not, however, a summary of the data of the Harvard Project. These data will be reported by various authors in books and scholarly papers now being prepared for publication. These works in progress include an effort to summarize systematically the main findings of the Project with regard to the sociopolitical attitudes and the daily life experience of the Soviet citizen. That volume, by Alex Inkeles and Raymond A. Bauer, will be essentially the second volume of our final report, intended as companion, supplement, and supporting documentation for this book. Here, however, we are dealing predominantly with the conclusions derived from our questionnaire data and from the research team's experience in working directly with the refugees through many hours of intimate personal contact. The evidence for these conclusions exists in works already published and in unpublished manuscripts which were prepared under the research contract. To give some indication of the scope and depth of this supporting material we have in an appendix presented a complete list of the published papers and the unpublished reports prepared by the Project, and reference will be made to these documents at relevant points. Rather than summarize those materials, however, our intention here is to take a fresh look at the Soviet system in the light of those data.

This final report is not based on the special data of the Harvard Project *alone;* it draws equally on regularly published works on the Soviet Union. To a large extent it consists of insights which the new data have given us into the various published sources. The purpose of this report is to present insofar as possible a coherent picture of the strengths and weaknesses of the Soviet social system, with special emphasis on those sources of strain and those characteristic institutions and modes of behavior that might aid in anticipating future developments in Soviet society. At times it was necessary to rely largely on inference. We do not believe the reader will have trouble in deciding which of our propositions are based on firm data and which are "informed guesses." The merit of this work must lie not only in the degree to which we have succeeded in presenting a picture of the Soviet system that is consistent with our existing knowledge of that system, but also in the new understanding of old facts that comes from this picture, and in whether or not it will enable us better to comprehend and predict future developments in the Soviet order.

Finally, this report does not pretend to be a complete description or interpretation of the Soviet system. We have concentrated mainly on social and psychological aspects of Soviet society. These are the aspects on which the data of the Harvard Project shed most light. They are, furthermore, the aspects which in the past have received least attention from scholars and with which we, by virtue of our disciplinary training, are most competent to deal. The fact that we have given proportionately less attention to the political and economic sides of Soviet life does not mean that we intend to underestimate them. Political and economic factors are of immense importance in understanding the Soviet system. For this reason we precede the main portion of this book with a brief review of the salient political and economic characteristics of the system, so that the remainder of our discussion may proceed in an appropriate context.

Although we have valuable information on later periods, the conservative baseline for many of the *quantitative* data which we gathered from Soviet refugees is 1940. The question can properly be raised: even if the findings give a roughly correct picture of the Soviet Union in 1940, how much faith can be placed in them for 1955, after a victorious war, a turbulent postwar period, and changes in the top leadership? Certainly one cannot mechanically equate descriptions of conditions, or even attitude patterns, between two periods separated by such momentous events. Some of our materials probably have primarily a historical interest, indicating the background of the contemporary situation. However, we have tried wherever possible to correct our basic information for the changes of the past fifteen years. We were aided in this by some eighty life-history interviews, twenty clinical psychological interviews, and fifty-seven questionnaires with postwar refugees, some of whom left the Soviet Union as late as 1950, and by carefully following the

Soviet and American press and the writing of Western scholars.

In considering our data we have concentrated on both the relatively stable and the evolving characteristics of the system. No society is completely stable or completely changing. By and large, we have been concerned with those structural features of Soviet society which appear to have become pretty well stabilized by 1938. It is the consensus of Western experts on the Soviet Union that the main lines of this society have not altered appreciably since that time, even though there have been important changes in detail and emphasis. To the extent that the central features of the system have remained largely unchanged, and insofar as we can assume that the basic human material of Soviet society is not very different from the population of the prewar period, we can within certain limits assume that at least the general pattern of popular reaction to Soviet policy and institutions will in important respects be similar to earlier trends. Furthermore, as we shall point out, a detailed comparison of the responses of postwar as against wartime refugees indicated that most of the aspects of the system with which we are concerned remained stable. We are not, of course, unconcerned with or oblivious to change. The entire purpose of this work is to provide a basis for the assessment and, hopefully, the prediction of change. It is for this reason that we have in the course of our analysis given a great deal of attention to generational trends in our data as a basis for extrapolating to the new Soviet generation.[2] In addition, we have sought throughout the text, particularly in the last chapters, to assess the probable reactions of the population to the measures constituting the Moscow version of the "new look."

To the best of our judgment, developments since Stalin's death do not make our conclusions obsolete, but verify them. The changed and changing policies of the post-Stalin leadership indicate that the new Soviet leaders are wrestling strenuously with the very same problems that characterized Stalin's regime. In the concluding chapters we discuss these post-Stalin changes and hazard guesses for the future. Some ten months have intervened between the completion of the final draft of the original report and the present writing. In that period some important changes have occurred in the composition of the top leadership and in foreign and domestic policy. At the risk of appearing at some points merely dated and perhaps at other times foolish, we have chosen to leave the text in its original form at all points where our statements relate directly to current developments. Where appropriate we have added a footnote describing subsequent developments and indicating where we were clearly wrong, apparently right, or neither. We do this in part to preserve the integrated quality of our original presentation, and partly from a desire not to appear to be more prescient than we actually are. We hope that in the process we are presenting interesting evidence for an evaluation of the predictive power of modern social science in this highly complex and difficult field of social systems analysis.

WORK WITH *Émigrés* AS SOURCES OF INFORMATION ON THE SOVIET SYSTEM[3]

Research on the Soviet Union has been handicapped by the absence of certain types of data, principally that bearing on the day-to-day life experiences of Soviet citizens, on the informal aspects of the functioning of Soviet institutions, and on the psychological characteristics of the Soviet population. Considering the impossibility of gathering information of this nature within the borders of the Soviet Union, the most obvious source of such data — granting certain elements of bias and selectivity — is the Soviet emigration, those persons who either fled from the system or chose to remain outside the Soviet Union after having been caught in the currents of World War II. Before our project began, there had been partial utilization of this source by a few individuals, by several agencies of the government, and by the Survey Research Center at the University of Michigan. But such studies either covered limited objectives, or their findings were restricted by security classifications. In the spring of 1950, the Russian Research Center of Harvard University accepted support from the United States Air Force for a more systematic exploration of this source of information. This decision was made on the basis of pilot studies made by senior members of the Harvard faculty in the summer of 1949.

Between September 1950 and September 1951, hundreds of interviews were conducted and thousands of questionnaires administered to Soviet *émigrés* in Europe and the United States. The basic interview was an extended life-history interview which took from two to four days to administer. It covered the individual's work and educational history, his family background and relations, his sources of information — reading and listening habits and attitudes toward them — his social and political attitudes, and the history of his relations to the regime. In addition to this interview, each respondent filled out detailed forms on his personal and family budget, plus two additional items. One of these was a psychological test consisting of incomplete sentences for the individual to complete, which were designed to tap many of his personal values and certain aspects of his personality. The other contained some questions relating to his social and political attitudes and, although not so identified for the respondent, these were essentially "tests" designed to identify those persons who might be expected to bias their answers unduly in a pro-American or anti-Soviet direction. In all, 329 persons (53 of them in the United States) were given this battery of interviews, plus supplementary forms and tests. After a few months of experience with the oral life-history interview, a written questionnaire was devised to cover the same topics. This was administered to 2,718 respondents, together with the budget forms and the attitude and sentence-completion tests referred to above.

This main body of interviews and questionnaires was supplemented by 435 interviews and 9,748 questionnaires on such special topics as: the operation of the Soviet firm; the role of the Soviet doctor and the attitude of patients toward the Soviet medical system; the training and problems of the Soviet lawyer; life in the Soviet urban family; aspects of social stratification and mobility; the operation of the lower Party organizations; problems of the minor nationalities; and life under and reaction to the German occupation. Furthermore, of those persons who had been given the extended oral interviews, 60 were interviewed by clinical psychologists and were given a series of standard psychological tests designed to delve into deeper aspects of their personality. The data gathered by these various instruments are summarized in Table 1.

The bulk of the interview and questionnaire data was made available for statistical analysis by coding and processing accord-

Table 1. Numbers of persons from whom data were collected
by the Harvard Project on the Soviet social system.

Type of data	In West Germany and Austria	In eastern United States	Total
Extended life-history interviews, including personality and methodological tests	276	53	329[a]
Interviews on topics about which the subjects had special knowledge	418	17	435
Sets of protocols on individuals who were interviewed at great length and given five sets of clinical psychological tests	55	5	60[b]
General written questionnaires	2080	638	2718
Written questionnaires on special topics	7510	2238	9748
Manuscripts written on special topics	48	—	48
Interviews and psychological tests administered for control purposes to a matched group of Americans	—	100	100

[a] This number includes 80 interviews with postwar refugees.
[b] Includes a few incomplete cases of clinical subjects who were not given the full range of psychological tests, or who took the tests but not the interview.

ing to standard procedures. In addition, the oral-interview data were used qualitatively to piece in items of information and to give us a better understanding of the meaning of our statistical findings. In certain instances, intensive case studies were made of individual respondents in an attempt to get further insight into the life problems of Soviet citizens.[4] Since other projects had been based on interviews with refugees, however, the distinctive aspect of the Harvard Project lay mainly in the size of the group reached, the diversity of the subjects explored, and particularly the *statistical* treatment of a large body of data.

Quantitative analysis of data from *émigré* respondents, which must be presumed — at least for the sake of methodological safety — to be riddled with potential sources of bias, demands utmost vigilance in its use. Space limitations as well as the purpose of this document prevent outlining the full scope of the methodological precautions employed. This will be dealt with more extensively in a forthcoming book and has already been discussed in detail in one of the Project reports.[5] The fact that a sample is biased does not mean that nothing can be learned from it, but merely that data from the sample cannot be projected directly back onto the population from which it was drawn. Any sample, no matter how biased, shares some of the characteristics of the population from which it was drawn. Our major methodological task was to determine the sources and directions of biases and to take them adequately into account in our analysis.

The popular conception of the nature and extent of bias in a sample of Soviet refugees, however, considerably exaggerates the real problem. To regard our sample as representing only a tiny special and disaffected minority would be contrary to fact. Only a minority of our respondents (about 40 per cent) claim to have fled the Soviet Union voluntarily. In most instances they led the lives of normal Soviet citizens until their transportation to Germany as forced laborers or their capture as prisoners of war. Furthermore, judging by their answers to many questions and by what is generally known of the Soviet emigration, we estimate that from two-thirds to three-fourths of the persons whom we interviewed would have returned to their homeland if it were not for the fear of the suspicion and ill treatment with which returnees were being greeted in the Soviet Union.* If any objections arise about trusting our respondents' reports of the circumstances under which they left the Soviet Union, we need only point out that the time and situation in which they were interviewed would, if anything, have prompted them to

---

* Since the original report was written, the Soviet leaders have inaugurated a campaign to induce *émigrés* to return to the Soviet Union by promises of good treatment and resumption of their normal lives. Persons in close contact with the Soviet emigration in the summer of 1955 reported that this campaign was achieving some success.

bias their answers in the direction of claiming that they had fled voluntarily. Thus, whatever bias exists in these statistics would tend to make them *conservative* estimates of the proportion who left *involuntarily*.

Not all members of our sample belonged to the older generation. More than half — 58 per cent — were born or came to their maturity *after* the Bolshevik Revolution. Nor were they predominantly members or descendants of dissident groups who had been discriminated against by the Bolsheviks. The proportion who came from what the regime defines as "hostile class backgrounds" (i.e., parents who had privileged positions under the Tsarist regime) is roughly what one would expect on the basis of census data. Furthermore, they certainly do not report a history of unanimous, implacable opposition to the Soviet regime. The proportion of our respondents who admitted having been members of the Communist Party or the Young Communists was higher than the rate of membership in the Soviet population. (This was in part due to the fact that the sample included an unusual proportion of successful people, a point which will be discussed below.) About one-third of the sample stated that they had once *favored* the Soviet regime; and a close reading of the life-history interviews indicates that the proportion of our respondents who were onetime adherents of the regime was probably higher.

Except for the highest levels of the armed forces, Party government, and secret police, there is no major segment of the population of European USSR which is not represented in appreciable numbers. The total sample includes people of all ages and of both sexes who were peasants, skilled workers, white-collar employees, military personnel, ordinary workers, and intellectuals.

A stereotyped conception about Soviet refugees, which is not supported by our sample, is that they are "the failures of the system," people who were either psychological misfits or unable to succeed in Soviet life. Contrary to what one might expect, the members of our sample were unusually successful in the Soviet system. The fact that a very high proportion of them were well placed in Soviet life must be attributed in some measure to the way in which our sample was selected from the Soviet emigration. More literate people, obviously, would be willing to fill out a written questionnaire. What is most relevant, however, is that our respondents, when one takes into consideration where they started out in life, were unusually successful in advancing in the system, more successful in fact than would be expected of the Soviet population as a whole.[6] As for the notion that the refugees were psychological misfits, the very extent of their success in the system is a partial refutation of the idea that they were predominantly alcoholics, habitual criminals, loafers, or people who were constantly in trouble. This mistaken image of the refugees was further disproved by the psychological data collected, which indicated that the members of our sample showed no more evidence of instability than might be expected of any group of persons living under the difficult conditions of refugee life in Western Europe where the majority of the interviews were conducted.

While many of the prevalent conceptions of the degree to which a refugee sample is unrepresentative of the Soviet population are thus manifestly in error, we do not contend that the group of people whom we interviewed is directly representative of that population. It was necessary that we understand the sources, location, and direction of bias in our sample and take them into account in analysis and further that we should have enough people in each of the subgroups concerned in order to be able to make meaningful statements about these groups. In general, we had an adequate number of persons in all the meaningful subgroups with which we were concerned. Where we did not, as in the case of the highest elite, we had to rely on other data for our statements.

A considerable proportion of our staff's energy was devoted to the study of actual or potential sources of bias within the sample. For example, a study was made of the history of the Soviet emigration so that we might, insofar as possible, place our respondents with respect to the remainder of the Soviet population. Furthermore, the characteristics of subgroups within our sample were scrutinized for ways in which they might deviate from comparable subgroups of the Soviet population. Our peasants, for example, were found to come disproportionately from families which had been "dekulakized," i.e., dispossessed and discriminated against during the period of collectivization on the ground that they were "exploiters" of other peasants. An analysis of the characteristics of dekulakized peasants compared with those who had not come from dekulakized families not only offered guidance as to when in further analysis we had to take such factors into consideration, but also gave us a good deal of understanding of the impact of this experience on the attitudes and lives of peasants. Once such sources of bias were detected, not only could they be compensated for in evaluating the data, but they actually became valuable tools of analysis.

As a step in overcoming the fact that the majority of our respondents left the Soviet Union during World War II, a comparison was made of the responses of postwar refugees with those of closely matched wartime refugees. This study was prompted not only by the fact that we were concerned with the possibility of changes over time in the Soviet system, but also because it was widely conjectured that the wartime refugees, having last seen the Soviet system in a period of stress and instability, might overemphasize these aspects of the system. We found no evidence for this proposition.[7] There were some psychological differences, with the postwar refugees being somewhat more disturbed and unstable,[8] but it is not clear whether these differences arise because those who defect under conditions of relative stability are mainly a particular psychological type or because the nature of defecting under postwar conditions is a particularly difficult and disturbing experience. Probably both factors contribute. Nevertheless, the crucial point is that these personality differences are not matched by differences in attitudes toward either general social issues or specific features of Soviet life. We are led, therefore, to have greater confidence in the *current* relevance of the testimony given by a sample of persons predominantly displaced during the war, even though many had been away from the Soviet Union for more than five years before we reached them. In addition, we were thus reinforced in our belief that our instruments were tapping opinions which reflect relatively enduring features of the Soviet system.

To assess the possibility that refugees in Europe might bias their responses in an effort to facilitate their emigration to the United States, they were compared with people interviewed in the United States. Again, the results were encouraging. There *were* differences in the reported attitudes of the two groups, but their nature was such as to indicate that Soviet refugees in the United States had, in fact, undergone certain changes of attitude, and not that the refugees in Europe had consciously slanted their answers.[9]

As a general device or "test" for locating individuals who might be prone to bias their answers in an excessively pro-American or anti-Soviet direction, i.e., to "tell us what we wanted to hear," indices of "distortion" and "flattery" were included in the questionnaires and interviews. The number of respondents who might be considered suspect on the basis of their scores in these tests was a small minority of the total sample and, on the basis of staff studies, under the most pessimistic of assumptions they had a gratifyingly slight influence on the data.[10]

All of these checks, precautions, and methodological devices, however, cannot alone assure the worth of the conclusions drawn from these data. Even the most complete battery of methodological precautions would not be a substitute for judgment, caution, and intellectual integrity on the part of the analysts and interpreters of these refugee data. The steps we have outlined somewhat reduced the areas over which judgment had to be exercised and additionally gave us and the many analysts who worked on the Project guidance in the use of such judgment. Ultimately, however, as in all scholarly enterprises, the end product can be no better than the minds through which it was processed.

We feel that the Project provided the first systematic and comprehensive picture of how the Soviet system looks "from inside," that is, from the various vantage points of different groups and subgroups of individuals who had been participants in the system. This first extensive study of the subjective and informal sides of Soviet life enables us to assess with some confidence which groups and subgroups are most discontented and which institutions are most and which least liked or disliked and by whom. As we have already indicated, those findings are systematically summarized in a series of topical reports, most of which we hope to publish in time. In this report, however, we have adopted a different and, we believe, distinctive approach which departs from the usual topical mode of presentation. We have sought to describe the system in terms of a number of themes or repetitive patterns which cut across the fabric of Soviet society. We have utilized the discrete findings from our survey and, what is more, the insights into Soviet society which they suggest. They have not been presented alone but are woven together with the conclusions we have drawn from the more traditional studies of the Soviet Union by Western scholars. These two elements represent the warp and the woof through the interlacing of which we hope to reconstruct the fabric of Soviet society.

Part II

OPERATING CHARACTERISTICS OF THE SOVIET SYSTEM

2

A Brief Review of the Formal Characteristics of the System

In this part of the book we shall list, document, and discuss a number of operating characteristics illustrating the way Soviet society actually works, focusing our attention upon what really goes on and not upon official statements and ideology, except as these bear directly upon interpretations of the system in operation. Our list of operating characteristics is not exhaustive; and, although we believe these would very likely appear on comparable lists which might be drawn up by other students of Soviet affairs, they certainly should not be taken as *the* eight operating characteristics of the Soviet social system. They were selected because they emerged most clearly and strongly from our materials. In addition, these particular characteristics appear here because awareness of them is essential to understanding the data concerning the individual in Soviet society, where we feel our most distinctive contribution is made.

We do not claim to have "discovered" these operating characteristics, but we do seek to evaluate and, where necessary, redefine and reinterpret them in the light of our findings. Our basic material, therefore, represents a combination of "old" and "new" data and interpretations. The mode of analysis does, however, represent something of an innovation. Rather than focus on the conventional "institutions" (family, industry, political system, and education), according to which societies are ordinarily described, we try to depict a series of themes — or threads — that cut across the fabric of Soviet social behavior, giving it a stability or continuity of form and structure. This method will, of necessity, entail some repetition, but we have sought to give a different emphasis to the material wherever a theme recurs and to make the picture truly cumulative. We hope thus to expose central and repetitive patterns of action, a knowledge of which makes possible the forecasting of likely responses, under particular conditions, of various segments of the Soviet leadership and of the governed masses. Some of these operating characteristics are probably common to totalitarian societies — a minimum definition of which would be: a society in which those who hold political power attempt to coördinate for the attainment of their goals all the material and human resources of their society, extending even to the private feelings and sentiments of the populace. Others of the characteristics cited may be distinctively Soviet. At any rate, we think they are general enough and built deeply enough into the system to continue to be manifested for some time to come, despite the march of events and changes in the particular personalities in power at any moment.* These operating characteristics channel and limit action; they provoke reaction.

It is difficult, if not impossible, to assign a rank order of importance to these operating characteristics, since they constitute an interlocking system in which each has implications for others. They are organized here in a way designed primarily to facilitate exposition through a fairly logical sequence of development. We shall begin in Chapter 3 with the official doctrine, for its role is perhaps the most distinctive single feature of the system.

We take the "Soviet system" to be that distinctive total complex of traditional and Bolshevik institutions, values, and patterns of behavior which are manifested within the territory of the nation-state known as the Union of Soviet Socialist Republics. Since the main portion of this book, from Chapter 3 on, is devoted to an analysis of the operating characteristics and of the informal and generally less discussed aspects of that total complex, it is desirable that we should set down here briefly those main features of Soviet society which have long been widely recognized not only by students of the USSR but by informed lay-

* This assumption does not hold, of course, if there should be *radical* change in the general nature of the system or a revolutionary alteration in the composition of the leadership.

men as well. These "formal" characteristics constitute the setting within which most of the specific assertions to be made later will apply.

The Soviet government is officially proclaimed to be the most democratic in the world, federal in form, and based on the will and interests of the people. In practice, however, nearly absolute power is concentrated in a small, self-selecting, self-perpetuating clique. The Soviet system may be more accurately described as "total statism," rather than as either "socialism" or "communism." Under both Lenin and Stalin, power gradually came to be concentrated in the hands of a single individual who used the remainder of the ruling elite as personal lieutenants, as administrative agents, and as a select and secret sounding board. The evidence available to us suggests that, at present, no single person has attained the control exercised by Lenin and Stalin in their later years. "Collegial" forms of dictatorship are inherently unstable, and it is likely that in the near future Malenkov,* Khrushchev or some other leader, perhaps now little known, will emerge as a single dominant figure at the head of the system. We do not anticipate that collegial rule in the USSR, assuming that it is really operating in fact and not merely in form, will long persist. If it does, this would seem in and of itself to be an indication of rather fundamental change in the nature of the system.

One of the distinctive features of the Soviet governmental structure is the role of the Communist Party. In one sense it exists outside the formal governmental structure. "The government," as distinguished from "the Party," constitutes the administrative apparatus for carrying out the day-to-day functioning of the Soviet state and the Soviet economy. The top organ of the government is the Supreme Soviet, which nominally passes the laws of the Soviet state. In practice, however, all major policy decisions originate in the Party, and the formal governmental structure is merely the instrument for the execution of policy decisions. Not only does the Party originate policy, but it super-

---

* Malenkov suffered a substantial decline of fortune since this was written, but the point made is, of course, not thereby weakened but strengthened.

vises its implementation. All organs of the government, the army, and the secret police are permeated at every level by the Party. Not only are responsible members of the various agencies of the government ordinarily drawn into the Party, but the Party structure itself interpenetrates such agencies for the purpose of supervision and control. Thus, a colonel in the army would almost certainly be a member of the Party. Primarily, however, he would be a member of the military. Assigned to his unit would be a Party functionary — the "commissar" of popular legend — whose main obligation is to the Party and who acts specifically as an agent of the Party. The same picture, with some variation, would be found in the factory, on the collective farm, and in the secret police.

While the Party determines policy for the Soviet government, the top elite determines policy for the Party. The Party is, in effect, an instrument of the top leadership, organized on military lines and extending down through the lowest territorial and production units in the society. All Party units are formally, and to a great extent actually, at the complete disposal of the top echelon. These Party units serve mainly to execute decisions received from the top and to report upward relevant information required by the leadership. The Party apparatus constitutes a sort of government within the government, although in many areas and instances it exercises its powers directly. However, it is, in effect, the instrument for control over the government by a very small group of men at the summit of the Party. One of its main functions is to maintain rigorous control over all other power elements in the structure of the society, especially the army and the secret police. The government of the USSR is federal in form. But as with so much of Soviet society, blueprint and practice are in conflict. The "autonomous republics" do not decide even minor matters unless such decisions are clearly in line with policy set by the ruling group in Moscow. It is possible, however, that the persistence of the "federal" units has some practical significance in that popular sentiment may adhere to these regional units as well as to the USSR as a whole.

Not only do the top elite monopolize (or attempt to monopolize) power in the Soviet structure, but they restrict severely the autonomy of action of all other groups. Their actions and policy decisions have been outstandingly arbitrary, with the result that both legality and tradition in the Western sense have been of limited significance. Civil and criminal law have been operative throughout the Soviet period, but the elite have paid little attention to legal forms in the political sphere. Since the mid-thirties there has been a relatively continuous increase in public emphasis on the *forms* of law ("Soviet socialist legality"). In the civil and criminal spheres this emphasis has had some substance. In the field of politics the forms of law have been particularly emphasized since Stalin's death. There was a period of some months in 1953 when this note of legality was much muted, but the regime went to great pains to legitimize the secret trial and execution of Lavrenti Beria by invoking an obscure decree of December 1, 1934.[1] While the regime has not abandoned its monopoly of power or its freedom to act arbitrarily, it is apparently seeking to alleviate popular resentment of this arbitrariness by trying to create the impression that there is a rule of law.

The Soviet political system has been characterized by the exercise of an extremely high degree of force, which has become so intense at times that it can only be designated as terror. "The terror" (a phrase that recurs frequently in the conversations of Soviet refugees), must, together with the use of forced labor, be regarded as an integral and essential part of the Soviet order. The application of police terror reached its peak in the years 1937 and 1938. It has, however, been less intense since that time, and the post-Stalin leadership has shown some sensitivity to the Soviet people's hatred of this system of police terror and forced labor. There is no evidence, however, that gestures toward the reduction of the use of terror have as yet reached the point where it is no longer to be regarded as an essential aspect of the system. The iron fist may be gloved in homespun, but it remains poised. The people remain aware of it, and the regime still regards it as its key instrument of social control.

ECONOMIC POLICY

The state is virtually the sole owner of all means of industrial production, down to the level of ordinary hand tools. It operates the industrial economy through a system of hierarchically organized production units. The goals of production are set by centralized decision-making, with some participation by lower units. The broad lines of economic development are largely determined by the long-range political goals of the leaders, but consequent planning is based to a considerable degree on predominantly economic decisions. To effect the plan and to achieve the goals, a rigid system of resource allocation is utilized. The whole industrial economy has been strikingly characterized both by rapid growth, which, in large measure, continues, and by an associated pattern of continued change in its internal composition. The high rate of capital accumulation, reflected in the rapid growth of Soviet industry, has been effected largely by deflecting production from consumption goods.

Agricultural production is overwhelmingly concentrated in large scale production units with labor organized in an approximation of the factory system, except that payment (much of it in kind) depends on the earnings of the unit. Some of these units (*sovkhozy*) are state owned; the majority (*kolkhozy*) are nominally coöperatives. Decision-making is, in fact, highly centralized (although less so than in the factory), despite the claim that the kolkhozy are semiautonomous coöperatives. Tractors are neither owned nor controlled by the production unit, but by big government-owned and government-controlled machine stations (MTS). Through its control of the machine-gathered harvest and by obligatory deliveries of produce at fixed prices, the state regulates planting, produce, and distribution. The peasant, however, either sells on the peasant market the produce he obtains as wages in kind from the collective farm and from his own garden plot, or he uses it for personal consumption.

Relative to the situation in industry, however, agricultural output has seriously lagged behind and has undergone only a modest change in its internal composition. Except for the administrative postwar reform, which consolidated the collective farms into less than half of the former number of units, the organization of Soviet agriculture has remained unchanged. Consequently, developments in other areas, such as increasing industrialization, urbanization, and population growth, have outdistanced agriculture. The resulting gap has fostered frequent agricultural crises. Some Western students think that the problem has recently been exacerbated by government reliance upon the official Lysenko-Michurin theory and practice of genetics.* It has been suggested that recent attacks on Lysenko have been motivated by a realization of this on the part of the Soviet leaders. A more continuing difficulty in Soviet agriculture, however, is the endemic problem of giving the peasant adequate incentives for increasing production within the framework of collectivized agriculture.

To summarize: Since 1929, top priority has been given by Soviet economic policy to the expansion of industry. The development of the collective farm system was not primarily motivated by the goal of increasing agricultural production. In all probability, there has been less production under the collective farm system than would have been possible under a system of private ownership. The purpose of collectivization of agriculture was to extend state control over the peasants in order to maximize the amount of food which could be obtained directly from them. This policy was tied to the program of industrial expansion and capital accumulation. Related to this was the overall policy of diverting the smallest possible proportion of production to consumption. The program of expanding the industrial base of the economy as rapidly as possible, therefore, has led to a proliferation of political and economic controls with a resulting high degree of popular dissatisfaction, which has compelled the regime to increase controls still more. It may be said that Stalin's refusal to reduce his goals of economic expansion was at the root of most characteristic problems of Soviet life. The post-Stalin regime has shown some disposition (though a vacillating one) to contract its goals of economic expansion. If it were to do so, the result might be a basic change in the pattern of Soviet life.

COMMUNICATION

The Soviet system has gone far beyond the usual censorship pattern of authoritarian governments in making all forms of mass communication the direct monopoly of the regime, to be disseminated by state-owned media with Party-dictated content. Police surveillance has also been used, with incomplete success,

* Confirmed, implicitly, by Khrushchev's speech of March 1954.

to bring informal, private communication under control. The system is as comprehensive as possible and includes the fine arts, literature, and music. It is quite successful both in preventing foreign communications from reaching the population and in forcing the network to use only approved material. The system, however, appears to have only moderate success in eliminating things already there, like informal communications and old ideas.

SOCIAL ORGANIZATION

In many respects, the social organization of the Soviet Union resembles that of the large-scale industrial societies in the West. The occupational system is similar, in important ways, to that in other industrial societies, but one critical difference is that almost all individuals are employees of the state. This is associated with an extensive, although generally inadequately implemented, social-welfare program on the one hand and, on the other hand, the severe proscription of anything approximating an independent professional society or trade union. Even the church is not an independent, autonomous institution. Despite the proclamation that the Soviet Union is a "classless society," it is obvious, even from official sources, that Soviet society is highly stratified into classes somewhat similar to those in Western industrial society. Our refugee data indicate with surprising strength the extent to which the citizen's social class and his occupation determine both his opportunities for advancement and his attitudes toward the Soviet system. On many important questions, the individual's social position is more important for understanding his attitudes than are such factors as his nationality or whether or not he or a member of his family had been arrested. In theory, the class system is open. Mobility — i.e., moving from one class to another — has actually been extensive. However, certain avenues are blocked for those of "bourgeois" family background and for many others whose relatives have been proscribed as "enemies of the state." More recently, there has been a tendency for children of elite parents to receive educational and occupational preference. The family is the most important primary social group and, although it has clearly been deeply penetrated by the regime, it remains one of the institutions most impervious to regime influence: an island of "private feeling" in a sea of public surveillance. The school is probably next most important in influencing individual development, and here the control of the state is virtually complete. State control is also exerted through the ubiquitous Communist youth organizations.

SOME DOMINANT ATTITUDES OF THE REGIME AND THE PEOPLE

Subordination of the individual to the state derives from the principle of statism, and applications of this premise have penetrated every sphere of behavior in the USSR. Supported by the claim that it is executing "the will of history," the Soviet leadership is characterized by ruthlessness in handling people. Physical suffering, even loss of life, have little meaning if appropriate goals can be advanced through human exploitation. Only when lack of morale affects production or gives rise to disorders does the regime relax the pressures. This indifference adds to the flexibility of its pursuit of short-run goals. Events of the post-Stalin period suggest a decision to pursue at least a temporary policy of giving various conciliatory gifts to the populace.

On the whole, the regime's subordination of the individual to the state is accepted by the people, although they do not approve the tempo of the demands made upon them. The regime's purposefulness, activism, and steady looking to the future receive widespread approval. Soviet citizens expect governments to be stern and demanding. The regime's indifference to human suffering is, however, not approved and is one of the main bases for dissatisfaction and disaffection within the Soviet Union. The belief held by many citizens that interest in power alone motivates the top leadership makes it alien and repulsive to the average Russian. The majority fear but do not love the leaders, although at times they will make a profuse outward show of love following the traditional custom — which finds its place as well in Russian religion — of placating the all-powerful as the only way of winning benevolence. There is pride in the rapid industrialization of the USSR and in the present power of the Soviet Union on the world scene. There is willingness to accept a small clique which holds power and rules without much recourse to public processes of law. But full acceptance of such absolute control would be granted only on the condition that this power is exercised in a predominantly nurturant way with affectionate, "fatherly" care for the welfare of the masses. The main grievances, expressed by a wide variety of groups, are the failures of the regime to solve the agricultural crisis, to provide sufficient housing and adequate supplies of consumer goods, to ease the terror, and to relax the tempo of demands.

3

Creating and Maintaining Myths

All societies have their "myths," systems of beliefs or values that organize and synthesize the main ideas of a culture and rationalize or justify the total system. We shall not worry about "myths" that are more in the nature of synthetic folklore, such as Soviet stories that depicted Stalin as the just and even benevolent father of all the people. So far as major organizing ideas are concerned, societies differ primarily in the following respects: (*a*) how seriously the myths are taken; (*b*) whether popular and variant forms are tolerated or a single official mythology is demanded; (*c*) whether the myths are held to be true in a broad, symbolic sense, or there is emphasis upon the literal content of chapter and verse. In this perspective the Soviet system is outstanding in its demand that one and only one internally consistent ideology be taken with great seriousness and literalness. This is true even of those numerous aspects of the official ideology which are clearly contrary to fact. Typical, for example, of the regime's attitude is the ritualistic adherence to certain forms of Western democracy such as voting, election campaigns, and public meetings of the Supreme Soviet, which have no practical significance.

Basic Soviet doctrine in its most orthodox form is adhered to by only a small group of leaders and doubtless believed in full detail by even a tinier minority. Nevertheless, while there are wide variations in acceptance even within the Party, there is certainly a tendency* for individuals, as they rise in the leadership hierarchy, to conform — in their outward manifestations, at least — more and more completely to Soviet ideology. Apparent receptivity to indoctrination is, in actuality, a factor in

* With some there is undoubtedly also a tendency toward inner disillusionment as they see what really goes on in practice within the system.

promotion. Persons being groomed for advancement in leadership typically undergo at least one year of conditioning in Party schools at each of several stages in their advancement. That this conditioning, in spite of some cynicism, is on the whole remarkably effective is shown by the acts of the Soviet leaders as well as by their words. In the pattern of taking over the satellites, for example, there is a certain formalistic repetitiveness. It is apparent that most Soviet leaders are convinced that you just cannot do even "the correct thing" in the wrong way. There are no alternative ways of achieving the proper result under the same historical circumstances. Everything must be done "by the numbers." Much of the Soviet criticism of Tito was not merely cant. When they said he had no "sense of history" they meant it, even though for them the proof of his sense of history would have been mainly to follow blindly the Russian Politburo. It is true that the "take-over" pattern in satellite countries varied in important matters. At a more abstract level, however, the pattern was the same and was derived from basic Communist doctrine. The Soviet leadership's sense of security appears to be very intimately tied to ideological conceptions which are treated as if they were absolute and immutable ideas. It is true that change is built into the system — both in doctrine and in practice — but this applies much more to details than to fundamental premises and ideas. This persistence is particularly evident in the latent as against the manifest, or what has been called the "esoteric" as against the "exoteric," ideology of Bolshevism.[1] Indeed, one of the most persistent causes of failure to understand the workings of the Communist mind derives from our neglect of what Leites[2] has called the "unexpressed" content of Marxist-Leninist-Stalinist ideology.

The Soviet propaganda machine does not limit itself — as most other systems of political propaganda have done — to the technique of reiteration, hammering in, and to the suppression of complaints and disturbing information. There must be a positive and developmental side too.[3] It is true that incessant profession of faith is adopted by many as a major path not only to personal security but also to advancement at school, in work, and in every sphere of life. To conform, at least outwardly, is necessary for survival. But the regime wants more than conformity; it wants not so much "belief" (in the sense in which Christians would use that term) as positive identification with the Party as the trustworthy custodian of all fundamental doctrinal questions, an identification normally achieved through actively propagating and executing the Party program and its concrete demands.

There is no subject on which even well-informed Americans show greater misunderstanding than that of Communist ideology. The tendency, in characteristic American fashion, is to make extreme interpretations. Either: "Soviet ideology is an inflexible code, a sort of theology which dictates all plans and policies," or: "Russian Communists no longer believe this stuff. These are just words which are used ritually or for propaganda purposes at home and abroad. They pick the texts they quote to suit the purpose of the moment. They'll say the opposite next week if they feel like it." There are elements of truth in both of these views, but in this instance the full truth does not, as so often, lie somewhere between two extremes. Rather, an adequate statement requires conceptions that are outside the range of ordinary American experience.

It is true that many in the USSR are cynical toward the official ideology. Many more are apathetic. It is also true that what remains of the formal ideology is largely what has been found useful, with or without modification, in support of the maintenance and enlargement of power by the regime, at home and abroad. But this does not mean that the *method of thinking* has ceased to influence both the elite and the masses. Seeing the actions of the leaders from the fresh perspective afforded by the descriptions of the system given by the refugees, we are strongly inclined to agree with Leites and others that, despite changes in the formal ideology and in concrete policy goals, there has been a high degree of continuity in Bolshevik behavior, stemming from the persistence of certain "core" ways of thinking and acting, including those we have treated here as operating characteristics.

Moreover, the leadership's use of ideology for cynical manipulation does not mean that the regime does not take ideas as such seriously — quite the contrary. The amount of serious effort that Stalin put into the genetics and linguistics controversies and into his last book was strikingly high. It is as if the President of the

United States were to enter into controversies on esoteric matters in *The Quarterly Journal of Economics* and the *International Journal of American Linguistics.*

Ideology plays two roles in the behavior of the Soviet elite: (1) as a system of ideas to which they are committed; (2) as a doctrine to be manipulated by them in the pursuit of practical goals. Some ideological tenets are more "believed" than others, and, of course, there is great variability among individuals. There can be no doubt, however, that the Soviet ruling elite makes persistent attempts to maintain the *appearance* of ideological consistency. Even though policy may change its direction, the orthodoxy of every policy must always be established. The retention of the Marxist slogans "materialism" and "determinism" are a symbolic means of maintaining the legitimacy of contemporary Soviet policies and doctrines. But while in theology the main doctrinal tenets are the most stable elements, in Bolshevik ideology substantive doctrinal tenets are sometimes considered expendable if they conflict with the demands of the immediate action program of the Party. If necessary, the basic statements of Marx, Engels, Lenin, and Stalin are reinterpreted. When such alterations are made, however, argument or citation of appropriate textual quotations, or both, are used to preserve the air of continuity and consistency. The Communist devil is very apt at quoting his scripture to his own purpose.

In the realm of strictly political ideology, the retention of rules and beliefs which have no basis in present-day reality is apparently deliberate. Belief in the myth that practice and theory are one, for example, is thought necessary for the continued existence of the Party. Its basic dogma is that it alone is the custodian of Marxist-Leninist-Stalinist orthodoxy, and to admit departure from that orthodoxy would be to destroy the dogma. Moreover, there is the significant "vanguard theory," according to which the USSR is to lead the world into a "better life," and the Party in the Soviet Union is the vanguard of World Communism.

To ask simply, "Are the Communists 'sincere' in their beliefs?" is to ask the wrong question. As a recent study points out:

Nobody inside the Soviet Union expects the loyal citizen to believe in Marxism in the same way as he believes in the suitability of sowing a certain crop at a certain time of the year. Earnest foreign Marxists who have settled in the USSR have had to discover this fact at their own expense and the price they had to pay was considerable.[4]

The expression of values and political beliefs in a Communist society is not comparable to the expression of such values and beliefs in the West. In the USSR such expression plays much more the role which compliance with custom has played in the middle classes of a free society. Soviet citizens generally profess the official "religion" not out of deep conviction but to avoid public disapproval and the legal sanctions against nonconformist behavior, which are much more severe. Beliefs which are expressed for these practical reasons have, of course, persistence and functional significance quite different from those held on the basis of being deeply felt and thought to be "true." In the first place, such pragmatic beliefs are not easily modified by argument or exposure to "truth." The realistic fear of someone who lives within the Soviet system that deviation would weaken his chance of sheer physical survival acts as a kind of insulation and is far more powerful — at least in the short run — than abstract truth. Indeed, literal and complete belief would be an actual danger to the working of the system, for such belief leads to "idealist disillusionment" and disaffection.

Nevertheless, these same doctrines, which at first are held pragmatically, become so habitual that they are almost automatic, however cynically or semicynically they were embraced at first. And so — in spite of cynicism, apathy, and ritualistic lip service — Communist myths are still of genuine importance. We saw this with the *émigré* population. Of our intelligentsia respondents who were born after the Revolution at least 15 per cent* made constant use of the Marxian dialectic to explain and to predict; they accepted the inevitability of the class struggle, the assumption that historical laws are external to man, and the opposition

---

* This figure is undoubtedly artificially low. Our European interviews were going on shortly after the passage of the McCarran Act, and most of our respondents were quite aware that their chances of entering the United States would be adversely affected if they appeared to be Marxists in any sense. Hence, it is probable that many of them consciously refrained from the use of a Marxist vocabulary. The striking thing is the number of spontaneous usages of Marxist theory.

of "materialism" and "idealism." Clearly they had learned their lessons all too well, and Marxist doctrine had become part of the unquestioned stuff of their thinking. Yet these were individuals who, if asked the question, "Is Marxism valid as a system?" would reply — in most cases sincerely — "No!" There is a striking parallel here to attitudes toward Soviet institutions.[5] Former Soviet citizens are characterized by their across-the-board rejection of (and hostility to) the Soviet *regime*. Nevertheless, they reveal an acceptance of many of the institutional features of Soviet society. Similarly, these former Soviet citizens indicate, along with their disavowal of "Marxism" and "Communism," a retention of some basic Marxist notions. There is no doubt that a significant number of Soviet intelligentsia perceive nature and society through Marxist spectacles — often without realizing at all that they are wearing these spectacles.[6]

Certainly the Soviet leadership thinks that these myths are important and useful or it would not go to such pains to maintain them. Lower Party leaders who do not operate and talk strictly in terms of the Party charter are disciplined. Acts of the top leadership palpably in violation of the mythology are rationalized, though at the expense of time and money. Stalin's summoning of Party and government personnel to his office was elaborately treated as a shining example of collective leadership. Much fanfare was given to the tenth anniversary of the Eighteenth Congress, even though the Nineteenth Congress was at that time *seven years overdue*. Directives ignored for twenty years are still given ceremonial honor. Many younger Party members, who did not personally experience the pre-Stalinist days of the Party, are really convinced that myth and "Soviet reality" are largely coterminous. They do not interpret the myths in ways adverse to the regime. Taking the myths as their guide, they exercise "the right of criticism and self-criticism" to help the Party center discover weaknesses in the work of the lower organizations without creating either the possibility of undermining authority or the possibility of the organization of opposition. In their hands, Party elections serve as instruments with which the Party center can restrain the lower leaders from abuse of their delegated authority. Although it is true that Party elections are generally "means of registering assent, rather than forums of free choice," Party members have, on occasion, with-held their assent to the election of persons recommended from above. On such occasions, punishment went to the persons re-jected in accord with the official mythology, which says that those rejected in this system are unworthy.[7]

The Soviet system lays enormous stress on ideology both as a doctrine and as a practical instrument. The "operating ideology" of the leadership at any given point in time is kept remarkably consistent. The more formal total theoretical system has, in fact, undergone change through time, but much effort is expended to rationalize these changes and preserve the appear-ance of continuity and consistency. There is good evidence that Communist ideology affects the thinking and the acts of leaders and of other intelligentsia who grow up under the Bolshevik regime.

4

Planning and Controlling

Authority is centered in a small group of men whose immediate objectives are clearly defined: stability and industrialization at home and expansion abroad. "Muddling through" is abhorrent to this group. Everything must be planned and rationally calculated. Nothing can be left to chance or to the natural tendency in healthy societies for varied strands of activities to fit reasonably together. This group is, in fact, sensitized to conflict and changing power constellations and often "plays by ear" and even muddles, but it likes to give the impression that everything is planned to the last detail. Therefore, a distinctive feature of the system is conscious emphasis upon rational planning.

Individuals and organizations through which the master plan is carried out sometimes become involved in a conflict of loyalties and work at cross purposes. For example, a member of the middle elite has certain responsibilities as a member of a Party unit and somewhat divergent duties as a bureaucrat. Conflicts that are actually or potentially serious are eventually referred to the top and resolved there. Let us review briefly how, in various spheres of life, planning and controlling from the top operates.[1]

INDUSTRY[2]

There is Party reporting and direct Party interference in management as well as supervision by separate chains of bureaucracies. The state not only owns the means of production but has organized production units into several hierarchical systems of authority. Centralized control is also effected through planning and allocating resources from the top. At present, authority over details appears to be less concentrated at the very top than under Stalin. A *Pravda* editorial of April 26, 1953, states that the authority of various ministries has substantially widened as a result of governmental reorganization in March. Ministries are said to have the complete right to allocate material and monetary resources within their basic allotments and to decide on all basic questions of activity and enterprise within the institutions subordinate to them. If this unified command within ministries is really in effect, it means that considerably fewer matters are referred upward to the Party Presidium or to the Council of Ministers.

In general, however, central control still very much prevails. Both labor and management are induced to work at a high level of effort through a system of rewards and penalties, through ideology, and through force. The regime's plans require a high rate of investment and a low rate of consumption. This planned low rate of consumption is certainly designed to divert capital to the expansion of basic industry, but it may also be intended to hold a maximum number of people in the labor force. Among the mass of the workers, the level of consumption is low enough so that a low rate of increase in real wages does not result in a withdrawal of labor. If the real wages of the masses were relatively high, there might develop the phenomenon common in underdeveloped countries of increased wages leading to a withdrawal of labor. Soviet practice maximizes the quantity of labor offered by the workers (overtime, and work by women and children) and also permits the high rate of investment that is necessary for the state's objective of a rapid rate of growth. Factory discipline in an industrial society requires a standard workday and workweek which limits the extent to which a worker can vary his hours of work in response to variations in wages. The widespread use of a progressive piecework system (as part of the regime's general policy of promoting competition for scarce goods) discriminates in the income offered for successive quantities of output. This restores flexibility in the worker's ability to offer more effort in an intensive sense, if not by working more hours. It also elicits a given quantity of effort at a smaller real wage. Among managers, too, the piecework aspect of the premium system obtains more effort for less pay. In order to encourage occupational mobility, higher real wages are offered to skilled workers and managers. Prestige factors and other social rewards combine with higher incomes to provide a successful incentive to people to upgrade their skills and assume the responsibilities of managers.

Controls against uneconomic and unlawful activities are thwarted because of the need to establish measures of the performance of supervisory officials at each level in the hierarchy. The most common measure is the performance of the enterprise over which the supervisory official has charge. But since unlawful activities are essential to successful performance, the supervisor is motivated to "look the other way." Those who have the best knowledge of the enterprise (such as chief accountants or chief engineers) are little inclined to control strictly according to the letter. Those who are motivated to impose the tightest controls (Ministry of Finance, Ministry of State Control) have the least detailed knowledge of what is actually going on.

There are, however, forces such as the priority system that limit the departure of resource allocation from the optimum set by the regime. In the case of the highest priority, the desired output will usually be approximated. The greater the failure to meet priorities, the greater the counteracting force of sanctions. There are many small violations of priority, but few large ones. If a sector of the economy begins to deviate in some aspect from the established standard, such as an increasing neglect of spare parts, a campaign may be instituted which restores the system to a more normal situation.

AGRICULTURE

Thus far, agrarian productivity has been least effectively controlled. The support of the peasants made a great difference in the Bolsheviks' rise to power in 1917. The peasants accepted the Communist Party because it promised to let them keep the land which they had seized in preceding months. However, subsequent relations between the peasants and the regime have not been happy. No group in the Soviet population has been as consistently, and often as bitterly, antiregime as the peasants. As a bribe to the serious resistance to forced collectivization, the Collective Farm Statutes of 1935 allowed each farm household a private plot of approximately one-fourth to one-half hectare. The regime has tried fairly consistently to whittle down these private holdings, partly to free more labor for communal work and partly to increase the peasant's dependence upon his proceeds from the collective. The leaders have a still more fundamental distrust of private agriculture because, according to Lenin: "Peasant small-scale production breeds capitalism and a bourgeoisie — every day, every hour — by a natural process and on a mass scale."

Production plans for the collective farms are drawn up by government groups and then formally adopted by the collective farmers at meetings where the plans are subject neither to real dispute nor to change. The chairman of the collective farm is "elected" by the general meeting *after* he has been appointed by the Party. Sometimes he knows nothing about agriculture. He is the Party's agent and his primary responsibility is to carry out the Party's tasks, not to consider the interests of the collective farmers. The interests and wishes of the members of the farms are important to him mainly as they affect the working of the collective. The chairman is "assisted" by "agricultural technicians," attached mainly to the machine tractor stations. Many of these "technicians" were regarded by our respondents as covert agents of the secret police. Recent decrees do not give much evidence that this particular form of surveillance of peasant agriculture has been relaxed. In any event, supervision *from the top* has certainly not been lessened. According to Khrushchev's speech to the Supreme Soviet in April 1954, there are 422 administrations, departments, and sections in the USSR Ministry of Agriculture. (And there are two other USSR ministries concerned with agriculture.)

As with industry, agricultural production on the collectives (85 per cent of all agricultural land) and on the state farms (9 per cent) is based on piecework wherever possible. Those who overfulfill quotas get more pay and bonuses. Conversely, inadequate production and absenteeism are penalized by loss of pay, fines, and expulsion from the collective. Payments, both in cash and in kind, are extremely low because the government, outright and through barely disguised indirect levies, takes a tremendous portion of the total annual revenue. And there are other inequities in the system. Payment is on the basis of "labor days." A farmhand must often work more than an actual day to get credit for one "labor day," whereas more privileged individuals — ranging from farm officials to those who drive complex machinery — are credited with two to three or more "labor days" for each actual day of work.

The agricultural system is currently in crisis. The Soviet press is full of complaints that individuals have considerably larger holdings than they are allowed; in some cases collective farms (especially in Georgia) become merely fronts for the illegal private enterprise of their members. Far more startling are the figures publicly announced by the Central Committee (September 1953) and by Khrushchev (April 1954). During the period 1940–1953, when the population of the USSR increased by fifteen million, there was a total decline in grain acreage of 3.5 per cent of the prewar average. Food production is the lowest and the average Soviet diet the smallest and poorest since the First Five Year Plan came into force in 1929.

It is clear that the peasants have met discrimination against them and their preferred forms of production by wholesale non-coöperation. They have also successfully taken advantage of the price inducements offered to milk and meat producers in September 1953, at such a rate that the government has been forced to release grain reserves that will take a year or more to replenish.

Nevertheless, official policy continues to demand that agriculture should be subordinated even more strictly to the state. Such concessions (including the 1953 economic inducements) as have been made to the peasants have been granted explicitly to induce them to help in their own subjection. Whether the planning and controlling of agriculture from the top can be carried on much longer in the present fashion remains to be seen. Khrushchev has appropriately been dubbed the world's most worried gardener at present. Thus far he has diverted blame from himself by attacking his lesser subordinates and by diversionary measures (mainly ploughing pasture land for cultivation). The fanfare attending his May 1954 visit to Kazakhstan would seem to commit him definitely to the betterment of agricultural production through bringing steppe lands under cultivation and other types of land reclamation. He has also made it clear (without completely disavowing Lysenko) that the Party requires more than pseudo science, and that the urgency of the regime's agricultural measures will not wait for the resolution of theoretical arguments.

COMMUNICATIONS

The dependence of the Soviet system on a proper flow of communications is particularly great because of the wide range of institutional activities that are planned and controlled. The regime relies upon propaganda as a means of reducing the cost of domestic and foreign domination. At home this is justified in the 1950 textbook of Soviet administrative law, which essentially states that it is a regime which for the first time in history takes upon itself the role of an organizer and political educator of the people. Stalin has called coercion "the prerequisite of persuasion." Lenin verbally reversed the order of the two measures. In fact, though a minority may genuinely want to comply in full, the two procedures all come to the same thing, for those who accept "persuasion" know that by so doing they avoid becoming members of the to-be-coerced minority. Again, according to the textbook, coercion is applied to the minority after the persuasion of the majority has been successfully carried through.*

To discuss the flow of communications in Soviet society we should distinguish several orders of information, and the two directions of flow. In the "upward" flow of communications there are two main categories of information: information on the basis of which policy and planning decisions are made; and information necessary for effective social control. Information relevant to policy and planning includes basic statistical data, knowledge of such matters as the state of morale and loyalty of the populace, and an assessment of conditions outside the Soviet system. Information relevant to control somewhat overlaps with the preceding, but more particularly it involves knowledge about specific acts which it may or may not be desirable to redirect. The "downward" flow involves "technical" information (i.e., information required by persons on lower echelons for making appropriate decisions) and propaganda (i.e., information intended by the regime to persuade and shape the attitudes of the citizen).

* The skeptical Western observer must note that the textbook reverses the factual "minority" and "majority" relations!

The Soviet system's highly centralized decision-making procedure and the completeness of control which the regime strives to exert over all institutions and individuals necessitate a huge apparatus for assembling, transmitting, and processing a vast amount of information. The sheer volume of data to be handled is a problem in itself. This problem is complicated by the fact that reporting of information is frequently coupled with responsibility for the very activities on which one is reporting. Control over information on one's own activities is essential for the survival of many people in the Soviet apparatus, and, as a result, there is an appreciable amount of suppression and distortion of upward-flowing information. We must infer as well — though the evidence is by no means watertight — that, as in all totalitarian societies, there is a tendency for subordinates to tell their superiors what they want to hear. There are many stories in circulation, most of them in essence fairly convincing, of the falsification of statistics and the suppression of derogatory information. If the most extreme of these stories were taken as typical, we would conclude that the information available to decision-makers would be so inadequate that the society could not long survive. The fact that the Soviet system has not collapsed must in itself be regarded as sufficient evidence that the upward flow of communications is adequate for its survival.

Among the major reasons for the apparent success of the leadership in maintaining at least the minimum flow of upward communication is its reliance on a multiplicity of channels. The top leadership has available the administrative-government apparatus, the Party machine, the MVD, letters to the editors of official organs, and other sources. In addition, the "functional" sections of the Central Secretariat of the Party have the responsibility of seeing to it that these channels are kept open. Thus, if one channel fails to provide adequate information, another may be checked against the remaining channels.

One of the categories of information which the regime requires is a reasonably accurate estimate of the state of morale and the political attitudes of the populace. The regime has deliberately rejected, as a matter of policy, the use of sample-opinion surveys as a means of getting such data,[3] and relies mainly on reports of the secret police, compliant citizens, Party agitators, and similar functionaries. Aside from the technical problems of procuring an accurate assessment of the popular mood by such methods, many of the general difficulties which characterize the upward flow of communications in Soviet society are found here. In many instances, the people who do the reporting are themselves held responsible for the state of public opinion. Also, it seems that higher-ups do not accept with enthusiasm negative reports concerning popular opinion. To this must be added the inherent bias that comes from assessing the attitudes of a population which dares not express them freely.

All of the foregoing indicates that there is considerable distortion in the upward communications in the Soviet system — and this is a system which places unusual demands on such communications. The amount of distortion that occurs has apparently not been sufficient to handicap the regime greatly in making decisions of broad policy. The deficiencies in the upward flow are most evident in more detailed decisions, and particularly in the regime's ability to control the behavior of the citizen with precision. Probably the area in which the regime's reporting system fails most frequently is in locating specific actions. If morale is bad, production is low, and graft is going on, this general deterioration will not escape the regime's attention and it will put appropriate corrective policies into effect. However, it may be difficult, for the reasons we have noted, to locate the precise persons whose morale is worst, the exact kolkhozy or factories which are falsifying their statistics, and the particular officials who are "chiseling."

There is a great deal of differentiation in access to technical communications in the Soviet system. Because of the high proportion of esoteric communications, certain groups are much more fully informed on regime policy and economic and military data than others. Party members get political briefings. Officers of the secret police, if they are highly placed, receive reports on the morale of the populace. Administrators and planners have better statistical data than do those on lower echelons. The general policy of the regime, however, is to give a man only as much information as is necessary for carrying out his job. In most instances, there is an acute hunger for such information on the part of persons in responsible positions. This stems partially from curiosity, but also from the fact that "technical" knowledge of this order is essential both for personal survival and for the proper execution of one's job. With respect to technical communication, then, the problem of the regime is, on one hand, to keep access to it restricted and, on the other, to get adequate information to responsible people. The regime errs on the side of supplying less information than would best serve the functioning of the system.

The problem of the dissemination of propaganda is entirely the reverse of that of the dissemination of technical information. The regime attempts to maximize exposure and access to propaganda, and its main difficulty, aside from the purely mechanical one of physical transmission of information, is commanding the attention and gaining the confidence of its intended audience. There are current complaints in the Soviet press over the poor quality of entertainment programs. This situation presumably cuts down the radio audience for propaganda. There is also a big element of self-selection in exposure to propaganda. In general, the less well-educated and less well-placed segments of the population and those most opposed to the regime tend to ignore the mass media. This is true to the point that the voluntary exposure of some groups is not sufficient to meet the regime's requirements in its efforts to get its propaganda messages across to the whole population. This indifference, coupled with certain limitations of the Soviet media — inadequacies of radio network, for example — are partially compensated for by the system of "oral agitation," [4] which exploits captive audiences.

Overcontrol and overcentralization are marked features of the Soviet system. There is fragmentary evidence which suggests that the post-Stalin regime realizes this situation and is attempting to make corrections. Some USSR ministries seem to have been given more independence. Even new ministries in the Federal Republics appear to have some autonomy. According to Khrushchev, at a meeting of the Plenum of the Central Committee of the USSR Communist Party on February 23, 1954, the local workers correctly estimated the problem of too much centralization in planning, and this interfered with the utilization of potentialities, restrained the creative initiative of kolkhozniks, and weakened their interest in improving the harvest.

This possible trend in the Soviet Union is one to watch with the closest attention. If it continues, even cautiously, one of the major vulnerabilities of the system will be reduced. As is so often the case, of course, this gain would be bought at a price, since permitting local autonomy somewhat dilutes the power of the center. This results, in good measure, from the fact that the practice of local autonomy breeds habits of independence and weakens the automatic character of responsiveness to orders from the central authorities. It is our strong impression of the top elite, however, that they are exceedingly, perhaps excessively, sensitive to this danger. If they must err, they will err on the side of overcontrol rather than by permitting too much local autonomy. We anticipate, therefore, that local initiative will be allowed to increase only slightly in order to permit greater efficiency, which may indeed result. But it will be kept under close check, and the new freedom of the local authorities will be sharply withdrawn at the slightest evidence of slackness in instantaneous compliance with commands from the central authorities.

5

Problem Solving, the Overcommitment

of Resources, and "Storming"

Under Stalin, and to only a slightly diminished extent under the new leadership, the goals of Soviet society have been set very high relative to available resources. This circumstance explains the existence — or at least the salience — of many of the operating principles of Soviet society and conditions of Soviet life already cited and to be mentioned. This overcommitment of resources has converted the Soviet Union into a rationed society with the characteristic shortages, hoarding, evasion of controls, and other features of such a society. It is only to a limited extent that the policy of overcommitment of resources may be regarded as an *explanation* of other phenomena in the Soviet system, since this very disposition to extend ruthlessly the human as well as the material resources of Soviet society was in itself a reflection of the same "Bolshevik mentality" that exhibits itself in other operating characteristics of the Soviet social system. However, if Stalin's successors deviate from his practice of pushing through objectives with minimum regard for the strain on the system, other features are likely to alter also. If present and future regimes take as their objective a society that runs smoothly rather than by fits and starts, they may also modify the application of police power and other aspects of control and may feel less necessity to maintain myths that deny unpleasant reality.

This is a mobilized society, existing in a state of perpetual emergency. It is a society which is continually being pushed by the regime toward certain goals. The metaphors used by Soviet leaders are suggestive of an armed camp: "fortress to be stormed," "campaigns to be carried through," "strategic retreats," and the like.

Planning and control from the top have, both as a consequence of this state of mobilization and as a technique of implementation of the goals, the extremely instrumental character of all official Soviet behavior. While final goals remain fixed, day-to-day decision-making and action are devoted primarily to the next successive step. Each step is thought of as part of the long-range master plan. All activity must serve the ends of the state as they are held to exist at a particular time and in a particular situation. Education, for instance, is never considered as an end in itself or as a means to promote the personal fulfillment and cultural development of citizens. From the standpoint of the regime, education is a way to train personnel to meet the manpower needs of an expanding industrial society, to allocate this manpower in a preliminary way, to grade and select within this manpower pool, and to develop loyal, reliable citizens. A postwar textbook describes "Communist education" as the preparation of the younger generation for active participation in the building of Communist society and for the defense of the Soviet government which is building that society.

Throughout the system there is tremendous emphasis upon the application of all knowledge, including science. Psychology, for example, is primarily the instrument for its applied aspect, education. Some informed students have held that the USSR deliberately concentrated almost exclusively upon applied science, counting on the West to do the basic research. The excellence of at least a few aspects of Soviet basic science shows this statement to be an exaggeration. In any case, there is little official prestige attached to, or support for, any activity, including those which are scientific or scholarly, that is not actually or potentially instrumental to the requirements of the state — i.e., "problem solving."

The word "instrumental" is also a primary key to the Soviet use of ideology. The leaders draw selectively upon the body of Marxist-Leninist-Stalinist doctrine to sanction their policies at a given time or to promote their purposes in a certain situation. This is specifically illustrated by the Soviet practice of "turning Marx upside down" to justify policies concerning the family and social stratification. The regime's relationship with the Orthodox Church and with science is another case. The official position is that Marxism-Leninism-Stalinism is being constantly revised and tested against experience. Ideology is mainly a means, not an end. Nevertheless, this is not the whole story. Members of the elite, however cynical and opportunistic they may become, speak so habitually in Communist jargon that they eventually become prisoners of their own vocabulary. There is good evidence that, in some respects, they take for granted some of the premises and concepts of the doctrine which, consciously, they are using as an instrument.

At any rate, this system of belief, with its seeming paradox of rationalism-intellectualism combined with distaste for and distrust of free intellectual inquiry and empirical data, remains of key importance to those who would understand Soviet action. The Soviet system of belief, alike in its rigidity and its flexibility, is typical of the bipolarization in the system. Bolshevik leaders do not disregard either ideas or empirical data: their attitude is ambivalent. They like to have their position supported by empirical findings, but when scientific discoveries conflict with action programs and "consistency" of doctrine, they will sometimes override science by rationalization or evasion. The carefully maintained rigidity of ideology is intended to support the pretensions of Marxism as an "infallible scientific system." The ceaseless ideological blarings also have the purpose of convincing all citizens that they can achieve nothing without the sophisticated tutelage of the Party and state, which are guided by these unchanging premises and concepts.

A distinctive aspect of Bolshevism is the highly elaborate ideological rationalizations which have been evolved to justify and implement a closely coördinated program of act and thought control in science. For the Bolshevik, thought and act, idea and practical consequences are so closely linked that the distinction between them is almost an artificial one. Probably more than any other group of men in modern times, the Bolsheviks have stressed the pragmatic consequences of ideas. Interpretation by Westerners of Kremlin intervention in science and the arts has usually taken one of two lines. It is maintained, on the one hand, that such intervention is a blind imposition of dogma and, on the other, that it represents a complete disregard for ideas and ideology in the interests of immediate practical utility. Both interpretations miss the essential point of the relation of ideas to action in the Soviet system.

To some extent, the impression that intervention in the arts and sciences represents blind imposition of dogma results from a failure to understand the "problem-solving" operating characteristic of the Soviet system. It is true that consistency of ideology is highly valued, as the proponents of the "blind-imposition" interpretation implicitly maintain. But much of what looks like farfetched dogmatism is usually far-reaching pragmatism. For Bolshevik pragmatism, coupled with ideological rigidity, often leads to a preoccupation with basic premises that seems at first glance far removed from practical problems. But any form of "deviance" is an immensely practical issue to the Soviet regime. The Bolsheviks know that deviant ideas will ultimately lead to "undesirable" actions. Premises must be examined lest the ideas stemming from them threaten orthodoxy.

A word of caution might be in order here. Soviet ideological dogmatism is precisely compatible with the "problem-solving" pragmatism. The assertions of historical laws, which will inevitably bring about the victory of Communism because history moves in dialectic jumps, are dogmatic. But to bring about these ends, the Bolshevik "vanguard" (of history and, therefore, of the future of mankind) has to "solve" the problems *correctly*. This correct solving of problems — because "the future is a Communistic one" — is equated with the ability of the Party to make the most of its strength and power. While there is nothing dogmatic about the solving of problems, the criterion of pragmatic desirability of consequences is dogmatically determined: it is all behavior which promotes the Party and Communism.

The contention that even the most abstruse of Bolshevik assertions have a practical intent is in no sense an acceptance of the opposite explanation — that such attention to ideas and ideology is "*mere* expediency." The very fact that such complicated rationalizations are fabricated, and that official high-level intervention in intellectual activity is so extensive, is in itself a sufficient demonstration that the Soviet elite take ideology seriously. Even though "practicality" takes precedence in the long run, the

Bolshevik attitude toward science cannot be understood except on the premise that ideas are practically important.

Explicit theory per se and new theory are less important in the present Soviet scheme than they were. The constant stress is upon action. However, a fairly consistent and simple philosophy of life underlies this hyperactivity. Not only the leaders, but to a considerable degree the people of the USSR, are outstanding in the present world, and indeed in history, for their conviction that all problems can be solved by human ingenuity and effort. Lip service is still paid to the Marxian theory that the processes of history unfold according to inevitable laws and that a conscious Party leadership can only speed up ineluctable destiny. In practice, however, the leadership acts as if events could be controlled by a rational calculus and by resolute effort. Neither God's will nor irrational and unconscious processes have any real place in the thinking of the ruling elite. Rational self-consciousness, control of the environment, and — more recently — moralistic exhortations of the *individual's* will are mobilized to "solve" problems in succession: industrialization, collectivization, mechanization of agriculture, and the like.

Stalin came to power in the midst of a conflict over which of two premises should be dominant in controlling Soviet society and, more specifically, in the expansion of the Soviet economy: the premise of Bukharin and others that society had to be viewed as a coördinated pattern of events, the equilibrium of which could not be unduly disturbed without dire results; and the premise with which Stalin became identified, that better results could be obtained in expanding production if maximum efforts were made toward this aim and considerations of coördination and equilibrium were secondary. Another way of stating the Stalinist formula is that maximum productivity can be achieved from a social group if maximum pressure, incentive, or coercion is applied to each of the component parts. A system maintained according to this formula, since it operates on minimal reserves, is subject to fits and starts, to malcoördination and waste. But the total loss is assumed to be less than that involved in setting aside the reserves of materials, machinery, and manpower that are required to avoid the fits and starts. Needless to say, either premise pushed to its extreme can lead to a grossly inefficient system. However, the Soviet system which has evolved in the last twenty years has been based strongly on the second premise — of maximum exertion of the component parts and maximum commitment of resources. It has been reasonably stable and effective, but, by virtue of the dominance of this premise, the system has developed distinctive institutional features and patterns of behavior.

The characteristic Soviet approach to problems is that of "storming," i.e., tackling (on the domestic scene) one or a limited number of objectives at a time and hitting them hard, largely ignoring side effects. The regime's notion of how to effect social change is still based on a direct *assault* on goals with only a secondary consideration of cost and consequences.* This procedure involves running roughshod over individuals and groups which stand in the way, and it exacts from the Soviet citizen a maximum of exertion. This produces:

(*a*) Alienation of the groups which were injured in the process of social change;

(*b*) Deprivation and discontent among loyal citizens who paid the cost, along with those who were discriminated against, of rapid social change and economic expansion;

(*c*) Pressure toward illicit behavior (theft of state property to alleviate low living standards, illegal procedures for meeting responsibilities) which in turn results in: (1) a sense of guilt and resentment against the regime; (2) a general tightening of controls; (3) punishment of offenders.

The use of the methods and resources of a totalitarian society for the control of disaffection and for producing social change increases discontent and disloyalty. The very methods used to control disaffection — arrests, intense spying, an all-pervasive distrust, bombardment with propaganda, and so on — become additional irritants to those who are not loyal, and on occasion

---

* It might be argued that, although this was true of the Stalin era, it is not accurate as a description of the new leadership. Although we acknowledge some toning down in the violence of the attack on objectives, we feel the basic approach remains the same and point as evidence to the "assault" on the agricultural problem launched by Khrushchev through the breaking to the plough of millions of marginal acres of steppe land.

turn even the loyal citizen from the regime. It also, however, creates favored groups who have an interest in preserving the status quo.

The method or strategy of the regime is not to reduce discontent, but (1) to isolate it and suppress its manifestation; (2) to exploit as fully as possible all motives other than those specifically and systematically thwarted; (3) to deflect blame onto scapegoats.

At least on the domestic scene, Bolshevik leaders are characterized by their propensity to undertake a massive program to mobilize totally every conceivable resource, including critical reserves. This allows minimum room for normal error and maximizes the chances for crises and almost complete breakdowns. In particular, the leaders apparently expect that where real shortages exist the necessary resources can somehow be squeezed out by exacting extra effort from people, with the result that human resources are particularly overcommitted. Under these circumstances, tensions, pressures, and resentments are developed to the fullest extent.

There can be no question of the immensely instrumental emphasis within the Soviet system. "Problem solving" is a tendency (though an important one), rather than a literal fact. In particular, notice should be taken of the regime's persistent habit of keeping an alternative policy in reserve. There is evidence that the proponents of alternative policies appear in high positions after the "storming" techniques of the other faction have failed or only incompletely succeeded. It is useful for Western students to be aware of these alternatives that are sometimes visible just beneath the surface of the day's campaign.

6

Refusal to Allow Independent
Concentrations of Power

In any complex industrial society there are and must be diverse organizations. Hence, in the Soviet Union individuals have varied memberships: in the Party, in the family, in youth groups, in military organizations. Such groups may be foci of alternate loyalties of the individual and may serve as concentrations of power which are not easily or firmly kept under the control of the central Party nucleus. We have, at various points, maintained that a totalitarian society by its very nature impels its citizens consciously or unconsciously to develop *sub rosa* loyalties as a way of getting some psychological independence and to use and, to some extent, create independent concentrations of power as a defense against the excessive demands of the regime.

Alternate loyalties and independent concentrations of power are obviously closely related, both in their functions and in their close association with the existence of diverse organizations within the framework of the totalitarian system. Both constitute a threat to the regime's desire for total control, one by alienating the citizen's allegiance, the other by giving him a measure of independence through affording him the power to control some sphere of life relatively free of the intervention of the regime. While thus closely related, the problems of alternate loyalties and of independent concentrations of power also have rather different implications for the system, and, therefore, we will treat the problem of alternate loyalties in detail later in connection with the general problem of political loyalty.

The refusal of the regime to permit autonomous concentrations of power can be documented from every area of Soviet life. The mutual interpenetration and infiltration of Party, secret police, and government bureaucracy is well known, as is the lack of independent trade unions and professional organizations. The two basic techniques of the regime in controlling potential seats of independent power are to bureaucratize potentially independent institutions — to capture them from above and to subject them to additional controls outside of the ordinary line of command, often by infiltration with Party personnel, or more frequently by bringing key personnel into the Party and subjecting them to Party discipline.

THE ARMY[1]

As with all professions, there is in the military a centripetal force of common interest, a common set of values, combined with the need for some autonomy in the conduct of exclusively military matters, that produces a certain drift toward independence of control. Because of this drift toward independence, and since the army is mobile and possesses its own internal communication system, the regime inevitably has a primary concern for control over the military.

Many observers of the Soviet scene have stated that no effective solution to the problem of the conflicts between the Party and professional authority can be worked out so long as responsibility is assigned to the Party for the success of the professionals' functions.[2] Unless the regime decides that the Party control apparatus in the army can be dispensed with and that all political control can be assigned to the cadre officers themselves, the political workers in the army are under constant pressure to interfere with the cadre officers.

At the moment, the regime's need for an effective military establishment, together, perhaps, with its need to secure the "affection" of the military in this period of instability among the ruling group, results in the enhancement of the military's authority. But, even now, political interference in the army persists. It is attacked, of course, but the very presence and persistence of these attacks attest to the continuing interference. Moreover, if the political controls should be more drastically reduced than at present, the fact remains that it is the police even more than the political controls which are the cause of the cadre officers' most intense reactions. One can adjust more easily to interference, bureaucratic frictions, and the frustrations and resentments which they generate than to fear and anxiety about the unknown. It is precisely the latter which the MVD produces among the officer corps.

To date, there is no clear evidence of any decisive letup in the police controls of the MVD and its special military sections. There have been some transfers of functions and troops from the MVD to the Ministry of Defense — probably the result of the conflict within the ruling group — but these do not imply that the MVD is being deprived of its secret and pervasive military surveillance functions, nor that these functions are coming under military control. Nevertheless, the possibility that the top military personnel is assuming an increasing political role within the ruling group does further complicate the situation and could alter it, especially if the top military should actually enter the ruling group. But, short of military hegemony within the ruling group, which few observers suggest as current or even imminent, it is likely that, precisely because the political role of the military command is increasing, the ruling group as a whole, and certainly its "antimilitary" component, is going to be even more concerned with maintaining its MVD surveillance controls throughout the military organization. It is an open question whether the military can thwart a continuation of MVD controls. Meanwhile, these police controls persist in the military organization, with the result that the cadre officers' major complaint also persists and there remains what Fainsod has described as a "gulf" between the officers corps and the regime.

Direct control of the military by the political power from "above" has been reflected in the fact that the government ministers — and indeed many leading marshals and admirals — have been mainly Party functionaries in uniform* rather than career military people. The control from "within" by the special sections of secret police is, of course, supplemented by the

---

* Zhukov, in his role of Minister of Defense, is a notable exception, reflective of a changed role for the military which is commented on further below.

effort to recruit officers into the Communist Party. Thus, according to Marshal Vasilevsky's statement at the Nineteenth Party Congress (1952), 86.4 per cent of all officers in the grade of captain and above were Party or Komsomol members.[3] This means that most officers are directly within the control of Party discipline. In this regard, it is apparent that the regime's efforts to enlist the cadre officers — almost en masse — into the Party are directed to the aim of imbuing the military's increased authority with the proper Party spirit. It is doubtful, however, that this will work, since the cadre officer who is also a Party member tends to be first and foremost a professional army man. His Party membership and involvement may be more nominal than real; the same has been true of civilian professional personnel. Consequently, when the regime grants increased authority and autonomy to the cadre officer (even if he is a Party member), it tends to stimulate his professional independence. On the other hand, insofar as political orientation is concerned, the experience of Party membership may become very significant in the case of cadre officers.

Despite the persistence of these controls, one can safely assert that the military were never a more significant group than at the present time. Indications are that this significance is likely to increase rather than decrease in the immediately foreseeable future. There is evidence that the relative prestige and power of the military in Soviet life have increased in the past two years. Although some Western commentators have undoubtedly made too much of certain single incidents, such as the role of Marshal Konev in Beria's "trial" or the hypothesis that the army forced a public announcement of Beria's execution (Zhukov's "toast to justice"), the fact remains that many fragments of evidence all point in the same direction. There is also evidence that the regime is concerned about the military and its identification with the regime. There is the recent prominence given by *Pravda* and other Soviet newspapers to the role of the military forces. This suggests that the military has been conceded greater political importance.* It is also suggestive that the amnesty decree of March 28, 1953 made much more precise reference to the

* We note, in this connection, the role played by Zhukov at the "summit" meetings in 1955.

release of prisoners sentenced for minor military offenses than it did in the case of other categories of prisoners. More deference to the military is also indicated by the fact that when political workers were reëstablished at company level in 1950, they were drawn from specially trained junior military officers. And on the other side of this coin, the regime felt it necessary to reintroduce political officers at this level. Finally, the published reports of the "deaths" of 112 *young* general officers between 1948 and 1953 make tempting the speculation that the regime has had concrete grounds for worrying about the senior officer cadre.

It may be worth while to add to the points already mentioned a number (although by no means a complete listing) of bits of evidence, all pointing in the direction of the rising power of the military and of the regime's respect for this category of Soviet society:

(1) The 1954 Supreme Soviet includes all commanders* of the military districts with three exceptions.

(2) Six of the 129 members of the Central Committee of the Party (and 20 per cent of the candidate members) are in uniform.†

(3) In the 1954 Supreme Soviet the representation of the armed forces has *increased*, while that of the secret police has declined.‡

(4) The MVD has surrendered control over atomic matters to the army.

Over and above these recent trends, there are some sheer situational factors that are of great importance. In the nature of military organization, the armed forces have greater potentialities for independent action than any other category in the USSR, save the Party and possibly the secret police. They have certain strictly professional characteristics. They have had, on the whole, more experience with the West and for professional

---

* It is true that only those who are considered politically reliable receive top military commands.

† Of the total, only four were either members or candidate members in 1939.

‡ While the Supreme Soviet has almost no real power, its composition indicates symbolically the thinking of the regime and the general state of affairs.

reasons must continue to obtain tough-minded and (relatively) unslanted knowledge about the West. Both because of their professional characteristics and because they are more closely identified with the people than other elite groups in the USSR, they are more likely in crisis situations to respond in terms of national, as opposed to regime, interests — *if* they are convinced another option is open. Finally, the people, and indeed certain elite groups not completely committed to the regime, are psychologically more ready to cast their lot with the armed forces than with the other two groups that have the potentiality of independent movement (the Party and the secret police).

But the Army did serve them [the people] in defending their frontiers and homes against the invader. And the Army is part of them and they of it, since all able-bodied males serve in it, and in it are better fed, clothed, and housed than at any other time in their lives. Finally, the Army is thought of for defense rather than for a deeply feared aggressive war. The people trust the Army more than they do the Party or the Police, and around it they could be most easily rallied." [4]

The most reasonable estimate of the situation appears to be the following. The military elite is now in the strongest political position it has enjoyed, but this is not a position of partnership with the Party elite. The military's position in relation to the MVD is the strongest ever, but again a qualification is in order. Since the Party elite is not likely to hand over power to the military, or, more subtly, place its head in the military's cannon, it will, in Fainsod's words, very likely "depend on a reorganized MVD and on its own Party controls in the armed forces to nip in the bud any military conspiracy." [5] The military's political role, to the extent that it represents a serious bid for power, is more potential than current, not only because of the presence of the Party and police controls, but also because of the lack of any impressive evidence of the military elite's desire for power.

To all this, one significant qualification must be made. In the event of war, and previous to a clear consolidation of power in the hands of one of the political elite, the threat of the military is likely to be at a maximum. Prior to the last war, Stalin's leadership was unchallenged. Party and police controls were particularly strong, and the military were just coming out of the foxholes they entered at the time of the military purges or, as in the case of many of the current leaders, they were just emerging from the lower ranks. Top and bottom, but particularly on the top, they now are probably a much more confident group of men than their counterparts of nearly fifteen years ago. With war, a good bit of signal-calling falls to the military leadership by necessity. In any country, the challenge to civilian control of the military forces is then necessarily greater. Thus, if the Soviet political leadership falters in any way, it is likely that the military will fill the breach, not because it aspires to political hegemony,* but rather to protect and maintain the nation and because such a move by the military in wartime would stimulate the fewest inhibitions on its part.

THE FAMILY

The institution over which central control is exercised least effectively is the family.[6] In many respects the family is most immune to the pressures of the regime. It thus constitutes the single most significant seedbed for the generation, preservation, and transmission of antiregime attitudes and information which the regime would like to suppress. However, the regime sees the family also as an institution which has important possibilities for the transmission of proregime attitudes and information and for the shaping of the character of the younger generation in directions consonant with its aims. For these reasons the regime has made a major effort throughout its history to exercise control over the family and to direct its activities to the regime's ends. Since the family is probably the single most important semi-independent enclave in Soviet society, a rather detailed look at the forces which act to reinforce and those which tend to destroy the solidarity of the family is instructive.

* There is some evidence that officers of high grade, even though they may not be fully committed to the Party, are sufficiently indoctrinated to feel that they are relatively ignorant of "the laws that govern political and social processes." They express themselves as feeling "provincial" compared to the Party theoreticians who know "how the world operates." The lack of ambition to assume governing powers exhibited by the military elite thus far may be traced in part to this attitude.

The family in Soviet urban society is both a social group in which the pre-Bolshevik and sometimes anti-Bolshevik traditionalistic values of the population are expressed and reinforced, and a group beset with internal tensions owing to the penetration of its traditional way of life by new values associated with the special features of the Soviet system. Thus, when the regime took actions contrary to the interests of the members of a particular family, these actions tended to become the target for united opposition. Project data reveal that the most frequent reaction to the arrest of a family member was an increase in family solidarity. The data also suggest that, regardless of the actual arrest experience of people in the family, the feeling of being threatened by the terror served to draw the individual closer to his family and thus to enhance solidarity among family members. In the same way, reactions to some of the more radical features of the officially sponsored prewar ideology — such as the injunction to children to report on the political attitudes of their parents — were generally hostile and had the effect of uniting the family in opposition to the Soviet system.

Other regime-sponsored values, which clashed with traditional attitudes but which had a differential rather than a uniform impact on the individual members of a family, tended to become sources of tension. Such tensions led in turn to the emergence of adjustive mechanisms which acted to protect the integrity of the family as a group. For example, Bolshevik ideology, as dispensed through mass media and the school system, had a marked impact on children's thinking, and young people typically came to espouse a greater portion of officially endorsed values than did their parents. This constituted a severe problem for the Soviet urban family, and some kind of modus vivendi had to be achieved. Analysis indicates that a common solution chosen by Soviet parents was to conceal their own opposition to such values and to "go along with the times." In this instance, the regime has effected an indirect triumph in overcoming the family's independence from external control. Further, the frustrations created by material deprivations appear to have increased interpersonal tensions within the family, although age and class differences affect these reactions to some extent.

RELIGIOUS GROUPS

Organized religion is a source not only of ideas and values which may be (in fact, in most instances actually are) in conflict with those propagated by the regime, but also a potential source of independent control over the thinking and ultimately the behavior of the faithful. The early policy of the regime was to attempt to destroy such independent loci of power. In more recent years the regime has attempted, with marked success, to capture control of them.

Roman Catholicism, except perhaps in some of the newly annexed western territories and in Lithuania, has little organized strength. Protestantism is confined to ethnic minorities and scattered splinter groups such as the Evangelical Christians in the Ukraine. Jews are under attack and disorganized, and the Moslems until recently got limited favored treatment, including much-publicized pilgrimages to Mecca. The Orthodox Church, on the other hand, has new power through the annexation of the Uniate Church and subordination of Orthodox communities in the satellite countries — but it is a power that is strictly at the service of the regime. Gone is the neutral position of the thirties, when the line of the Orthodox Church was "Render unto Caesar the things that are Caesar's." Passive loyalty and obedience are no longer enough in the eyes of the Orthodox Church: there must be an active and indeed a fierce patriotism — which often leads into Pan-Communist as well as Pan-Slavic imperialism. Consider this 1946 statement published in the official *Journal of the Moscow Patriarchate:*

On the 10th of February our great, united multinational Soviet people will . . . tell who of the candidates of the block of Communists are worthy to become members of the Supreme Soviet of the USSR . . . Inspired priests will step forth on the dais and will bless their spiritual children to hasten forth from the church to the ballot boxes. They will bless them to give their votes to the candidates of the block of communists . . . Why? Firstly, because the ministers of the church as well as all her members are at one with and inseparable from their own people. Secondly, because in the entire world there are no conditions more favorable for the flourishing of the Holy Church of Christ than those which are found in the

Soviet land. All the faithful know that the candidates of this block will preserve these conditions and will even improve them, if this be possible.

Indeed, where, in what country, is the church so free from the fetters of the state and from political intrigues, where does the state, while demanding nothing from the church, surround her with such attention? . . . [Nowhere else on] earth are there or can there be better relations [between church and state] than those relations which obtain in our country . . . This is why all the Orthodox Russian people will joyously give their votes to the candidates of the block of communists . . . And in this they will be at one with the entire people.

It does not follow, of course, that all or even many Orthodox Christians, including the editor of the *Journal of the Moscow Patriarchate*, are as enthusiastic about Communism as the above passage would imply. But, at least, the Orthodox Christians are presently caught in a conflict of loyalties, for resistance to the regime is punished by excommunication from the church which they believe represents their hope of salvation. This penalty, for instance, was applied to all who joined the Vlassov movement or otherwise aided the Germans in their struggle with Stalin.[7] Priests were unfrocked, and countless thousands were excommunicated. To the devout Christian, this is a deterrent to active disloyalty, whatever his private convictions about an atheistic state may be. Finally, under the instigation of the Orthodox Church, the leaders of all denominations are presenting a united proregime front as evidenced by the May 1952 "Conference of All Churches and Religious Associations in the USSR for the Defense of Peace." This was attended by at least one Roman Catholic bishop, bishops of Evangelical-Lutheran churches, Jewish rabbis, "Old Believers," and Moslems.

Indications are that the Christian religion will lose strength steadily.[8] During the past decade, the regime has shown limited "tolerance" to the Orthodox Church but no toleration for religious liberty. The tolerance itself may be the belated recognition of the slow pace at which religious sentiment will change in the Russian people, coupled with the realization that a "loyal" church, strictly supervised by the government, constitutes no real threat to the regime. Meanwhile, the elite carry forward their long-range program of "freeing" young Soviet citizens from "religious prejudice." Our data indicate that the intelligentsia and white-collar groups have steadily become more irreligious. With continued exposure to the secularizing effects of urban living and working, ridicule from Pioneer and Komsomol age-fellows, repeated assertions by teachers of the exclusive validity of the "scientific" approach, and emphasis on this life's material possibilities, it seems likely that rejection of religion will increasingly become a pattern among workers and peasants. Many of the Project's life-history respondents state that, although religious themselves, they refused to complicate their children's lives by instilling their own (but regime-disapproved) notions and ideals. Even in families where the parents continue to practice their religion, the religious heritage is not transmitted.

This is not to say that some individuals do not turn to religion later in life as a result of disillusionment with Communism. But the main trend strongly suggests that religion will constantly become less important in the USSR. The process of modifying the behavior of the masses is a slow and difficult one for the regime, but in the religious sphere the regime seems to be winning gradually — not a complete victory but a victory nevertheless. Possibly the state could have virtually stamped out religion in the younger generation by now. Recent stories in the Komsomol newspaper, however, suggest that religious activities even among the youth of industrial centers are tolerated. The building of new churches by workers is chronicled. The regime has eliminated the more blatant features of its antireligious propaganda. Apparently, the leaders have decided that it serves their purposes better to "capture" or harness religion to its own ends. Religious observance, channeled into an expression relatively harmless to the state, may serve for some religious people as a substitute for working off discontents which might otherwise be directed against the regime or, at least, against fulfillment of its specific demands. Nevertheless, the churches remain the only places where people hear a doctrine other than the official one.

Most recently, beginning with the summer of 1954, there has been a resurgence of the Soviet campaign against religion. Apparently, the regime was disquieted by the attraction that religion continued to have among a limited segment of the youth, or it felt that the strength of its position had increased to the point where it could resume a more vigorous attack on religious beliefs and practices in general. It is not inconceivable that there may be more twists, turns, and reversals in Soviet policy toward religion before the final word is said on this matter.* Despite some occasional exaggerated statements in the American press, there has never been any indication that the Soviet regime has abandoned its long-run antagonism to religion. Nor, again contrary to the wishful interpretations of some Western writers, is there any indication that religion has a wholesale attraction for Soviet youth. Some American sources have taken Soviet criticism of the religious practices of a limited number of Komsomols as an indication of a religious revival in the younger generation. There seems to be absolutely no doubt on the basis of our data that the interest of the Soviet youth in religion continued to decline until as late as 1950. Our data do not extend beyond this point, but there is no reason to believe that the trend has been substantially reversed in the last few years.

SCIENCE

Most scientists in the world feel allegiance to a relatively independent community which, theoretically, acknowledges a duty to a nonpolitical and nonnational ideal. To the extent to which a scientist has allegiance to these supranational ideals and responds to their special set of demands and pressures (even within national boundaries), his efforts may be channeled in "undesirable" directions — "undesirable" being defined in terms of the needs of the totalitarian state. The scientist may also prove to be a locus for the generation of independent ideas, arrived at by empirical and logical effort, which challenge the existing ideology. As a result, the regime's intervention in science must have two prongs: act control and thought control. Active interference on the part of the political leader with both the acts and the most abstract theoretical publications of scientists is well known. There have been scientific purges as well as prolonged oral and written discussions, which such figures as Stalin and Zhdanov have entered into vigorously. Some scientists escape into the so-

---

* Since this report was written, there have already been several indications of such twists and turns, reflecting the unsure tactical position of the regime on this issue.

called "inner emigration," a flight from the politicized areas of life. If this flight leads, as it often does, to preoccupation with practical problems of applied science, it tends to be approved; but if it leads to greater concern with the nonapplied aspects of science, the regime will condemn it as "formalism."

NATIONALITY GROUPS

Any tendencies toward genuine autonomy are as zealously watched and fiercely isolated and suppressed as any other sources of conflicting information and opinion. One of the charges against Beria was that of inciting nationalism. The "nationality policy" of the USSR, as expressed in the 1936 Constitution, provides for a great deal of "home rule" and for cultural autonomy. This policy has often been hailed by the innocent abroad as one of the genuinely constructive achievements of the Soviet regime. In fact, however, as we shall see when we discuss the nationality problem more fully, the governments of the individual republics have no autonomous power, and the central authorities are constantly on the watch to prevent any tendencies of the local Party and governmental leadership from establishing relatively independent organizational bases in the national republics. Since Pan-Slavism is not merely condoned but in effect actively fostered, any trend toward a Pan-Islamic or similar regional focus is sharply curtailed.

THE PROFESSIONS

It is characteristic of the professions in nontotalitarian societies that they are self-governing bodies, setting up their own rules of conduct and having their own organization for the enforcement of these rules. In the Soviet Union, professional organizations, of doctors,[9] lawyers, and even of writers, are instruments of the government used to control members of the profession; they are not self-governing institutions.

TRADE UNIONS

Totalitarianism was firmly established with the beginning of the Five Year Plans in 1928 and 1929. One of the most decisive steps in the process of establishing control over Soviet institutions was the conversion of the trade unions from being, to some limited extent, organs of the workers for expression of their interests into being exclusively organs of the government for the control and regulation of the workers. It is not surprising, therefore, that refugees who have worked in Soviet factories regard the trade unions as a branch of the government.

INFORMAL GROUPS

The preceding examples dealt rather exclusively with the regime's efforts to prevent ongoing institutions — family, church, science, the professions — from operating free of central control. In addition, there are *ad hoc* informal groups which spring up as loci of independent power. These so-called "family groups" (see the discussion of informal adjustive mechanisms in Chapter 8) consist of people who form cliques based on common interests and functioning as mutual protective associations. One of their main functions is to permit members of the groups to operate somewhat independently of the center. While these family groups also have a positive function for the system, the regime is generally highly disturbed by this practice of "familyness," and constant attempts are made to root out such practices in factories, on farms, in the government, or wherever they occur. The concern of the regime over "familyness" seems out of proportion to the reality of the situation and appears to be based on a pathological fear at the prospect of a portion of the system being outside its control.

The same pattern — with small variations — exists in all areas of Soviet life. The regime relies upon external controls and force rather than upon adequate motivation. In the USSR it is a cardinal point of policy to structure the individual's life in such a way that situations offering him a choice occur as seldom as possible.* Since the regime realizes that in times of "peace" it can seldom rely on the masses for support on the basis of sentimental allegiance, primary emphasis is placed on a rigorously stratified reward system to insure full effort and on coercion to enforce conformity. The regime deliberately centers much *internal* atten-

* This does not mean that he cannot move upward in the class and occupational hierarchy, only that the regime tries to control fully who moves where.

tion on itself with occasional emphasis on major bureaucratic scapegoats (e.g., Beria) and more often on minor ones. Since it so clearly defines itself as the source of *all* power and decision, it gets the blame as well as the credit. To meet this situation the regime needs scapegoats, so that it can claim that plans and policy were correctly formulated, only to be sabotaged by traitors or imperfectly executed by inefficient individuals. Even the scapegoats, big and small, are pictured as deviants from what the regime claims are *its* high standards.

The political apathy of most citizens and concern for their own safety keeps them from actions disloyal *in intent*. However, the regime fully realizes that acts which are not intentionally political or disloyal may have consequences unfavorable or dangerous to the regime. Because of both their addiction to rational planning and their conviction that "everyone who is not completely for us is against us," the ruling elite has bent every effort to achieve a tremendous amount of centralized control and surveillance. Their success is, however, incomplete.

7

Terror and Forced Labor[1]

More than any other modern state, the Soviet Union uses political terror and forced labor as an integral part of its political and economic system, and does so on a vast scale. Political arrests have been a marked feature of the regime from the time of the Revolution. While they have occurred at all times, the rate of arrests has increased and decreased in successive waves that accompanied various political, economic, and social crises. They reached their peak in the late thirties during the Great Purges, known as the Yezhovshchina, after Yezhov, who was then head of the secret police. However, large waves of arrests have taken place even in the postwar period: one, of people who were suspected of collaboration with the Nazis during the war; another, following the famine of 1947. Presumably, there have also been reasonably large-scale arrests in connection with events since Stalin's death.

The outstanding characteristic of Soviet arrests is not solely their high incidence, but the wide range of offenses that are considered political, and the prophylactic use of arrest. The term "political arrests" is something of a misnomer, since in recent years a very small proportion of such arrests are for direct political actions — unless one were to judge the telling of a joke against the leaders to be a political action. The regime itself has extended the definition of "political" to a wide variety of acts that might otherwise be regarded as nonpolitical crimes — such as theft of grain from a kolkhoz or material from a factory, or negligence in the handling of expensive machinery — as a pretext for stricter enforcement and more drastic punishment.

Furthermore, arrests for specific crimes are surprisingly few. Particularly in periods of large-scale arrests, a high proportion are what Gliksman calls "prophylactic." A person may be arrested not because he has done something, but because his "objective" characteristics suggests that he *might* do something — e.g., a member of his family may have been declared an "enemy of the people," he may have lived in German occupied territory under compromising circumstances, he may have been a member of a group which has fallen into disfavor or the associate or protégé of some deposed political figure, or in the earlier years of the regime his "social origins" may have been suspect. Any sign which may point to a person's loyalty being *potentially* weak — even if only because the state has done him an injustice — can serve as the basis for a prophylactic arrest. These prophylactic arrests are intended to isolate and control the potentially dissident persons who might either commit some overtly disloyal act or spread disaffection to their associates.

An additional effect of widespread arrests either for trivial offenses or for prophylactic purposes is the creation of an atmosphere to which Soviet refugees refer as "the terror." Anxiety over the possibility of arrest for a slight offense, a mistake of judgment, some event over which one has no control, one's associations, or, in some instances, on an apparently arbitrary basis, acts as a very effective means of social control over the behavior of the mass of the citizenry. "The terror," the threat of running afoul of the law, and particularly of the secret police, acts in the Soviet Union very much like an electrified fence in a cow pasture. Like the cow who has once been shocked, the Soviet citizen carries constantly in his mind the image of the secret police as a source of danger. He may, as many interview data suggest, even exaggerate in his own mind the very real danger of the secret police as a device to keep himself from straying too close to the boundaries of improper behavior. One is almost tempted to speculate that, if the secret police ceased to exist, this organization's image as "the terror," built into the citizen's mind, would act for some time as effectively as if the secret police still existed.

The strong feeling of the populace about "the terror" is indicated by the fact that it was spontaneously cited by our respondents more frequently than any other as the aspect of the Soviet system they would want to change. Furthermore, fear of repression was the reason most often given for not returning to the Soviet Union. It is testimony to the potency of "the terror" that some arrested persons actually felt a sense of relief and relative security once they were sent to forced-labor camps. The worst had happened and there was no more "unknown" to fear.[2] Descriptions of all aspects of life — school, work, family, recreation — are saturated with complaints about terroristic political controls and fear of the secret police. Thus, the creation of an atmosphere of terror and the prophylactic use of arrest has the effect of isolating, containing, and suppressing potential expressions of dissent or acts of disloyalty. Our evidence clearly indicates that a relaxation of the threat of the secret police would do more than any other single step to improve the morale of Soviet citizens.*

Of the persons who filled our questionnaires for the Project, 22 per cent reported that they had been arrested one or more times, and 62 per cent reported that some member of their family had been arrested.† It is impossible to say to what extent the experience of these respondents represents an overestimate or underestimate of the proportion of the Soviet population which underwent the same sort of experience, since there was a greater tendency for people who had been arrested to escape if they could, and a simultaneous decrease in their opportunity to escape (some of them having been executed or having died in camps). Nevertheless, those statistics and the qualitative testimony of our respondents, combined with the information given by Western observers, attest to the pervasiveness of arrest in Soviet life. Such arrest does not alienate the individual from all Soviet institutions, but it does increase markedly his hostility toward the regime and doubles the possibility that he will flee the Soviet Union voluntarily — apparently partly as a result of feeling that his future position is insecure.[3]

---

* There is some evidence that, in modest degree, such an easing of "the terror" has occurred. Whether it is sufficient to make a qualitative difference in the general atmosphere is not clear. We firmly believe, however, that it has not been abandoned as an instrument of policy and that a more active arrest policy would unhesitatingly be reinstituted if conditions seemed to require it.

† This family arrest figure, of course, includes a substantial but undetermined amount of double counting when, as was often the case, several members of the same family filled out our questionnaire.

Arrests and forced labor are closely related to the working of the Soviet economy. In only a limited number of instances is a person "convicted" of a political crime executed. (The word "convicted" must be kept in quotes since in many cases judgment is passed by administrative action, rather than by court trial.) A person may be executed if he is of such political importance that his continued existence cannot be risked; or the execution may serve some "educational" function for the populace, such as a warning against certain types of behavior; or it may foster certain myths — for instance, that violators of "Soviet social legality" will be dealt with harshly, as were recent victims of the post-Stalin regime. The vast majority of "convicted" persons, however, are either sent into "corrective labor camps" or exiled to regions where their labor will be useful. Camps are located in terms of economic needs. The secret police, with this immense pool of labor at its disposal, has come to dominate a significant sector of the economy.

The extent to which forced labor is used and its obvious close coördination with the needs of the economy, together with the apparent arbitrariness of many arrests, have caused a number of scholars to suggest that arrests in the Soviet Union were made predominantly on an economic basis, to supply the secret police with needed cadres of workers. There are a variety of reasons for rejecting this overly simple hypothesis. One of the most persuasive is the series of case histories of persons possessing skills badly in demand in the economy as a whole who were used for manual labor. A reconstruction of the history of forced labor in the Soviet Union suggests very strongly that the simple need for workers was not the primary factor in its development. In earlier periods it is clear that there was an enormously inefficient use of imprisoned persons. Engineers, doctors, and others with skills desperately needed throughout the economy were used as manual laborers. As time progressed, there were increasing attempts to bring the system of forced labor in line with the needs of the economy, and individuals seem to have been used in fields more congruent with their level of skill.

Certainly there is little reason to deny the possibility that, on some occasions, the judgment of the secret police in making arrests has been colored by manpower needs in the economic projects under its jurisdiction — that a needed engineer, for example, might have a somewhat harder time demonstrating his innocence. However, even in the postwar period there has been continued evidence of failure to utilize prisoners' skills.

There seems little doubt that the political motive for arrests is primary, and that the economic use of forced labor represents an attempt to utilize the resulting available pool of manpower. The situation is somewhat akin to that in an American army of draftees. Most doctors, many engineers, and a few lawyers will end up working at their professions within the military organization. But *most* lawyers, professors, scientists, and other professional, semiprofessional, and skilled workers will be occupied with general military duties — as infantrymen, record clerks, truck drivers. In the USSR not defense but the "internal security" of the regime lies behind this forced labor "draft," but there is the same lack of discrimination in placement of personnel as in the American military draft.

The number of persons in forced labor in the Soviet Union has been a source of endless speculation and argument by scholars. Because of the wide variety of categories of persons who might be included under this label — labor conscripts who are accused of no offense, but have been drafted for a regular period of service; persons banished or exiled and forced to work in certain geographical areas; persons restrained in geographical mobility after serving a sentence in a camp; and persons actually serving sentences in camps — estimates have run as high as 25 million and more. It is patently impossible that this number is actually in any strict sense under confinement, since it would constitute a preposterously high proportion of the male labor force (the overwhelming proportion of camp inmates being men). However, it seems quite certain that the number of persons actually in "corrective labor camps" at any one time is in the vicinity of several million and may, in fact, be higher. The addition of the above-mentioned categories of exiles would presumably multiply this figure, since they would include large numbers of members of Baltic and other nationalities who were forcibly transported. It is obvious from these minimum figures, from the overwhelming testimony of Soviet refugees, and even to some extent from official Soviet sources that forced labor and the camp system are salient aspects of Soviet life. The proportion of families in which some member has at some time served a sentence is apparently close to the proportion of American families who have had a member in the armed forces.

8

Informal Adjustive Mechanisms

The clear objectives of the regime and the means it has chosen to achieve them (overcontrol, overcommitment, overcentralization, refusal to permit independent concentrations of power) have led inevitably to the development by the people of informal adjustive mechanisms. To be sure, no organization anywhere works exactly as it is supposed to. But in the Soviet Union the discrepancy between the official code and what actually goes on is particularly glaring. The existence of such "deviant" ways of behavior is absolutely essential to the survival of this system.

If one were to accept the idealized blueprint of the Soviet order, he would see a society in which all resources were allocated to the service of an over-all master plan, and in which the efforts of men and machinery were completely controlled and coördinated for the execution of that plan. Even men's thoughts, their very characters, would, according to this blueprint, be molded to fit into the master plan. In practice, however, we find a fairly wide range of deviant behavior, of spontaneous, informal patterns of action which are independent of, and in some measure contrary to, official policy and plans. These informal processes and patterns of deviant behavior (deviant, that is, by the official standards of correct behavior) find their origin partly in the fact that complete control over any complex social order is inherently impossible. But their genesis must also be sought in precisely those aspects of the system which are designed to prevent "spontaneous" — that is, unplanned and uncontrolled — processes. They result from excessively rigid and centralized controls, too close planning in the allocation of resources, and the extreme demands which are put on individual citizens in the performance of their assigned tasks.[1]

Even at the very core of the system the structure is not as monolithic as the myth alleges. The gap between theory and practice is glaring in Party operations. The Party structure is complex and unwieldy. Theoretically, the Central Committee, elected by a Party Congress largely composed of local, regional, and republican Party representatives, designates a Presidium responsible to it. In fact, the Presidium controls the Central Committee, which in turn controls the subordinate Party organs pervading all levels of Soviet political, economic, and social life. These lines of authority seem simple enough: they run straight from top to bottom. But more often than not, important Party members bear direct responsibility for economic, administrative, or other matters. The Party chief on any level (city, region, republic) may be less influential than the economic, administrative, military, or other official on that level — also a Party member — whom he is "controlling." Only at the very top is their authority unqualified, and even there its distribution is temporary and precarious. If one traces out the overlapping of authority in a single sector (say the armed forces), one sees that the balance of power is so involved and so delicate that it can be maintained in equilibrium only by informal mechanisms. Marshals, generals, officers, and field officers operate in two and sometimes three chains of command (military, political, and administrative) and their status is seldom equivalent in the separate chains. The Party Central Committee has a military section which is at the same time the chief political administration of the Ministry of Defense, in charge of Party and political activity within the armed forces.

The deviant behavior which results from these pressures is not always motivated by a desire to avoid one's responsibilities, but may as often be a result of a man's attempt to do the job set before him. It may be selfish in intent, prompted by the desire to make a good record, to earn premiums and bonuses, to avoid punishment or demotion. In the case of persons devoted to the interests of the regime, it may simply be an attempt to cut through red tape in order to get something done under seemingly impossible circumstances. Any combination of these motives may be present in any specific instance.

One of the most pervasive of the informal modes of operation which characterize the system is called *blat*[2] — the use of "good connections" in order to obtain goods and services not readily available through official channels. Thus, the manager of a warehouse with whom a factory director has a good blat relationship may supply him with needed materials or machinery. Blat seldom involves bribery or direct dishonesty. On the simplest level it may mean no more than cutting red tape to get speedily that to which one is in the long run legally entitled. In general, as with all such informal mechanisms and relationships, blat is based on the idea of reciprocity. It is assumed that one will do similar favors in return.

Managers engage in simulation of successful performance by producing an assortment of goods other than those called for by the plan, reducing quality, and falsifying reports. These are all disadvantageous to the system, having only one minor compensating advantage: the turnover of managers due to discharge for poor performance is reduced. Managers also resort to evasions of the plan in order to provide themselves with resources. Blat has a great positive usefulness to the system in providing for those marginal cases with which bureaucratic and centralized planning are unable to cope in sufficient detail. In the absence of blat the incidence of underfulfillment and the fraction of idle resources would be much greater. On the negative side, blat redirects resources into channels which are contrary to the stated objectives of the state.

While these actions of managers result in a pattern of output somewhat divergent from the optimum from the state's point of view, there is a fairly successful device for managers to keep down the cost of production for the pattern of ouput they do produce. If the plants were not already operating at about their optimum point, increasing the output might lower the unit costs — but a few managers find themselves in that happy situation. This is so because plans are set at so high a level that the enterprise operates at increasing cost for the marginal increment. Since the manager is motivated to overfulfill the plan, he can do so and stay within the planned cost only by lowering his cost curve, i.e., by improving his production technique. The effectiveness of this device is generally high, but it is weakened by three considerations: (1) the "safety factor" in the cost target permits the manager to overfulfill the plan to a certain extent without improving his production technique; (2) since costs are considered secondary to output when the two conflict, a manager may press ahead to achieve higher production no matter what the cost, with resultant disorganization and waste that is very dysfunctional; (3) certain institutional rigidities, springing from the system of rationing, discourage factor minimization and therefore militate against cost minimization.

So-called "family groups," which we have already mentioned, develop among persons thrown together by common interests. Thus the manager, the Party organizer, and the production engineer of a factory, some local Party officials, and certain officials of the Ministry in charge may be bound together by common interest in the attainment of good production records for the factory. Not only do they help each other by legal means, but each inevitably becomes involved with the others in responsibility for illegal or quasi-legal methods that must be used in order to attain the production goal. "Family groups," besides aiding each other in a positive fashion, cover up for and protect each other. The immediate effect of "familyness" is to afford protection against excessive demands from above. While the primary motive behind such groupings may be self-interest, sometimes certain jobs get done which would not otherwise be possible. More likely, failures to meet excessive demands are concealed.

In the Soviet industrial system, output targets are set as high and input targets as low as possible. Stocks in the warehouses are inadequate, and managers have great uncertainty concerning the delivery of their planned inputs. Planning is inexact, partly because of bureaucratic inefficiency and partly because of technical problems of aggregating production functions, time lags, and predictions of future outputs. Because of these conditions, managers take advantage of what is called "the safety factor," i.e., they underreport production capacity and hoard materials and labor. Although such practices represent behavior contrary to the express wishes of the state, they have some advantages for the system: (1) they introduce greater flexibility into the system and hence greater responsiveness to emergency demands; (2) they reduce the number of bottlenecks that would otherwise develop; (3) they reduce the incidence of underfulfillment.

The above examples, drawn primarily from industry, could be multiplied from every other area of Soviet life. Physicians, in such a society, find themselves caught between the conflicting claims of individuals and the state. In practice, Soviet physicians wink at a good deal of malingering on the job and protect people from punishment. By mitigating the pressure of the regime upon the individual, the physician actually brings an element of stability to the system.[3] The same role is played by many officials up and down the line in their treatment of persons who seek educational opportunities or jobs from which they are, in theory, barred by social origin or close relation to "enemies of the state." If, in literal fact, every individual on the black list were prevented from any kind of advancement, the result would be a substantial reservoir of disaffected people, and the state would be deprived of their services — except in forced labor camps. In practice, most of the debarred persons eventually evade the regulations, either temporarily or indefinitely. The situation causes them some trouble and risk, but the informal mechanisms permit a reasonably satisfactory adjustment.

Despite the complicated measures undertaken by the regime, the upward reporting of many facts is blocked by the connivance of local officials. The web of mutual interdependence is such that there is group solidarity in suppression and distortion of information. These flaws in the upward flow of communication can be determined directly from the testimony of *émigrés* and from official complaints and exposure in Soviet publication. We seldom know when such forbidden behavior was undetected or unreported, or when the information was simply not used.

Dissatisfied with the tight controls which the regime exercises over information, even loyal citizens may make use of informal extralegal channels.[4] Their motives may vary from sheer curiosity, through concern for personal safety, to a desire to do one's job more effectively. Complete suppression of informal, officially disapproved communication is, of course, impossible. While the regime generally takes a negative attitude toward them, these informal patterns do, in some ways, function for the system. They reduce some of the frustrations that the populace feels because of the regime's practices, and individuals in responsible posts often get facts that permit them to perform better. Actually, it is also likely that the regime itself deliberately uses these illicit channels from time to time to spread rumors that serve its purpose.

Informal mechanisms originate in most instances in the efforts of individual citizens to solve their own problems within the framework of the system. What, however, explains their persistence in the light of the tight controls and severe punishments with which the regime responds to deviant behavior in general? The answer lies in the essentially ambivalent attitude of the regime toward such informal mechanisms. In theory, it is violently opposed to them. Two related factors, however, inhibit the suppression of these processes. The first is the fact that they unquestionably permeate the system from top to bottom. While every official may disapprove of them in principle, there are few who do not approve or condone some of them in practice. Every bureaucrat sees in some operation for whose success he is responsible the necessity of cutting through red tape. Secondly, he knows that other officials also disapprove *in principle;* therefore, he does his best to prevent the spread of information about such informal mechanisms as are operating within his own bailiwick.

Even when information about such informal mechanisms reaches those in higher positions — and there can be absolutely no question, judging by the treatment of such topics in the Soviet press, that higher-ups are aware of their pervasiveness — there is no consistent disposition manifested to suppress them ruthlessly, as the regime has done with other practices to which it is opposed. The attitude of the leaders seems to be that such practices are "bad" and should be kept under control, but they also seem both to feel that these abuses are inevitable and to sense that the entire system might bog down if they were completely suppressed.*

---

* It is also conceivable that the regime not only *expects* that the official system will be violated, but calculates that the guilt engendered by such violations will act as a spur to performance and to conformity in other respects. The numerous violations of rules necessary to effective management also provide those on top with a fat dossier which the manager knows is always there to be used against him if those on top decide his time has come.

The regime's ambivalent attitude probably conforms pretty well to the reality of the situation. As with so many other aspects of the Soviet system, these informal mechanisms may be regarded either as a strength or as a weakness, depending almost entirely on the time perspective which one takes. It is possible to conceive of them as being very considerable detriments in the short run. For instance, scarce supplies may be drained off from priority activities via blat. Attempts to shake the slack out of the system of production may be prevented by "familyness." The network of informal communications may be the channel for the leaking of vital information. If, on the other hand, the regime should at any time be lured into tightening controls over such mechanisms too drastically, the system would probably soon be in trouble. In the long run, a certain amount of such deviant behavior must be tolerated. But, if the controls are too lax, these mechanisms will probably result in excessive featherbedding, and in evasion of the regime's schedule of priorities. Their main disadvantage, from the standpoint of the regime, is that they may inhibit its flexibility of action over the short run, and may in fact make it impossible to execute certain programs rapidly enough to make them effective. But, precisely because they may prevent or cripple certain programs in the short run, they may also save the system over the long run. They act very much like automatic compensators preventing excessive commitment of the system to one course of action at any one time.

A word of caution must be entered against a frequent interpretation which is made of such mechanisms. They are usually viewed only as evidence of the breakdown of the formal mechanisms of planning and control and therefore exclusively as a sign of weakness in the system. What is overlooked in this interpretation is that the informal mechanisms take over and keep things running at places and times when the formal mechanisms are inadequate. It is true, however, that the regime is constantly faced with decisions whether to impose tighter controls or to let the informal mechanisms run their course.

Informal mechanisms, while definitely adjustive for the society, create prevalent patterns of interpersonal relationships that contravene the official code. Faced with the task of getting things done under impossible conditions of bureaucratic regulation, having his fate lie in the hands of some official of the Party or government, the Soviet citizen has learned that it is extremely important to assess the man with whom he is dealing. A superior or official who shows his hand and who expresses his emotions directly is a safer man to deal with than a person who is coldly impersonal. He is a human being, subject to human emotions, and potentially responsive to one's own plight.

Most societies are held together by face-to-face group loyalties. It is characteristic of the Soviet system, however, that such loyalties are deemed intolerable. Soviet publications are filled with attacks on "familyness." Intermediate authorities in the Soviet hierarchy have full *responsibility* for their subordinates, but they have *no claim to the primary allegiance* of these subordinates.[5] To pursue the matter even further, not only are the intermediate authorities not entitled * to allegiance, but one of their duties is to serve as a target onto which the criticism for the failures of the system can be deflected. By permitting criticism of the bureaucrats, the top Soviet leaders attempt to keep the loyalty of the citizenry focused on the leadership. Thus, in their efforts to prevent the development of loyalties to intermediate authorities, they both necessitate and facilitate the emergence of a supreme idealized leader. The destruction of local group allegiances, however, necessitates creating the image of a leader of sufficient stature to command the loyalty of the populace over the heads of those officials with whom they are associated in day-to-day contact. According to the myth, nothing ever gets properly accomplished unless the top leaders concern themselves personally with everything: Stalin himself had to watch and discipline the very highest bureaucrats. To this degree, therefore, the system will have a real problem so long as the present form of "collegial" rule persists.

* Formally. In fact, some intermediate authorities can command allegiance from their subordinates, either because of their personal qualities or because of their opportunities to hire, promote, and fire. It is precisely because of these downward allegiances that purges spread through networks. Conversely superiors must, to some extent, keep their subordinates happy lest the latter report the former for actual or claimed malfeasance.

9

Rigidity–Flexibility

The long-range goals of the leadership appear to be highly stable. This fact plus the tightness of the operating system generally makes for major elements of rigidity. Certain courses of action persist on the domestic scene long after events seem to argue most persuasively for a change. An example is the postwar agricultural policy which resulted in the killing of cattle by peasants. This result was entirely contrary to the regime's aims, but it took five years after the facts were established to reverse the policy. Rigidity is likewise enhanced by the doctrinaire and dogmatic nature of the ideology. Finally, rigidity is further created and reinforced by the extreme character of the control system and the fixed nature of the communications network which prevents critical information from reaching the top. It is not so much lies as half-truths ("slightly slanted reality") that are reported upward. Within the USSR the distortions from different organizations reporting on the same or overlapping topics are probably slanted variously enough so that the top echelon will note and investigate the discrepancies. However, the network abroad, though undoubtedly widespread, cannot, in the nature of the case, provide as many somewhat independent cross checks for the Kremlin. There is abundant testimony of informed and competent witnesses that the ruling elite get information from the West regarding matters of politics, popular attitudes, and economics that is slanted predominantly in congenial directions. This would appear much less the case as far as technology and science are concerned, for here the objective facts rapidly become public knowledge which it would be dangerous for Soviet agents and diplomatic staffs to report in distorted form.

To turn to the other pole: *tactical flexibility.* The massive elements of rigidity arise from the total nature of the system and specifically from the almost compulsive trend toward "rational consistency." Since Communist leaders use ideas and values instrumentally, relative emphasis is modified or shifted to suit immediate purposes — *so long as a façade of consistency is maintained.* Hence the leadership is characterized by extreme flexibility in many of its short-run goals in a way that has been much noted and marveled at in the West. This flexibility is facilitated inside the system by the absolute control of power and of mass communications. Nevertheless, this facilitation is more than offset internally by the established features of the system which cannot be reshaped in the short run. Moreover, the rigidity tends to increase with the age of the system. There appears to be great dependence today upon a generation of higher bureaucrats who tend to be self-perpetuating. However, there is a sufficient supply of these self-perpetuating higher bureaucrats so that some individuals can be purged without much disturbance to the overall functioning of the system.

Short-run flexibility shows its greatest development in the sphere of foreign policy.* One of the most basic characteristics of Soviet foreign policy is that the rulers pursue diverse policies simultaneously, though with different emphasis. Western observers have sometimes been misled by this fact. They have assumed flexibility throughout the system. Even though foreign policy is more flexible than domestic policy, the relative rigidity of domestic policy in itself places limits on the flexibility of foreign policy.

Indeed, there is another condition under which Soviet foreign policy becomes rigid. This happens when the opponent makes a major move that is completely unexpected, altogether outside the range of possible alternatives previously calculated by the Kremlin. The leaders were stunned by the German attack in 1941. Molotov talked almost like a child to the German ambassador, complaining that he could not understand, that the USSR

* The recent (July 1955) tone of conciliation in Soviet foreign relations, including Khrushchev's extraordinary visit to Belgrade and climaxed by the "summit" meeting, is only the most recent striking example of the assertion made above a year earlier.

had fulfilled all its obligations to Germany.[1] It took a considerable time for the Bolsheviks to regroup. The Communist leadership almost certainly did not expect that the United States would intervene militarily in Korea in 1950; prompt American and United Nations action temporarily paralyzed further Communist moves. It took some time for the Communist bloc to replan and regroup. There is an old Russian proverb, still frequently quoted in the USSR, which says, "The dancer cannot dance unless he can start from the right corner of the stove." Some evidence[2] suggests that the Communist elite places unusual reliance upon a most careful advance diagnosis of the intentions of the opponents. Rapid and skillful improvisations will be made by the Soviets as long as the antagonist behaves within the range of foreseeable possibilities. But if an altogether unanticipated gambit is undertaken, the Soviet leadership is blocked. Their "rational calculus" has been in grave error. They go into a huddle and revise it, often reversing previous policy to draw upon the views of a faction of the top leadership which has been temporarily in a minority or out of favor with the dictator. If one studies situations (such as Brest Litovsk; Poland, 1920; China, 1927; Germany, 1941) where the calculations of the ruling elite have seriously miscarried, one finds many abrupt reversals which resort to different versions developed by opposing groups of the top echelon.

At any rate, internally and in foreign policy, there have been enough sudden alternations both between rigidity and flexibility and between two drastically contrasting courses of policy and action to justify our listing *cyclical behavior* as one of the distinctive operating characteristics of the Soviet system. The propensity toward abrupt reversals and the drawing upon views very recently in disfavor is undoubtedly related in part to the strong instrumental bias of the Soviet system. That is, if something fails or does not work satisfactorily, another approach which the Politburo had temporarily discarded may be tried in the hope that it will work.

In any case, there is a strong tendency to veer to extremes in whatever direction is being followed at the moment. Push a program (whether it be farm collectivization or a purge) about as far as humanly possible. Then either relax considerably or go off hell-bent on the opposite course. These cycles expressed in pronounced form can be seen throughout Soviet history in a wide variety of contexts: the economic policies of the regime's earliest years versus the NEP (New Economic Policy), the shifts to and from "left" and "right" on basic ideological and planning questions during the twenties; opposition — alliance — war with Nazi Germany; Zhdanov-Malenkov; the recent purge of the doctors and anti-Semitism; the vagaries of postwar agricultural policy. The existence of such "cycles" in Soviet behavior should not, however, be understood as associated with lack of form and plan in the execution of policy once the new phase or cycle has decisively been entered upon. On the contrary, once the line is set, there is a marked tendency to operate mechanically, or, as we have expressed it elsewhere in this study, "by the numbers."

Behavior within lower Party organizations is a nice illustration of cyclical behavior in the specific form of an alternation between rigidity and flexibility. The top leadership tries to use these lower units as an instrument for providing some flexibility. The lower Party organs are thus supposed, through criticism and self-criticism, to uncover errors and shortcomings, to keep the center properly informed, and to show initiative. Yet the rigidity of the top leadership itself has steadily narrowed the areas in which initiative can be applied. Lower Party functionaries and rank-and-file members have learned from bitter experience that they had better be cautious rather than independent. Overcaution and apathy are then treated by shock therapy from the center. There are shake-ups in personnel and wholesale disciplinary actions. A new surge of energy sweeps through Party work, but it can be expected to signify nothing more than the beginning of another cycle which will lead back to cautious or apathetic bureaucratism.[3]

Within the total system, then, there tend to be sudden sharp alternations more than slow and gradual adjustments. There is "coexistence of contradictions," and almost any official attitude may be suddenly replaced by its opposite.

10

Caution at Major Risks
in Foreign Affairs

The narrow escapes from complete disaster which marked the Russian Civil War and World War II with Germany made a deep impression upon the psychology of Soviet leaders. They are, as all the world knows, aggressive enough abroad, but their aggression has thus far been carried out piecemeal under circumstances which they had carefully — and usually correctly — calculated as favorable. At times (as in the instances of the Berlin air lift and Tito's defection) when there appeared to be genuine risk of all-out war, they have pulled in their horns. Expansion — but only within the limits rigidly set by the overriding requirements of the security of the regime — has been the consistently predominant motive of Soviet foreign policy — at least in Europe. Only once in the whole of Soviet history (the invasion of Poland in 1920)* has the leadership undertaken foreign aggression *during a domestic crisis in the USSR.* And the record shows that this decision was narrowly made after much controversy. Many Western commentators have fallen into the error of projecting Communist analyses of fascism onto the USSR. The Marxist contention, probably correct, has been that the fascists had to solve domestic crises by foreign adventures. Fascism and Communism are similar in many ways, but in this respect Communist behavior (thus far) is consistent: the internal security of the home base comes first and must be strengthened as a basis

* And some scholars have argued that Poland precipitated this war.

for further expansion.* The Soviet leadership is apparently reluctant to undertake aggression *on or near the borders of European USSR* unless the domestic situation is well in hand and the foreign situation propitious (e.g., the Finnish war in 1940, and the seizure of Baltic states). Whether or not there appears to the outside observer to be any threat of war, propaganda stressing the danger of outside attack is carried out in the Soviet Union at a consistently intensive level at all times in order to solidify home morale and in order to identify opposition to the regime's demands with "treason" to the motherland.

It is not suggested that this propensity for caution so far as major adventures are concerned will continue indefinitely. Indeed there are three factors which indicate modification:

(1) The fact that the present leadership has even less personal and direct knowledge of the West than had Stalin's generation;

(2) The vast increase in the territorial base controlled or strongly influenced (China) by Moscow;

(3) A lessening of the disproportion in industrial productivity between the Communist bloc and the West.

If, as some authorities predict, Communist industrial production of goods that are militarily important reaches parity with the West by about 1965, the regime's caution may largely vanish. On the other hand, an equally good argument would suggest that, if the USSR remains stable until 1965, and attains real industrial might and a higher standard of living, both the regime and the people might have too great a stake in the *status quo* to willingly risk taking the initiative in global war. There are also factors which the Soviet government, like all governments, must consider. A global war with nuclear weapons is not at all likely to end in "victory" for either side. Not conquest but annihilation must be the objective of a war with no holds barred. Assessing

---

* It will be apparent to many that the current (mid-1955) Soviet *détente* fits very closely the pattern sketched here. As the magnitude of domestic problems became fully apparent, the response of the Soviet leaders was hardly one of becoming more aggressive. On the contrary, the apparent increase in the conscious acknowledgment of domestic difficulties was paralleled by a decrease of Soviet aggressiveness abroad, although it must be acknowledged that in this development other factors, such as the uncertainty of the new multiple leadership and the firmness of the Western response to Soviet tactics, may have played the major role.

either motivations relative to such a holocaust or vulnerabilities under it is extremely difficult. It has been argued that the threat of the extensive and thorough destruction of cities is much greater to the Soviet regime, since the markedly antiregime peasants would become the main sources of power in being or regenerative potential. This is certainly relevant, although it is to be doubted whether it requires refined considerations to impress on the Soviet leadership the general inadvisability of war with nuclear weapons, win or lose — assuming those words would have much meaning in such a conflict.

In any case, it can be forecast safely for the immediate foreseeable future that the USSR will be more prudent in taking risks that might involve survival than would other totalitarian states of comparable power in comparison to potential enemies. The regime has its enduring goals — and this must never be forgotten — but there is no present evidence that the regime will chance defeat in order to attain these goals *quickly*. Among other things, there is still too much of a residuum of conviction that, with patience, victory can be won the easy way: through the "internal collapse" of capitalism or through internecine wars among "imperialist powers."

In general, one can anticipate that those resistant to a premature* general war will be drawn mainly from the following elite groups: those who have had firsthand experience with the West and know its power (a significant part of this group consists of top military leaders); those who really believe the Marxist theory of the inevitable decay of capitalism; and those who, in terms of personal background, have still a small affiliation with Western values. Probably the majority of the upper elite hold a position something like this: they are committed to external expansion but with a long time-scale in mind, a willingness to wait, and a substantial vested interest in avoiding any external action that would endanger their internal security. Finally, there is the factor that the overwhelming majority of the Soviet people view with horror the idea of another war in the near future and would have

---

* There is, to be sure, always the danger that the Kremlin will miscalculate as they did in the North Korean attack in 1950. They may decide that war is no longer "premature" on the basis of inaccurate information from abroad.

little motivation unless they felt sure the motherland had been attacked first.

Of course, the steady position of Communist doctrine is that the foreign policy of "imperialist powers" is shaped by the blind forces generated by "the internal contradiction of capitalist economy." This is the picture of Western countries which the present regime attempts to disseminate both at home and abroad — with the additional imputation that the United States, in particular, blocks and refuses to accept the peaceful overtures of the Communist bloc.*

We have, up to this point, concentrated on presenting what we feel to be particularly characteristic and, in a sense, distinctive in the Soviet approach to problems of foreign affairs. We do not mean to suggest thereby that an understanding, much less a prediction, of Soviet international action can be attained *solely* on the basis of a knowledge of Soviet long-range goals, the special characteristics of its leadership, the nature of the social system, or all three in combination. On the contrary, we share the feeling that too often efforts made to understand Soviet (and indeed our own) foreign policy woefully neglect to give adequate weight to the fact that it is conducted by the Soviet Union as but one state acting in a system of states. Many acts of the Soviet regime in the realm of foreign policy are primarily *reactions* to earlier actions of the United States or to anticipated actions of this country, as indeed many of our acts are primarily reactions to Soviet acts. To recognize this, however, and to give full weight to the necessary and expectable adjustments to the realities of international power politics, which might be made in any foreign office, does not rule out the tremendous role of distinctive national styles of playing the foreign-policy game. Even less does it account for differences in long-range goals and objectives. We do not believe that Soviet leaders are acting as

* As a result of the "summit" meetings the United States did have an unusually good press in the Soviet Union, the central papers actually affirming that we are interested in peace. It is not to be expected, however, that the day-to-day line of the Soviet press, although no longer vituperative, will change *basically* with regard to capitalist and particularly United States foreign policy.

any power group would act if it were in control of foreign policy for the Russian land mass; nor are they acting as would any other power group in another great state elsewhere in the world. To choose but one marked example, we have already noted the considerable difference that has existed between the Soviet and the Fascist approach to war, with the latter regarding war as a way of resolving domestic tensions. As in the case of other great powers, the Soviet regime must adjust to the balance of international politics and react to the actions of its chief competitors in the power struggle. But this formula, even if fully spelled out, hardly begins to make Soviet foreign policy comprehensible unless the analysis takes into consideration the indispensable distinctively Soviet elements such as the caution we have discussed here.

Part III

THE INDIVIDUAL IN SOVIET SOCIETY

11

Soviet Policy Toward the Individual

The fact that the interests of the individual in Soviet society are placed second to and far below the interests of the state should not lead us to assume that the regime is not concerned about the individual. The very nature of the Soviet system makes the body of citizens, collectively, the key resource of the regime, and thereby a matter of great concern. Because of the overcommitment of resources characteristic of Soviet policy in recent decades, the regime treats the mass of the population as the most flexible of its resources. Economy and efficiency in handling physical resources such as coal, machine tools, and agricultural produce can be effected, but there is some clearly evident physical limitation on how far they can be extended. There is, however, no equally precise and apparent limitation on the degree to which the human contribution can be stretched, and it can be said, with only slight exaggeration, that the tendency of the regime has been to treat people as *the* flexible resource in the system. Cutting back the individual's consumption requirements has been one of the key sources for capital accumulations. His efforts have been the flexible element in the regime's production plans, as the leaders have followed the policy of forcing the individual to extremes of exertion by maximizing both the rewards and the punishments that exist for him. They have made him individually responsible for the failure of the system, yet oblige him to give the *regime* credit for its achievements. Many of the "rewards" are placed in an ever more distant future. Nevertheless, there is reliable testimony that at least some of the Soviet people are still motivated by these apocalyptic promises, however much they may grumble privately over the inadequacy of their present standard of living.

The degree to which the regime holds the individual responsible for the functioning of the Soviet system is based on: (*a*) the regime's refusal to reduce commitments except under extreme pressure, and (*b*) an implicit belief in the adequacy of the institutions which the regime has set up. In essence, the regime holds that all official goals are attainable, and that existing institutions are adequate. It is, therefore, up to individuals to attain these goals within the framework of existing institutions. Goals and institutions tend to be revised only after every effort has been made to accomplish a given task by exerting greater pressure on the individual citizen.

The official formulation of the relationship of the individual to the state has been given an appearance of spurious continuity by adroit verbal manipulation. Throughout the history of the Soviet Union, the regime has stressed harmony between the needs of the individual and those of the state. Immediately after the Revolution, this statement meant that a social order would be developed to serve the needs and interests of the individual citizen. In more recent years, it has come to mean that a type of citizen will be developed who serves the needs and interests of the state.[1] This aim is accomplished (or attempted) by elaborate concern for character training and social control. The regime is not *indifferent* to the welfare of its citizens, but its concern for it is dictated by the relevance of their welfare to the functioning of the system and the accomplishment of the long-range goals of the regime. The leaders go as far as they think they can in pressing armament programs, industrialization, and collectivization of agriculture. These things come first as long as the morale of the people does not become so low as to threaten these programs.

One of the salient features of the operation of all Soviet institutions is the extent of the demands and responsibility placed on the individual — the extent to which, with a minimum of assistance and resources, he is expected to accomplish a task. While he is expected to follow correct procedures, his failure to deliver the goods is almost invariably considered to be a worse offense than violation of correct procedures.

Not only is the continuance of the system dependent on the individual in a crucial sense, but the survival and happiness of the

Soviet citizen is equally dependent on other individuals. In many situations, the sole hope of the citizen is to find some person who will help him out of a difficulty. Hence, the Soviet citizen becomes a specialist in a very esoteric form of communication in which, with an initial minimum commitment of himself, he assesses the degree to which he can place confidence in the other person. Material from projective psychological tests shows in an interesting way how Great Russians of Soviet origin are very concerned with the characteristics of the "other" as opposed to a preoccupation with the self.

The role of the individual in Soviet society may be viewed in contrasting perspectives, from the point of view either of the functional requirements of the system, or of the individual citizen pursuing his own needs and interests within the framework of the system. Obviously, regime policies and the response of the citizen form an interacting system in which each affects the other, and each in turn responds to the other. We have outlined those broad aspects of official policy that are the essential determinants of the lot of the individual in Soviet society. In the following chapters, we shall discuss the citizen's response to his life situation and to the Soviet system, and then return to consider, in summary fashion, the interrelationship of regime policy and the behavior and attitudes of the citizen.

12

Sources of Satisfaction
and Dissatisfaction

It is extraordinarily difficult to give a balanced picture of the sources of satisfaction and dissatisfaction in the life situation of the citizens of any country, or to convey in any meaningful sense how happy or unhappy the populace of a country is from day to day. Even if we restrict ourselves to the most important factors of satisfaction or dissatisfaction, an inherent difficulty remains. The most effective sources of satisfaction and dissatisfaction are such commonplace aspects of daily life that they are unlikely to be seen as systematic elements of the society. This is particularly true of sources of satisfaction. By and large, satisfaction is taken for granted. It results from such casual activities as eating, work, recreation, rest, sex, and association with other persons. *Dis*satisfaction is, in most instances, some violation or failure of legitimately anticipated satisfactions — *absences* of food, rest, sex, and good interpersonal relations. We are likely to be aware of violations of satisfactions, whereas we take their fulfillment for granted. The result is that any analysis of sources of satisfaction and dissatisfaction tends inevitably to overstress the elements of dissatisfaction, since it focuses selectively on the violation of that which is taken for granted and which would not come to our attention except for this violation. In any society, including the Soviet Union, it is a rare individual who spends the bulk of his time being either consciously miserable or consciously joyful with the business of keeping alive, and satisfactions and dissatisfactions are pretty much imbedded in the events of the day.

Therefore, it is an impossible task to state precisely how satisfied or dissatisfied a group of people is. However, even after we have made due discount, the *émigrés* made an extrordinarily large number of complaints about their lives in the Soviet Union. One gets the impression that the Soviet populace is quite dissatisfied, judged by the standards of most Western countries. But there are very marked group differences in the level and nature of satisfaction and dissatisfaction. Children of the intelligentsia lead a happy life by almost every standard, and many refugees give a glowing picture of their childhood and youth. Many skilled industrial workers seem to have had a considerable amount of job satisfaction. The older peasants, on the other hand, appear to lead the most miserable life of any group, and yet it is spotted with certain distinctive satisfactions — those derived from religion, for example — and is free from some of the anxieties that beset the intelligentsia. It is not possible, therefore, to talk about levels of satisfaction in any absolute sense. We must content ourselves with drawing a topographical map on which it is possible to identify peaks, plains, and valleys, but on which sea level is unknown.

Since this is the first point at which we shall introduce conclusions based on the statistical findings of the Project, it may be well for us to comment briefly on our use of these data. First of all, we do not, of course, assume for a moment that the distribution of answers gotten from our sample represents the distribution which would have been obtained from a random sample of the Soviet population. In some instances, however, we assume that our sample provides a *conservative* estimate of what would be found in the Soviet population. For example, when 80 per cent or more of our respondents indicate they would retain a Soviet institution such as state ownership of heavy industry, we believe it reasonable to assume that at least as high a proportion of the Soviet population would favor such an institution. More often, however, we are concerned with patterns of responses, and, in this connection, we assume that the pattern of responses is the same as would be found in the Soviet population. Thus, if our respondents complained more bitterly of housing conditions than they did of food shortages, it seems likely that they were reflecting the priority of complaints that existed in the Soviet population at the time. Or, if an overwhelming majority of the intelligentsia indicates satisfaction with working conditions and only a small minority of rank and file workers does so, it seems reasonable to infer that the same relationship holds in the Soviet population. The actual statistics presented from time to time in the text are introduced for purposes of giving the reader some idea of the order of magnitude of the findings with which we are dealing, rather than precise estimates of attitudes presumably held by the Soviet populace. For many purposes, such descriptive phrases as "most," "more," or "fewer" are used where "a minority" or "a majority" could be, and sometimes have been, substituted.

The reader will remember that our *statistical* findings must be assumed to refer conservatively to a date no later than 1940. However, since we are not concerned here with precise estimates of the distribution of opinions and experiences in the Soviet population but with patterns and gross estimates, it would take really major changes in Soviet society to affect the conclusions which we draw from these data. Of course, we have not assumed that such major changes have not occurred without evidence to support such an assumption. We have, as indicated in the first chapter, interviews with eighty postwar refugees, some of whom left the Soviet Union as late as 1950. In these interviews we made a special effort to learn about changes which had taken place in Soviet life in the years following World War II. Furthermore, we have, as a matter of course, tried to keep abreast of more recent developments via the Soviet and American press and the accounts of visitors to the Soviet Union. In our use of the Project's statistical findings, we have tried to indicate, wherever relevant, whether or not changes in Soviet life would be presumed to have modified the conditions which our data reflect, and in what direction these changes will have occurred.

Throughout this chapter, it must be remembered that we are discussing sources of satisfaction and dissatisfaction in the life situation of the Soviet citizen. As we shall indicate in Chapters 13 and 16, satisfaction and dissatisfaction in one's daily life can by no means be equated with loyalty and disloyalty to the society in which one lives or to its leaders, nor with allegiance to or disaffection from the institutions of that society. A Soviet citizen may experience a good deal of day-to-day discontent without attributing it to the type of society in which he lives or to the policies set by the people who run it. Another citizen may "have it good" and still be alienated and disloyal. The relationship between alienation, disloyalty, and dissatisfaction will be developed gradually in following chapters. In this chapter, however, we are dealing only with day-to-day satisfactions and dissatisfactions, and the reader should not infer that these are necessarily effective sources of loyalty and disloyalty.

THE POLITICAL IMPACT

Pro-Soviet apologists depict the Soviet citizen as strongly identified with the regime, highly dedicated, proud of the system's achievements, and deriving great pleasure from this relationship. Refugees tend predominantly to picture the populace as opposed to and oppressed by the regime, and as suffering constant unhappiness in relation to the political order. A careful reading of the evidence favors, in general, the position of the refugees, with the reservation that there are subgroups in the population who conform to the image created by the apologists. Our information indicates that those whose balance sheets are weighted toward a predominance of satisfying experiences are largely the young and the well-to-do.

While they are still in school and have not yet come in contact with Soviet reality, young, and in general more highly placed, Soviet citizens often derive very real psychic gratification from a romantic identification with the Soviet order which they see as a dynamic system, making tremendous strides forward in building a new and better world and standing strongly in opposition to "reactionary capitalist forces." This form of gratification would appear to reach its maximum in late adolescence when the individual is most predisposed to such romantic identifications and before the citizen has observed the disparity between the realities of Soviet life and the idealized picture given him by official spokesmen. Such romantic identification is more prevalent among highly placed youths who are better able to escape firsthand contact with the seamier side of Soviet life, but probably is fairly typical of almost all Soviet youth. In any event, the majority of our respondents seem to agree that this early identification with the Soviet regime is characteristic of *most* Soviet youths, and presumably will increase with the years as the proportion of people who have directly experienced other forms of social and political organization decreases. A potential crisis in this identification comes when the youth are put in closer contact with the reality of Soviet life. However, our data indicate that the bulk of the youth pass through this period of potential crisis without a substantial, enduring decrease of loyalty. However, even among those of our respondents who clearly had experienced a good deal of youthful gratification from a romantic identification with the Soviet system and the regime, their post-crisis loyalty was qualitatively different, being based more on acceptance of and accommodation to the realities of Soviet life. While in many cases they retain an identification with the goals of the regime, there is less starry-eyed idealism in this identification.

Aside from the minority who, at any one time, find satisfaction in identification with the regime, the mass of the Soviet population appears to suffer rather uniformly from the fear of punitive action by the regime and from resentment at the intensive politicization of all areas of life. In proportion to the degree of responsibility that is associated with their jobs, even those devoted to the regime experience constant anxiety that they will suffer some penalty, ranging from reprimand to execution, for some real or imagined offense that cannot be foreseen or controlled. This anxiety reached its peak during the period of the purges of the thirties. People who lived through these years retain a good deal of this fear from their memories of these purges. Even before Stalin's death, however, this sort of tension seems to have decreased. Substantial portions of the population resent the fact that they are discriminated against because of their social origins or their accidental association with some person or event. This, again, is a decreasing source of discontent. Additionally, the populace is irritated by repeated, forced exposure to regime propaganda, and in many cases are forced to reiterate this propaganda even when they are opposed to it. One significant result of the penetration of politics into all aspects of life is the feeling of intense resentment at having no area of privacy. Again these sources of dissatisfaction are not necessarily correlated with disloyalty. Some of the most pro-Soviet of our respondents, for example, justified the all-pervasiveness of Soviet propaganda, but in the same breath complained of its boringness.

Objectively, all of these unsatisfactory aspects of Soviet politics seem to be most strongly associated with the upper positions in Soviet society. All respondents see the more highly placed and generally more desirable jobs as being most exposed to the danger of political arrest. The upper groups are unquestionably in greater internal or personal conflict because of their closer association with, and participation in, regime policies and actions. Nevertheless, in most instances, the lower classes express about the same degree of disturbance concerning danger of arrest and the interference of politics in their daily lives. Apparently, differences in the objective situation are offset by the greater tendency of refugees from the lower classes to experience diffuse, undifferentiated hostility toward everything associated with their lives in the Soviet Union. Furthermore, the lower classes, particularly the peasantry, have been subject to waves of arrest of an episodic nature. While all classes, therefore, express about equal concern with political danger and the politicization of life, these feelings are more directly linked to an occupational role in the case of the upper classes. This is reflected not only in the consensus of our respondents that more highly placed jobs are more dangerous, but also in the fact that persons holding such jobs complained more about political interference *in the work situation,* even though they did not complain more about politics in other areas of life.

Reaction to such aspects of Soviet political life ranges from a low order of chronic irritation and discontent to out-and-out hostility to the system. The most important political danger is to be arrested oneself or to have a member of one's family arrested. The citizen ordinarily reacts to this experience with a good deal of hostility to the regime, and with about the same amount of hostility whether he himself or a member of his family was arrested, since an arrest in the family can have quite drastic consequences for all of its members. Significant, however, is the fact that this hostility is not directed toward many of the institutional aspects of the Soviet system, such as government ownership of industry: people do not change their social and political attitudes, but merely become angry with the existing regime.

There are indications here that, as with respect to other sources of dissatisfaction in the Soviet order, the younger generation is beginning to take the intrusion of politics in daily life more for granted than did the older group. This is most clearly expressed in the reaction of our respondents to political interference in the work situation. Older respondents were more likely both to mention this factor and to consider it a major problem.

These political sources of dissatisfaction have been singled out for separate consideration, but it will be seen in the discussion that follows that the terror and politicization penetrate all aspects of day-to-day existence, even though the terror is decreasing in intensity.

DAY-TO-DAY CONDITIONS OF LIFE

By the standards of Western society, the day-to-day conditions of life in the Soviet Union are distinctly unrewarding. Yet, intergroup differences in rewards, and especially in feelings of satisfaction, are perhaps as striking as is the generally low level of reward and satisfaction. While the Soviet intelligentsia lack much that their opposite numbers in Western society have, the picture of life in the Soviet Union that is given by refugee intelligentsia makes it clear that they would have considered their day-to-day existence satisfactory and enjoyable if they had been freed from the threat of punitive political action and from excessive politicization of their lives. The manual groups, however, recall their lives as continually dreary and unrewarding.

MATERIAL CONDITIONS

All groups complain about material conditions. Yet there are, of course, substantial intergroup differences. Manual groups uniformly see themselves as worse off than the majority of the population (even though they obviously constituted this majority) and considered their material conditions to be generally highly unsatisfactory. However, in regard to some conditions — food, in particular — a majority of the intelligentsia even reported that they considered their conditions "satisfactory," a considerable concession from a refugee group.

Complaints about material conditions can, for the most part, be supported from official Soviet sources. Refugee respondents, however, reveal an interesting priority of complaints with respect to the three main items in their standard of living. Clothing is the source of greatest complaint, housing follows, and food is last. We base this order of priority on the relative proportion of persons in each social group who regarded each of these items as "satisfactory" in their own life experience.

Even among the intelligentsia a majority of respondents complained that clothing was inadequate. They reported that a professor's new suit would cause a stir in an academic gathering. The quality of clothing was frequently suggested as a good basis for distinguishing a Party member from a non-Party member. Stories were reported about lower-class children who could not go to school for lack of clothing. Lower-class respondents, particularly peasants, characteristically told of having to wear extremely poor and old clothing which had been repaired many times.

Housing is one of the perennial Soviet problems. Actual shortages of housing facilities are most marked in cities, where there is fantastic overcrowding. The main complaint against urban housing, however, was not so much the actual crowding as the resulting lack of privacy. In the villages, complaints tended to concentrate less on lack of space and more on the state of disrepair of the houses.

The Soviet population has endured several famines, including one in the postwar period. Except for these periods, however, complaints about food are concerned with the extremely high cost and short supply of a large range of items, circumstances which force on the general population an unvaried diet in which bread and potatoes bulk extremely large. Only the privileged escape the necessity of extreme economy in the use of food and the resulting dull and uninteresting diet. Khrushchev admitted in September 1953 that there were fewer cattle in the USSR than in 1941, and far fewer than in 1928. The grain crisis at present appears to be as severe as the cattle crisis and indeed has been partly caused by the means used to "solve" the latter.

An informed guess, based on what is known of the condition of the Soviet economy at the end of the war and developments since that period, is that the material conditions of the Soviet population have not improved appreciably since the late thirties,[1] and, therefore, that the standard of living described here is substantially that which obtains in the mid-fifties.

In our data there are indications, however sparse, that the younger generation may be coming to accept lower material conditions as natural phenomena. The older folk in each social group are about twice as likely to blame their poor standard of living on the absence of consumer goods, while in the younger group about one person in six sees his poor standard of living as a result of not having enough wage earners in the family — a response that is virtually unheard of in the older generation.

WORK SATISFACTION

The work situation in the Soviet Union ranges from one of frustration and dissatisfaction for the manual groups to one of gratification for the members of the intelligentsia and the white-collar workers. The general problem of standard of living colors work satisfaction. When asked to rate the desirability of jobs on various factors associated with working conditions in the Soviet Union, our respondents revealed that the level of pay was the strongest factor determining the attractiveness of a job. It is interesting as a side light on Soviet working conditions that there was, in the opinion of our respondents, an inverse relationship between the over-all desirability of the various jobs we asked them to rate and the degree of political safety they attributed to these jobs. The most desirable jobs were those that paid most and were simultaneously dangerous. An interesting implication of this finding is that, concerned as our respondents professed to be over political safety, this was not a sufficient consideration to offset their over-all evaluation of the attractiveness of various jobs. Until pay rises beyond a critical point, it is the dominant factor in shaping attitudes toward the work situation. When asked what they would want most in their work situation, workers and peasants select good pay as the element they desire, while nonmanual workers want interesting work — a luxury that one can consider only after the more basic consideration of income has been taken care of. Fewer than one person in six said he preferred interesting work to good pay in the job situation, whereas the relationship was reversed among the intelligentsia, eight citing interesting work for every one who mentioned pay. This trend illustrates graphically the differences in the life situation of the several social groups in the Soviet Union. The proportion of persons in each social group citing pay as opposed to interesting work is a good index of the point in the system at which preoccupation with standard of living ceases to be an all-consuming consideration. Obviously, it is not only a scale of lesser or greater assurance of basic livelihood that is reflected in these data, but also a shift in the type of work associated with the various class positions and in the values associated with membership in these groups. In every group, those persons with higher pay were more likely to be satisfied with their jobs.

A majority of the nonmanual groups were satisfied with virtually every aspect of their work situation. Compared to persons with other occupations, they considered their pay to be excellent or good and their jobs to be worthy of prestige. Work norms were not considered particularly unreasonable. The work environment was generally pleasant. The nonmanuals were satisfied with their superiors. They felt that they achieved, on the whole, whatever they most sought in the work situation. Most important, however, they enjoyed their work (82 per cent of the intelligentsia, 74 per cent of the employees). Members of the intelligentsia, in particular, enjoyed their work. As numerous accounts indicate, many of them found in their work a means of escape from the unpleasantness of other aspects of the Soviet system. They referred to their work as their "internal emigration." Only on one point do they have a distinctive complaint to make: they resented other persons being advanced beyond them on political grounds.

While members of the intelligentsia and the better-situated employees are not particularly discontented with their income, they have been at various times in the past few decades quite dissatisfied with the unavailability of consumer goods for which they have the money to pay. Under such circumstances, the system of economic incentives seems to bog down for these better-off groups, and the regime is faced with the problem of giving them adequate motives for exerting themselves. This consideration appears to have been behind Malenkov's aborted consumer-goods program.

The picture which the ordinary workers and peasants give is an inversion of that given by the employees and the intelligentsia. On every one of the above-mentioned points they regarded themselves as deprived or dissatisfied. Two-thirds of these groups, for example, reported that they did not enjoy their work and did not regard their job as having prestige. Naturally, they said they were underpaid.

The skilled workers fall between the other manual and the nonmanual groups. The profile of their reactions to the several aspects of their work situation is such that we cannot say that they were predominantly either satisfied or dissatisfied.

On one point there was complete agreement by an overwhelming majority of all groups: the attitude of their co-workers was friendly. This quantitative finding is also supported by qualitative descriptions of the work situation and is only one of a number of instances in which refugees indicate that friendly personal relations were one of the rewarding and alleviating features of Soviet life.

The peasants have a pervasive and distinctive complaint: they want more economic autonomy. Complaints about lack of autonomy are not unknown among other groups. The intelligentsia, for example, occasionally complain about restrictions on their activities which kept them from doing the things they wanted to do. But these complaints are minor compared to the peasant's inexorable opposition to the regimentation of his activities by the collective farm. Minimally, he wants more time to work on his private garden plot, but beyond that he wants passionately to return to a system of private farming.

SCHOOL EXPERIENCE

School experiences parallel quite closely the work experiences of our respondents. The upper classes get a great deal of direct satisfaction from their school experiences, enjoying their studies and the friendship of their fellow students, and see the schools as training them for a specific life career. They tend to be more satisfied with their opportunities to get as much education as they want. The lower classes do not, by any means, regard their school experience as an unmixed unpleasant experience. There is some tendency among the older peasants and workers, however, to consider it a waste of time which was forced on them and which kept them from working and helping at home. The lower classes are less sanguine than the upper classes about their opportunities for education. To some extent, their optimism on this score seems to be increasing with the expansion of the Soviet educational system. The perceived opportunities of the lower classes, however, do not seem to be advancing at the same rate as those of the upper classes. In other words, all groups see their opportunities as improving, but the upper classes feel their opportunities are increasing at a more rapid rate. Continued expansion of Soviet schools will unquestionably make access to primary and even secondary education routine for all classes in the reasonably near future. It remains to be seen, however, whether apparent trends toward more rigid social stratification will not make it even more difficult for the lower classes to get a higher education.

FAMILY[2]

Family life is an area of strongly mixed experiences for all classes of Soviet society. To some extent it is for everyone the final refuge from the hardships of Soviet life and from Soviet politics, but because Soviet politics and the harsher aspects of life intrude into the very life of the family, the citizen is often frustrated in his attempts to find satisfaction in his family circle. The chief sources of frustration in the enjoyment of family life are: conflict between parents and children over the political beliefs of one or another member of the family; lack of privacy because of inadequate housing; irritability of family members because of poor material conditions and anxiety over situations outside the family; lack of time to spend together because of excessive fatigue or because of the amount of time spent at work and shopping. Thus, the family is, to some extent, a refuge from these external events, but these events in themselves put a strain on family life. This is not as paradoxical as it may seem. When the individual brings his problems home to the family, the other members may be able to help him, but in so doing they must also share his problems. Perhaps the most striking example of this is the need of Soviet citizens to find some area where they can express freely their political feelings. Yet many persons withhold free expression of their opinions in the family circle for various reasons — distrust of some members of the family, concern for the reaction of children in the family, or simply because they do not want to burden the others with the responsibility of sharing these opinions. The evidence available suggests that the family serves as a source of support most effectively in the upper-class groups, both because of stronger cultural values toward mutual support and because the upper groups are better able to avoid physical dispersion.

The relations of family life to the regime can be understood only in the light of Soviet economic history of the past twenty-five years. Since 1929, the USSR has been in the process of rapid industrialization, with particular emphasis on the development of heavy industry. This program has resulted in a nation-wide shortage of skilled labor. It has also meant that the bulk of the Soviet population was forced to subsist at a low material level.* The regime has met this situation by distributing the available stock of consumer goods so as to maximize workers' motivation. Educational and occupational achievement have come to be highly rewarded through the system of markedly differentiated wage and salary rates, referred to above, by which the most highly skilled and responsible occupational positions are best paid. This arrangement has been put into the form of a slogan: "He who does not work shall not eat"; but a more accurate slogan would perhaps be: "He who works best eats best." It appears that the chief result of this policy has not been so much to arouse resentment at the "inequality of reward in a socialist system" as to promote and reinforce popular aspirations for education and occupational mobility. Such aspirations have been still further intensified both by the insistence of Soviet domestic propaganda on "the happy life in the Soviet Union" (a theme which strongly contrasted with the dire economic straits of the bulk of the population) and by the presence of considerable new opportunities for education and occupational advancement.

This set of circumstances — a low average living standard,

---

* However, the low living standard in pre-1940 USSR was not in itself (according to Project data) as important a factor in the political *disaffection* of the population as has been commonly supposed. For a discussion of the evidence for this, see Bauer, *Public Opinion Quarterly* (Autumn, 1955).

widespread occupational opportunity, differential reward by quality of performance, and high aspirations and expectations — has strongly affected the value structure and patterns of interpersonal relations in the family. For one thing, educational and occupational achievement seem to have become generally extremely important. Popular valuation of individual occupational achievement and mobility constitutes a point of strength in the system, for it contributes to the effectiveness of the mobilization of the work force and to a higher level of production — one of the main goals of the regime. At the same time, a family value pattern such as this is not without its disadvantageous aspects for the total system. What passes as occupational mobilization could also be seen as occupational "overinvolvement," consuming an inordinate amount of the individual's time and energy and depriving him of the chance to be a political activist, which the regime also desires him to be.

During the past twenty-five years many of the better jobs have involved personal risk, for failure was likely to bring punishment for "antistate activity." Also, a high-level job was likely to require the assumption by the incumbent of some degree of authority in the name of the more or less unpopular Soviet regime. Some persons hesitated to incur such liabilities. But various members of the family were involved in different responsibilities, and, in addition, the regime was not always equally unpopular among all members of the family. Moreover, one or more members of the family may have been unable (as opposed to unwilling) to achieve the occupational or educational goals which the other members of the family valued. Such discrepancies between values and behavior, or conflicts between values in themselves, led to family tensions. Analysis of Project data shows that there was tremendous pressure in most families to improve material living conditions, and that a major source of family tension was caused by the failure of one or more family members to keep up with this expectation. Thus, a correlation is found on all socioeconomic levels between economic deprivation and family disruption. Conversely, in the families where material living conditions were felt to be relatively satisfactory, interpersonal relations were more solidary.

INTERPERSONAL RELATIONS

Interpersonal relations are a focal point in the Soviet citizen's quest for pleasure and satisfaction in an otherwise often unrewarding existence. In a variety of situations respondents expressed the satisfaction that they derived from warm, friendly relations with people around them — friends, co-workers, members of the family, fellow students. This must be considered together with the constant complaints which were made about mutual suspicion and protestations that "you couldn't trust anybody." The summary conclusion that we draw is this: Russians — and possibly all of the Slavic nationalities in the Soviet Union — value warm interpersonal relations to an unusually high degree. The need for free, uninhibited social intercourse is both frustrated and accentuated under Soviet conditions. The desire to express pent-up feelings impels the individual to seek out confidants. The fear of talking makes him less likely to talk. The result is not a cessation of confidences, but rather the development of techniques of screening and assessing people in order to decide how much they can be trusted. There seem to be several steps of relation that are established: (1) Relations are carried on at a strictly formal level with suspicion or hostility circumscribing strictly what one will do and say. This probably characterizes most *initial* contacts and persists wherever one has a reason for continuing suspicion or fear. (2) Perhaps the most usual type of relation, one that characterizes contacts with co-workers, colleagues, and most friends, is that of limited friendliness and frankness. Politically delicate subjects are avoided; other topics are treated openly, and there is a warm and frank relation. (3) Intimate, confidential relations in which political confidences are exchanged are rare and are confined to some members of the family and a very few friends. There are unquestionably persons who share such confidences with no one.

The important conclusion is that, despite the barriers which the regime places in the way, warm interpersonal relations remain one of the very real sources of satisfaction in Soviet life.

RECREATION

Again, we find great class differences in patterns of recreation and the degree of satisfaction derived from this source. There were three active sources of interference with opportunity for recreation: lack of time; lack of money; lack of facilities. For the urban intelligentsia, lack of time is most important. For urban workers, money was more important. Lack of facilities (movies, libraries, theaters) was primarily the complaint of rural dwellers.

Attendance at movies, theaters, and concerts, and the reading of books and magazines increase regularly as one moves up the social ladder from the peasantry to the urban intelligentsia. There are, however, interesting qualitative changes in the pattern of recreation. Dependence on formal recreation seems to increase up through the employee group. The intelligentsia are characterized by a lesser dependence on such formal sources as the movies and theater, although their absolute use of such means of recreation is very high. In addition to formal recreation, they rely on family activities, vacations taken together, and friends. They tend to rely more on their own resources.

As far as arts and literature are concerned, the regime and the public are in constant conflict. The regime attempts to use these media as strictly political instruments. The public and most artists try to escape politicization.

THE PACE OF LIFE

An aspect of day-to-day conditions in the Soviet Union that appears to be an important source of dissatisfaction is the general pace of existence, referred to by refugees as "the tempo." This derives from the regime's efforts to spur the populace to maximum production with minimum resources. Complaints concerning "the tempo" involved high work norms, overtime (without pay, usually, for white-collar workers), long and difficult hours spent in transit to and from work (also substantiated by the Soviet press), compulsory attendance at meetings outside of regular work hours, precious time spent queuing up for scarce goods, and strict laws of labor discipline which made one liable to strong penalties for being late for work. Urban groups of all classes were depicted as being under extreme pressure because of the laws of labor discipline. Even high officials were said to be anxious over arriving a few minutes late for work. The pressure of the laws of labor discipline was at a maximum in the early forties. Enforcement of these laws has been relaxed progressively since then, especially in the post-Stalin era, apparently in response to popular resentment. In the past few years the laws themselves seem to have vanished from the statute books.

Lack of time is one of the important reasons cited for paucity of recreational opportunities. The peasants complain constantly about lack of time to work on their plots. Urban groups, particularly the intelligentsia, said that excessively long work hours interfered with family life.

VIOLATION OF OTHER ALLEGIANCES

There are a number of subgroups in the population in whom the regime generates a good deal of hostility and discontent, because it violates the allegiance of these people to other groups. In the past, church members and religious people constituted such a group. This conflict has been somewhat diminished in the last decade. The members of the various national minorities remain perhaps the most significant category of people who experience discontent on this score. The sources, the significance, and the extent of their dissatisfaction are discussed in Chapter 22.

As we have indicated at various points in this chapter, the picture of the sources of satisfaction and dissatisfaction in the life situation of the Soviet citizen is a changing one. Not only are conditions changing, but so are the expectations and aspirations of succeeding generations of Soviet citizens. The youngest people in the Soviet population take for granted many deprivations and more politicization of their lives than do the older people. Furthermore, almost all the conditions we have described have improved or are improving to varying degrees. The worst era of political terror preceded World War II. Even though politics permeated every area of Soviet life during the last years of Stalin's rule, the penalties for failing in one's job or for political incorrectness were less drastic than in the thirties, and they were imposed less arbitrarily. The post-Stalin regime seems to have gone even further toward relieving this source of tension. The pace of life, the "tempo" referred to by Soviet refugees, seems to have been slackened somewhat by the post-Stalin leaders. The standard of living of the Soviet population has increased markedly since World War II, though not rapidly enough to satisfy the Soviet people. It is questionable, however, whether by 1955 the standard of living of the Soviet population had risen appreciably beyond that of the prewar period. But it should be remembered that these conditions exist not because the Soviet leaders are powerless to rectify them, but primarily because they have in the past been unwilling to cut back their goals of industrial expansion and have preferred to produce guns instead of butter. A relaxation of international tension and an abatement of the armaments race — objectives which the Soviet leaders at the moment seem to be working for — would clearly make it within their power to satisfy many of the desires of their subjects. Not only would it be possible to raise the standard of living, but it would also be possible to relax the pressure on the populace and the use of police terror as a key instrument of social control. Whether or not the leaders will take these steps is, of course, problematical.

Solution of the agricultural crisis and relief of the discontents of the peasantry, however, is another matter. The very institution of the collective farm seems in itself to stand in the way of increased agricultural production and to frustrate the economic aspirations of the peasantry. It is likely that even with the best of intentions for "improving the lot of the people" the Soviet leaders will find it very difficult to do so without abandoning, in some large measure, the present system of collectivized agriculture. And this they do not seem disposed to do.

13

Attitudes Toward the Soviet System

In the preceding chapter we described the major sources of satisfaction and dissatisfaction in the daily life of the Soviet citizen. In this chapter we shall be concerned with the way in which these sources of satisfaction and dissatisfaction and other factors affect his attitudes toward the system per se.[1]

We have often been tempted to state that the alienated Soviet citizen accepts the system and rejects the regime.[2] By this we mean that hostility is focused selectively on the men who run the system, rather than on the institutional forms of the system. This statement, while generally true, is not precise. Certain institutional features of Soviet society, especially the collective-farm system and the secret police, are virtually unanimously rejected by Soviet refugees and seem to be sources of doubt and questioning even for loyal Soviet citizens. Furthermore, many Soviet *émigrés* regard the system, in a global sense as embracing the Communist Party, its rule, and the secret police, with such overwhelming hostility that they will reject the notion that there is anything desirable in the Soviet system. When directly questioned, these are the same persons who say that they would "keep nothing" of the Soviet system. On further investigation, however, it develops that they actually favor many of the institutional features that we ordinarily associate with the Soviet order. The most accurate statement concerning their position is that "the Soviet system" is a concept which has a sliding definition. It includes whatever they reject of the Soviet order. For many refugees, any feature of the Soviet order that they favor is automatically defined as not part of "the system." In any event, hostility to the Soviet order does not mean a categorical rejection of everything

Soviet, and especially does not mean a dislike of all of the institutional features that we might associate with the Soviet system.

In this chapter we shall review the evidence of the refugee Project to answer such questions as: What does the Soviet citizen accept and reject of the Soviet system? What type of society would he like to live in? Despite their alienation from the Soviet system, the testimony of our refugee respondents was very valuable in suggesting answers to these questions.

"WORST FEATURES" OF THE SYSTEM

Certain economic and political features of the Soviet order are rejected with such strength and unanimity by all groups in our *émigré* sample that when we add this fact to our other information about the Soviet system we must conclude that they are a source of great strain for even the loyal Soviet citizen.

Hostility toward the political aspects of the Soviet system is not focused on specific institutional features, but rather on what can only be summed up in the general term "absolutist terror." This feature of the system is linked, of course, with the secret police. However, for many Soviet *émigrés* it is not the existence of a secret police which they resent so much as the abusive use of police power. They believe that some form of secret-police system is necessary for the maintenance of social order, but they do not want the police power to be exercised arbitrarily to establish a rule of terror over the citizenry. Absolutism and terror blend into each other, but with various individuals the emphasis on the two tended to shift. Some gave more stress to the political terrorism represented in arrests and other activities of the secret police, such as forced collectivization. Others gave primary emphasis to the absolute hegemony of the Communist Party, the arbitrary way in which decisions are made and the disregard of public opinion, interest, and welfare. There is less complaint about absence of legality and a lack of representative government than there is about the lack of justice in carrying out policies, the inhibition of personal freedom, and the violation of public welfare.

Except for the system of police terror, no feature of Soviet life is opposed by Soviet refugees (and apparently by the Soviet population) with nearly so much directness and pervasiveness of hostility as is the collective-farm system, which is virtually unanimously opposed by all groups among the *émigrés* and is cited as a feature of the system to be eliminated before anything else. Harsh and unappealing working conditions, absence of opportunity for initiative, lack of private property and enterprise, and the depressed standard of living — especially the absence of adequate housing and consumer goods — are often mentioned as unfavorable aspects of the Soviet economy, but they run a very poor second to the system of collectivized agriculture in the opinions of respondents from all social classes.

"BEST FEATURES" OF THE SYSTEM

The features of the Soviet system which win approval may be divided into three groups: welfare aspects of the system; state ownership and control of the basic economy (except agriculture); and general accomplishments of the Soviet system.

There is little conflict or ambiguity in the approval which Soviet refugees show for the welfare features of Soviet society. This approval is freely and spontaneously offered and continues to be held under direct questioning. The Soviet system of education (except for the intrusion of politics in the schools) and the public health system, with its program of medical insurance, are cited spontaneously with approval even more often than the collective-farm system is mentioned spontaneously with disapproval. This is certainly an indication of a high degree of acceptance. Workers' benefits are also mentioned quite frequently, although they seem to be more important to the workers and peasants than to the nonmanual groups.

Although they receive markedly less spontaneous support than the welfare features of Soviet society, some economic features are also substantially supported by the *émigrés*. The lesser degree of spontaneous support seems to reflect a difference in salience rather than lack of consensus, since upon direct questioning representatives of all social groups exhibit virtual unanimity in approval of state ownership of heavy industry and related economic enterprises. Centralized economic planning is also agreed upon. So is coöperatively or government-owned agricultural machinery, but, of course, only for use on *privately* held and worked land. The manual groups are about evenly split on state ownership of light industry, but the nonmanual groups are predominantly opposed to the extension of socialization to this sector of the economy. Strong emphasis is placed upon the industrial development of the country. But noticeable approval is expressed for the regime's fostering of science and art, of physical culture and sports, and of the theory of equality of all races and nations.

Particularly among the younger respondents, there seemed also to be considerable pride in the military strength of the Soviet armed forces. This pride was most often revealed when respondents who had once supported the system discussed the lives they led while they favored the regime. Not only do Soviet *émigrés* acknowledge such attainments of the Soviet system as industrial growth and military strength, but they take substantial pride in them, especially in the development of heavy industry. There is, however, a tendency among the refugees to dissociate these accomplishments from the regime, and to say either that the people accomplished this and the credit is theirs (and not the regime's), or, alternatively, that the regime forced the people to purchase these attainments at an unnecessarily high price in human misery. It must be assumed, however, that substantial segments of the Soviet population share this pride in the strength and accomplishments of the Soviet system without the attendant distaste of the leadership that is expressed by the refugees.

Former Soviet citizens are characterized by strong sentiments of national patriotism, but this is primarily love of motherland rather than pride in anything specifically Soviet. They appear quite ready, however, to acknowledge substantial accomplishments during more than thirty years of Soviet power. From 60 to 90 per cent of all groups grant that during this period production of agricultural machinery increased, literacy was extended, and medical care was made more accessible. The affirmation of improvement in the realm of the theater and concerts was also substantial, although less marked. The lower manual groups — workers and peasants — run about 20 per cent behind the nonmanual groups in their readiness to acknowledge such accomplishments.

EVALUATION OF THE REGIME

Soviet *émigrés* tend to merge most of their reaction to the frustrations and deprivations of everyday life in the Soviet Union — and much of their resentment against various features of the system — into intense hatred for the Soviet *regime*. Hostility is directed against the regime primarily as it is symbolized by its formal leaders, secondarily as it is symbolized by the Communist Party and the MVD, and to a much lesser degree as it is symbolized by the rank-and-file memberships of those bodies.[3]

Even Lenin, who is associated by refugees with the generally positively evaluated NEP period, is regarded by three-fourths of all social groups as having been basically harmful to the Soviet people. Between two-thirds and three-fourths of all groups advocate violent death for the Soviet leaders if they are overthrown, and much the same proportion recommend that the leaders be handled without any legal procedure. The greater tendency to violence is always characteristic of the lower class or manual groups. Similarly, when the harmfulness of various social groups is assessed, about 90 per cent of all respondents, regardless of their position, say the Communist Party members did the most harm.

ASPIRATIONS — THE IDEAL SOCIETY

We have discussed the sources of satisfaction and dissatisfaction in the life situation of the Soviet citizen and the selective reaction of the Soviet *émigrés* to the Soviet system. On the basis of these and related findings, we can outline the image of an ideal society in which the Soviet citizen would apparently like to live.

In general, Soviet citizens appear to aspire to an economic system that can best be characterized as "NEPism." The period of the NEP (New Economic Policy, 1921–1928) is viewed by large numbers of the displaced persons as a kind of golden age of Soviet development. Their ideal assumes a welfare state with cradle-to-grave economic protection and assistance for the citizen, who is to be *guaranteed* maximum job security, health protection, accident insurance, aid in attaining an education and improving his living standards, and so on and on. To effect these goals Soviet citizens assume that the government must control industrial production and associated economic activities, and that it must support and foster science and technology. It seems to be accepted as natural that the general economic direction of the society will come from the government, rather than through the market, and that planning is necessary to coördinate the total operation.

While thus coördinating economic activity and putting a floor under economic security, the government must foster initiative (within certain prescribed limits) and not hinder the operation of personal motivation and the exercise of personal choice so long as that does not lessen the ability of others to enjoy the benefits of life in the welfare society. This concept is most marked in the attitude toward agriculture, where the collective-farm system is viewed as intolerable and as something which must be replaced by a system of individual plots, individually owned and worked, even if with collective or coöperative forms of machine operation and perhaps marketing. Similarly, in industry and the professions there must be room for initiative, free choice of jobs, and small-scale entrepreneurship in consumer-goods production and marketing. The purpose of economic life is viewed by the citizen as the betterment of individual economic welfare, and the pace and form of activity must always be subordinated to this welfare function.

In the political sphere, the basic expectation is an analogue of that in the economic realm. A strong central government is assumed to give the nation direction and purpose, to provide the stimulus for improvement and advancement, and to make possible the economic features of the welfare state which are so strongly desired. Such a government must have the characteristics of a just but benevolent father.* It may be autocratic, indeed is almost expected (though not necessarily desired) to be. But it should not be *sternly* authoritarian and certainly not total-

---

* We have already mentioned that Stalin, quite aware probably of this Russian trait, took great pains to appear as such a ruler. Now and again, he would select an "unimportant" Russian comrade far away from Moscow and single him out for a personal answer to questions, complaints, and grudges — doing so always on the front pages of *Pravda*. Our impression, however, is that his more truly characteristic behavior almost completely prevented any widespread acceptance of Stalin as benevolent.

itarian. It must look after the needs of its people and nurture them, but it must also see to it that basic values are preserved, that morality is maintained, and that malefactors — "enemies" of the common good — are punished. If a government has these characteristics, it should be honored, obeyed, loved, and respected. The test of the right to govern lies in governing in the interests of the people as they themselves define their interest. Such a good government is by definition a legal and right government, and one need not bother too much about fine points of law and the observance of fixed rules and regulations. If the government is harsh, arbitrary, and uninterested in public welfare, it loses its right to govern no matter how legal its position and no matter how close its observance of the letter of the law.

Government should, of course, be representative and probably elective, but largely in the sense indicated above, i.e., it is more important that it should respond to the wishes of the people than that it should be selected by them. If it is a good government, paternal, nurtural, friendly, and helpful, political parties and factions have no special place or meaning, although its right to govern should be periodically affirmed by a demonstration ballot. Such a government must restrict itself to fostering the welfare of the citizen and punishing the transgressor against the morality of the people in such areas as religion and the press. It cannot invade the privacy of the home. It should restrict neither a man's movement from job to job and place to place nor his right to associate freely with others and express normal free opinion and disagreement.

Where conflict arises either between organizations, between individuals and government or private organizations, or between individuals alone, Soviet citizens show a predominant concern with seeing that justice is done and good relations maintained rather than with the strict observation of legal norms. By implication — and in contrast with at least the formal values of Anglo-Saxon society — the government may do almost anything with approval so long as it seems to act in the public interest and to benefit the individuals, even though the government may in the process be grossly exceeding its formal legal or constitutional powers. As in most Western societies, however, the upper classes are more likely to be concerned with questions of formal legality and due process than are the lower classes.

LIMITS ON GOVERNMENT POWERS

Despite their acceptance of massive and widespread government powers, it should not be assumed that Soviet citizens value relatively unrestricted government power as an end in itself, nor should it be assumed that they want security at any price. While they strongly favor social-welfare benefits, there are definite limits to the price that Soviet citizens are willing to pay for them. For example, the proportion who would choose job security at the cost of lessened opportunity is at least 10 per cent less in all social groups — and 30 per cent less in the intelligentsia — than the proportion who would pay this price. More striking: if the price of security is a government which does not give the individual personal freedom, no more than 15 per cent of any group is willing to make this particular bargain.

Soviet citizens want government control not as an end in itself, but mainly because they see it as the natural way to facilitate both group and private interests. They do not accept such control if they see it as significantly limiting personal and private initiative. We must not forget, however, that, in general, they do *not* have the American tendency automatically to see government control of the basic economy as eliminating *all* private initiative. At the most, half, and in some groups such as the upper classes only a third, are willing to have the government control light (consumer-goods) industries. Although this attitude undoubtedly reflects bad experience in this area under the Soviets, it also stems from a desire to keep this sphere open to private initiative. Further, and most markedly, the Soviet citizen feels that the government should stay out of what are essentially a man's private affairs, particularly those involving his home, his friends and family, his clubs and cliques, his unions and professional societies. In such areas the government is expected to help, but is not supposed to control.

So far as the formal declaration of belief in civil liberties, such as freedom of the press, assembly, and religion, is concerned, former Soviet citizens show a marked and uniform propensity to declare themselves in favor of them. When specific limiting conditions or concrete situations are mentioned, however, a good deal of the support for civil liberties melts away in favor of varying degrees of government control and intervention. Less than half of the respondents feel the government has *no* right to intervene if the purpose or effect of an assembly or statement is verbal criticism or attack on government. Sentiment for civil liberties is weakest by far in the lower-class groups. These response patterns would be subject to serious questioning, because of imperfections in the wording of the relevant questionnaire items, if it were not for the fact that the general direction of sentiment which they indicate is also suggested by the qualitative analysis of spontaneous answers on the life-history interviews. These show that the concern over formal civil liberties, as they are understood in the West, is not very salient, and the allegiance to appropiate institutional forms is weak. Apart from freedom from arbitrary arrest, civil liberties for the Soviet citizen seem to mean largely freedom from state intervention in private affairs such as those internal to the family.

14

Attitudes Toward the West

A discussion of the attitudes of Soviet refugees (and to some extent of the Soviet population) toward the West tells us something of the impact of Soviet propaganda on the populace and of the social values of Soviet citizens, both of which are extremely important considerations in assessing the relation of the citizen to the Soviet government. At the time of writing (summer 1955) the treatment of the West in the Soviet press reflects the "new look" in Soviet foreign policy. The picture of America and the West is less hostile than it was in most of the years since the close of World War II. We have, however, limited our discussion to the period of the Cold War insofar as it relates to the content of Soviet propaganda and the success it had in conveying to the Soviet population its chosen image of the West. We do this for the reason that this period is essentially a test period of Soviet propaganda in its capacity for creating the most negative possible image of the West. Furthermore, there is every possibility that later — or sooner — Soviet propaganda will return to this line, and that we will have once more to think of Soviet public opinion under conditions least favorable to us. Therefore, our treatment of the attitudes of Soviet citizens toward the West as reflected in the testimony of Soviet refugees refers to the height of the Cold War. Even if Soviet domestic propaganda of the next few years should treat the West more kindly, the elements which we shall describe are revivable. In addition, many of the popular attitudes held at that time reflected relatively enduring images of the West based on deep-rooted culturally and historically conditioned values and orientations.

Information from refugees and from the accounts of Western travelers who have talked with Soviet citizens in the USSR indicates that Soviet propaganda is a powerful force in shaping the images which Soviet citizens have of America and of the West. Many *émigrés*, when asked what picture they had of the West while living in the Soviet Union, gave a picture that could have been lifted in its smallest detail from the pages of *Pravda*. Postwar Western visitors to the Soviet Union (Barghoorn, Stevens, Rounds, MacDuffie[1]) report many conversations with Soviet citizens in which the latter volunteered opinions about America in such a context that these opinions could not be suspected of being efforts at camouflage. In the majority of instances, they indicated a complete acceptance of official propaganda with regard to foreign affairs. Thus, the question of what images the Soviet public has of the United States and the West generally splits into two questions: What images of America and the West are to be found in Soviet propaganda? To what extent is Soviet propaganda accepted by the Soviet public? The latter question is, of course, the key one, and one that is impossible to answer with any precision. Unquestionably, there is widespread skepticism about some of the content of Soviet propaganda, even on the part of loyal citizens. However, as we mentioned previously, indications are that the *foreign* news put out by the regime is accepted more readily than domestic news, chiefly because the Soviet citizen has a scant basis on which to check the inaccuracy of what he reads about foreign countries. Refugees who emphasized that they read between the lines on domestic news nevertheless accepted a great deal of the regime's propaganda about the West, though apparently they had a general feeling that they lacked the basis for genuine judgment. The tendency to be more accepting of foreign news than of domestic news was reinforced by the experience of Soviet citizens with the German invaders. Having assumed initially that the official image of the Nazis was just more propaganda, many found that, for once, reality more than confirmed official propaganda, and since that time they have been more trusting of the picture of the outside world given by the official press. It is, therefore, safe to assume that the image of America and the West held by the majority of Soviet citizens in any social group will be importantly influenced by the one found in the Soviet press. This is even more true of the younger generation than of the older one.

The main elements in this picture have been derived largely from the statements of refugees and the reports of Western postwar visitors to the USSR, rather than from the press itself. Therefore, they should represent those elements of the official picture which have taken hold most effectively. Barghoorn's systematic treatment of the image created by the press, however, keeps us from overlooking any salient points.

The main elements in the attitudes of Soviet citizens and Soviet refugees toward the West are listed below. The method we have employed in presenting them is to set forth first the position taken by Soviet propagandists and then introduce what evidence we have as to the form in which it is accepted by the Soviet citizen, and the results of contact with the West on the attitudes of refugees.

1. *America* (and the capitalist West in general, but to a lesser degree) *is aggressive and bent on world domination.* A consideration of the successive time periods covered by various sources suggests that in recent years the Soviet regime has succeeded in getting this point of view established in the minds of the majority of Soviet citizens. A court official interviewed by MacDuffie, for example, said: "The United States has sent so many soldiers to foreign countries that if you had just one soldier at each base, you would still have a big army . . . We have no soldiers near the borders of your country." [2] A multitude of similar quotations could be collected from the reports of recent visitors.

This propaganda point has been established by dissociating the American government from two symbols which Soviet citizens apparently still value: the American people and Franklin D. Roosevelt. The Soviet press has insisted that United States postwar policy is a betrayal of the friendly policy of President Roosevelt, and that the government and its foreign policy do not represent the American people. There is also evidence of a considerable amount of good feeling remaining for the American people, whom the Russians see as friendly, peaceful, and quite like themselves in character. Russians assume that government and people are or can be entirely distinct, as in their own situation.

There are some people who reject categorically the picture of

America as an aggressor, but indications are that they are very much in the minority. It is our impression that such exceptions may occur among all social classes, but are much more likely to occur among older persons and among those persons who have had some contact with the West, either in person or through Western literature.

The notion of American aggressiveness loses meaning for Soviet refugees. Most of them regard the Soviet Union as the primary aggressor and are inclined to bewail the lack of aggressiveness of the West and of America. Repeatedly they complain that Western armies did not march against the Soviet Union at the conclusion of the war in Europe.

2. *America is respected for its technology and its material power.* The goal of "overtaking and surpassing" American production was a Soviet slogan from the beginning of the First Five Year Plan. It was and remains the supreme testimony to the respect which the Soviet government and the Soviet people have for American technical and productive capacity. This was reinforced by wartime experience with Lend-Lease. The extent of appreciation of American technology is so great that Barghoorn reports that "Willys" became a wartime synonym for "first-rate," and might even be used as a description of one's girl friend.

The high esteem which Soviet citizens have for Western and particularly American technology is strongly reinforced by their contact with the West.

3. *Capitalism is a decadent socioeconomic system which survives only by exploitation of the workers and under the artificial stimulation of armament production.* Quoting Marx, the Bolsheviks attempt to show how the accumulation of capital leads to gradual satiation of the investment markets and how, therefore, the capitalists are committed to move into foreign markets, thus creating pressures in all other capitalistic societies. Either they must wage war, or they will mutually attempt to dominate one another's markets and will, therefore, at some stage, have wars among themselves. The "capitalist bosses" permit social reform and certain benefits to the workers only to keep them from becoming united and revolting against the system. In this manner, the "capitalists" maintain themselves in power. This "evolutionary" rather than "revolutionary" attitude is the one

the Bolsheviks find the socialist most guilty of, blaming them for the continued enslavement of workers. For, after all, the capitalists do what is necessary in terms of their interests — but the socialists ought to know better than take the little "appeasements" in the way of social reforms being offered to them by the "capitalists." The capitalists are then the enemy; but the socialists are "traitors to the revolution." The notion of capitalist decadence is pretty well destroyed by contact with the West and the staggering impact of the Western standard of living.

4. *The standard of living of the rank-and-file citizen of Western countries is lower than it is in the Soviet Union.* Despite the respect which is generally held for American productive capacity, the regime maintains that the bulk of this production does not benefit ordinary citizens. Many, though probably not a majority of Soviet Russians accept this contention even though their own standard of living is low. Thus, a young engineer said:

> I saw that people lived very badly in the Soviet Union, but I heard on the Soviet radio that the workers in England and America lived even worse . . . they died of hunger, etc. Consequently, I thought that the people in the Soviet Union lived better than any other people did.

This image, however, is one of the most vulnerable in the over-all picture which Soviet propaganda creates of the West, since there is an appreciable number of people who can compare conditions in foreign countries. Also, wartime Lend-Lease supplies tended to make the United States seem to be a land of plenty. The older generation, having had firsthand experience with the pre-Revolutionary period and the NEP, and the more highly placed groups, being better educated and having better access to foreign information, are the groups most inclined to question Soviet propaganda about the low standards of living in other countries. However, considering how unrealistic this image is, it is surprising that even a minority of our respondents should have accepted it as literally as they did.

Émigrés were thoroughly and unanimously convinced that the Western standard of living is superior to that in the Soviet Union. It should be stressed, however, that even those persons who, while living in the Soviet Union, were convinced that

Western countries were better off, were unprepared for the actual magnitude of the differences that exist. In turn, *émigrés* in Europe obviously have a very poor idea of what the American standard of living is. This is evident both in conversations with refugees in Europe and from the reports of those in the United States who say that they were not really prepared for the extent of American wealth.

5. *Americans are "materialistic" and lack spiritual values.* Partly as an attempt to offset information about superior material conditions in the West, which seeps through the Soviet communications blockade, and partly to stimulate "social" motives in the Soviet citizenry in order to get them to coöperate in supporting the Soviet order for a minimum of material reward, the Soviet regime builds up the image of the West, and especially of America, as lacking in spiritual values. This stereotype is apparently accepted more by the intelligentsia than by the rank-and-file citizen. Granting the material superiority of the West, the Russian intelligentsia, today as of old, nevertheless insist on their own moral and spiritual supremacy. This belief is very deep seated, and indeed it may be that traditional Russian cultural values of dedication to the social group give some substance to it. In any event, the belief persists strongly even among the *émigrés*.

A large proportion of the *émigré* community continues to feel that we are lacking in spiritual and cultural values, in altruism, in dedication to society. The following remarks are representative:

I am firmly convinced that capitalism in such forms in which it has taken place in a series of European countries and countries across the ocean will never find a place in Russia. And simply because it is incompatible with the pure understanding of love for one's neighbors and dear ones, of fairness and justice, and mercy. Well, there you are. (A theater director, interviewed in Germany.)

Say you take the Germans and the Russians. Russians have a greater respect for society . . . And look how Americans would not fight to liberate the Russians. Russians, however, would fight to liberate other people. A kolkhoznik gladly helps to fight the capitalist abroad. (An officer, interviewed in Germany.)

In foreign literature the hero was always isolated, and that's how we reacted to it; we concluded that in foreign countries a man must live in isolation from his society. This is an abnormal situation. (An officer, interviewed in Germany.)

Another respondent made a violent attack on capitalism and the profit motive and accused Americans of not being patriots or devoted to their country.

Similar attitudes are expressed by refugees who had moved to the United States, and this coincidence seems to represent a genuine conflict between the values of Western — and especially American — culture and those of persons who have been raised in the Soviet system. This is to some extent a pre-Soviet reflection of a basic value of Russian culture but it has been exploited by the regime to enhance acceptance of its claims to "superiority." If anything, this attitude becomes stronger in the United States. The following is only one of many examples:

A Soviet schoolboy does not think of money, he has no other thought but of work. What else is there to do? He is more interested in the means of earning a living, not in ultimate personal benefits. Here, money is all important and that is why young people are not interested in spiritual and cultural life as much as the Soviet young people are. Sport is not a fetish in the Soviet Union as it is here. In this respect, the Soviet boy is better off. (A writer, interviewed in New York.)

6. *Westerners "are soft and can't take it."* This conclusion is based on a variety of convergent images. Our high style of living (an implicit contradiction to the notion of our inferior standard of living) makes us physically soft. We rely on technology to do our work. We do not have the spiritual stamina to push through despite obstacles. Finally, the Soviet people are purported not only to have great spiritual strength, but also the capacity to endure immense physical strain and deprivation. Thus, our superior technology would not save us in a test of strength between the Soviet system and our own.

It is difficult to say how widespread this stereotype is within the borders of the Soviet Union. By and large, it is more likely to be held by the young, and perhaps by the white-collar classes. It persists to a considerable extent in the emigration. The idea that Westerners are "soft" is at least greatly reduced in the minds of Soviet *émigrés,* although they continue to boast about the ability of Soviet people to endure hardships, and to accomplish through ingenuity and personal ability many things for which the Westerner depends on his superior technology. For example, they boast about the ability of Soviet mechanics to repair equipment without the elaborate tools and materials available to the Western mechanic.

I would also like to say that a Soviet citizen is not a jolly person, he is rather grumpy and ponderous. You won't see an elderly man playing ball with a child. A woman of 40 is already an old woman. But we can fight life better and the struggle doesn't fatigue us, we are used to it, we are hardened by it. (A female bookkeeper, interviewed in New York.)

Exposure to the United States does not reduce this latter feeling, and indeed we may be dealing here with a "hard fact," since Westerners who have had contact with Soviet citizens (the German general staff in comment on Soviet soldiers, for example[3]) have been repeatedly amazed by their ability to endure hardships and deprivation — whatever the explanation for this may be.

7. *All people are not treated alike in America. Certain racial and ethnic groups are discriminated against.* The Soviet propaganda system exploits mercilessly the picture of America as the land of racial prejudice and lynchings. This image seems to be widely accepted, especially among the more educated groups who are most thoroughly indoctrinated. Once more, the propaganda line exploited by the regime touches a deep-lying value of the Soviet people, who strongly favor equal treatment of all human beings.

Émigrés in Europe continue to think that America is a land in which minority groups are discriminated against. The following quotation is only one of many that could be introduced:

In the Soviet Union all races and colors are treated equally. This is much better than the unequal treatment in the United States given Negroes . . . e.g., Marian Anderson sometimes cannot get a hall to sing in there. This equal treatment of all races and groups is the strongest weapon of the Soviet regime. (A young typist, interviewed in Europe.)

This impression is very strong in Europe, but appears — on the basis of the fact that it is virtually never mentioned spontaneously in the United States — to be modified by contact with American life.

The previous points take Soviet official propaganda and attitudes held by citizens living in the Soviet Union as a point of departure. But as Soviet refugees live in the West, certain new attitudes develop spontaneously.

8. Former Soviet citizens are disturbed by what they consider to be the lack of awareness of Westerners, and most especially Americans, of the danger of Communism, and of the excessive political freedom that is afforded deviant political groups in the West. This impression becomes exaggerated as they move to the United States and one can scarcely hold a conversation with a group of Soviet *émigrés* in the United States before one of them expresses his anxiety that the American system is thoroughly penetrated by Communists and their agents and that Americans are excessively naïve in their treatment of left-wing political sympathizers. In part, this certainly reflects their indoctrination in the Soviet Union on the strength of the Communist and pro-Communist movement in the West, but it also indicates less concern with civil liberties and trust in the democratic process than is felt by most Westerners.

9. While Soviet *émigrés* are not too much concerned with political freedom, or at least do not approve of the type of political freedom they find in America, they very much approve of the personal freedom they find here — the freedom to move about and carry on their personal affairs with a minimum of government interference. One *émigré* told of a joke which a friend played on him when he arrived in the United States. The friend told him that only American citizens were allowed to live on the island of Manhattan. He accepted this as a reasonable regulation and located himself and his family in Brooklyn without ever asking a question. It was months later that he found that his friend had been joking. This type of freedom, to go where he wants, to do what he wants, is what the Soviet refugee sees as a positive side of America.

10. Attitudes toward the personal freedom permitted in America are not unambivalent, however. Soviet *émigrés* are frequently perturbed that in America people are not made to do things for

their own good. They object to the laxity of the American authorities in not exercising more control over the behavior of the public. One refugee complained of the lack of regulation in a New York hospital in which his wife had been confined.

Another thing, I came to visit my wife after a long ride through the dirt and grime of the New York subways. Nevertheless, I was shown in to my wife's bedside just as I was, in my overcoat, etc. In the USSR I would have changed my outer clothing for a hospital *khalat* [a long gown]. Also, there is no control whatsoever as to what the visitors might bring to the patient. (An actor, interviewed in New York.)

Another respondent, while complaining about the interference of the Soviet government in reading material available to Soviet children, thought that Americans went too far in the other direction.

On the other hand, when I arrived in America, I thanked God that we did not have the demoralizing comic strips, the cheap, vulgar literature that is available to children here. (An engineer, interviewed in New York.)

In America, youth is allowed to attend all kinds of films which make it sexually premature. (An engineer, interviewed in New York.)

11. Closely allied with their concern that Americans, even more than other Westerners, are not sufficiently convinced of the necessity of regulating individual behavior for the general good of the public, Soviet refugees feel that the American system does not make adequate provision for the social welfare of the individual citizen. They are dismayed by the absence of a comprehensive system of health insurance and of other social-welfare provisions which they took for granted in the Soviet Union and enjoyed in Western Europe.

Between a doctor and a lawyer an average person in America is always broke. In the Soviet Union it is quite different. The poorest and the richest received the same medical care. (An engineer, interviewed in New York.)

Furthermore, refugees in New York are much more favorably disposed toward the Soviet system of medicine than are Soviet refugees in Germany, who have access to socialized medical care.[4]

It should be emphasized that most of the *émigrés* said they had thought comparatively little while still in the USSR about the topics covered in this chapter. In the Soviet Union only the ruling elite have the freedom (or the time) to consider alternative forms of social life.

It would seem that Soviet cold war propaganda scored considerable successes in persuading large segments of the population to adopt a certain image of the United States and the West. Some elements of this image must be attributed to the regime's monopoly over the information available to its citizens. Such an element is the notion of Western and American aggression. Other elements, such as "Western decadence," reflect underlying attitudes and values which official propaganda was able to exploit. Many of these attitudes are to varying degrees reversible. But in some instances, for example, the notion of "Western decadence," such a reversal is likely to take place only when an individual has extended contact with the West, which is not likely to happen in the case of many Soviet citizens. Other of the attitudes toward the West which our refugee respondents reported, however, reflect such deep values that contact with Western societies is likely to reinforce them. They favor a more closely regulated society than they find in the West, and they miss in the United States features of the welfare state of which they approved (to the extent that they were implemented in practice) in the Soviet Union. The existence of such deep-lying attitudes suggests caution in estimating the probable degree of change in popular images of the West which might result from intensification of our own propaganda efforts or changes in the official Soviet line.

15

Some Aspects of Russian
National Character

Since its inception, the Soviet regime has sought to create a "new Soviet man" through its educational system and propaganda program. This is at best a slow and uncertain business, however, and the regime has had no choice but to work with the human material available to it. The effectiveness of many of the regime's policies and the resistance to much of its program have been influenced by the degree of "fit" between the new institutional system the regime introduced, on the one hand, and the persisting typical or modal personality trends among the people, on the other. Before turning to our summary statement on the political loyalty of individuals, therefore, we present some generalizations on characteristic personality manifestations among male Great Russians of Soviet origin* and our assessment of the relation between these trends and the adjustment of the individual to the Soviet system.

These observations are based predominantly on analyses of interviews and tests administered by Drs. Eugenia Hanfmann and Helen Beier.[1] The sample was small but rather homogeneous (males mainly under forty, primarily urban, well educated, occupationally well placed). We have also drawn upon the extended life-history interviews and sentence-completion tests from 330 subjects. In addition, to provide a suggestive standard for American comparisons and contrasts, we have utilized our American

---

* The expense and special problems of clinical studies of a foreign group obliged us to restrict our sample to Great Russians, but they constitute, of course, the most important single group in the total population.

control sample* and also our general knowledge, derived both from published studies and from personal observation.

Because the clinical materials will receive extended treatment in a forthcoming book by Drs. Hanfmann and Beier and in various technical publications,[2] a sketch will be sufficient for present purposes, which will present our impression of fairly typical or modal personality patterns among the Great Russian males. Obviously, not every Great Russian exhibits all, or even necessarily any, of these characteristics. They are, however, found frequently and regularly enough to constitute the more or less typical or modal patterns in the rank and file of the population. We do not assert that they are also characteristic for the elite. Indeed, as we indicate below, there is reason to state that those in the elite differ markedly in important respects.

In our clinical sample the modal subjects showed a great need for intensive face-to-face relationships, skill in creating such relationships, and deep satisfactions from them. They "welcomed others into their lives" but were not tensely anxious about the opinions of others nor compulsive about clinging to relationships once established. They see others in immense concreteness, yet make their judgments of their friends and acquaintances not so much on the basis of the individual's behavior as on an assessment of the person's qualities and attitudes. In other words, they value people in terms of what they are, rather than by what they have done. They are unthreatened by mutual dependence, whether in the family or in the peer group.

These Russians are expressive and emotionally alive.[3] They exhibit fewer defense mechanisms than do Americans of comparable age and occupational position. The issue between isolation and conformity is less pronounced than among Americans. Russians, as might be expected, do show greater fear of external authority. In general, they express fear, depression, and despair more frequently and openly than Americans. "They viewed the ambiguous situations presented in the tests in terms of danger and threat on the one hand, of privation and loss on the other." They accept the need for impulse control, but are nevertheless

* A group of Americans selected to match the Russians in the clinical sample in regard to age, sex, occupation, etc. which was given many of the same tests administered to the Russian group.

rather prone to excessive indulgence. They are, however, seldom
punitive toward themselves or others for giving way to impulses.
They are less perseverant than Americans and more acceptant of
the passive sides of their nature.

While a little puritanical about verbal discussion of sex, the
Russians exhibited little conflict in this area and showed less confusion about their sex identification than did the Americans.
Aggressive content emphasized the material realm: robbing, stealing, depriving. Among the Americans "aggression appeared more
often diffuse or displaced onto trivial external annoyances. The
Russians more often focused it on inimical and depriving people
and situations." Defenses of the Russians were not only less
prominent but also less stabilized; they were supplemented by
the utilization of the sympathy and support of others for the
expression and management of disturbing emotions.

Some other contrasts between Russians and Americans are
worth summary. American stress upon autonomy, social approval, and personal achievement does not often appear in the
Russian protocols. Russians demand and expect moral responses
(loyalty, respect, sincerity) from their group. Americans care
more about just being liked. Neither the Russian nor the American groups reveal marked needs for dominance or aggression —
two trends often emphasized in previous national-character
studies. Americans are more optimistic, former Soviet citizens
more pessimistic. In spite of the passion of the Russians for close
social interaction, they exhibit considerable mistrust of others.
They ask, "Is he wearing a mask?" "Where does he really stand
with respect to me?" But the dilemma is much more "outside"
in the relationship than within the self. Americans, on the other
hand, exhibit more acute self-awareness, self-examination, and
doubt of their own inner motivations.

Americans are appreciably more worried about their failures
in achievement, lapses in approved etiquette, inability to meet
social obligations. Russians are shamed most deeply by dishonesty, betrayal, and disloyalty. Americans are less aware of other
individuals as unique entities as opposed to performers of familiar
roles. The Russians value identification with and participation in
the larger collectivity more than Americans. At the same time,

they are less timid about expressing their individuality within the group. Yet they are extremely sensitive to public humiliation, to impersonal treatment by superiors, to what appears to them as violation of the dignity of the unique personality. In approaching new interpersonal situations, Russians characteristically take a very large view initially, then make a very detailed and specific analysis which usually takes an individualized and unstereotyped form. Russians and Americans both love material things, especially gadgets. The desire for "mastery" is stronger in Americans than in non-elite Russians, but Russians of all kinds often manifest great bursts of activity. Non-elite Russians are less likely to project their own hostile impulses onto others. They see mothers as nurturant and supporting and fathers as arbitrary and demanding more markedly than do Americans. Americans exhibit more inner conflict as to the dilemma of "rebelling or submitting."

The British psychiatrist, Henry Dicks,[4] in an earlier study partly supported by the Project, presented a description of the modal personality patterns of the Great Russian which, in most important respects, is consistent with the sketch given above. There were, however, some differences which deserve mention. Although both studies indicated that affiliation and dependence needs were very strong in the typical Russian, our data did not give clear-cut evidence to support Dr. Dicks's statement that orality is a central need and the oral character structure "typical" for the Great Russian. Nor did our materials suggest that the Russian people are psychologically driven to be submissive, although we did find them to have a strong desire for supportive and nurturant superiors.

The "modal national pattern" delineated above is found in its relatively pure form mainly among workers and peasants, is attenuated among those upwardly mobile, and almost disappears at the top of the social hierarchy. Our subjects reached only into the middle levels of the elite, and we did not have direct access to individuals who had been very close to the summit. The impression we obtained from those in our sample who were in the more favored groups in Soviet society was that they are notably less expressive emotionally and less committed to their primary social groups than those in less favored groups. They appear to be more capable of unconditional obedience, ruthlessness, and disciplined and orderly behavior. They are more persistent in their goal strivings, and are more prepared to shoulder responsibility for socially unacceptable actions. Drs. Hanfmann and Beier suggest that the marked discontinuity between those in advantaged positions and the ordinary citizens indicates a selective factor that is not solely a product of the better education and training of the elite.

The Party attempts — and has to some extent been able with small groups — to create the "new Soviet man": disciplined, working steadily and consistently, puritanical in conduct and motivation.[5] Prestige attaches to those who can master impulses and mood swings. The stress is on unlimited achievement, on restless organizing activity, and on tempo. The elite attaches great importance "to technology, machines, and other 'assurances of mastery' over nature and internal threats." There is a stringent taboo on depressive moods, pessimism, and sentimentality — all the "minor key" sides of Russian personality. There is also a persecutory anxiety which has two aspects. On the one hand, there is the compulsion to project tormenting fears onto foreign aggressors — "capitalists" and "imperialists." On the other hand, there is an identification with the "foreign aggressors" shown in the propensity to persecute the impulsive side of the populace. There is constant scenting of revolt, ill-will, and opposition in everyone's motivations. There is "intolerance of sloth, 'bourgeois' individualism, or easygoingness, and the progressive petrification of an ideological orthodoxy, in the world of beliefs, including the same kind of condemnation of subjective art which the Nazis once labeled *Kulturbolschewismus*."

Indeed, the psychological characteristics of the regime's ideal were largely developed to combat, control, or overcome many of the typical characteristics of traditional Russian personality. The attitude of those who attain this elite status, therefore, is often one of contempt for the ordinary citizen, and the great majority of the ordinary people experience a sense of alienation and often hostility in regard to the elite as personality types. This leads us, of course, to a fuller consideration of the relations between the modal Russian personality type and the Soviet system in which the average Russian must live.

RUSSIAN CHARACTER AND THE SOVIET SYSTEM

The scarcity element which predominates in Soviet society, the strictly rationed economy of materials, men, and the physical requirements of daily life, must be assumed to have aroused intense anxieties about oral deprivation in the Soviet population which would serve greatly to increase the impact of the objectively real shortages which have been chronic in the system. Indeed, the image of the system which most individuals in our sample appear to hold is very much that of an orally depriving, decidedly niggardly, and nonnurturant leadership. On the other hand, the regime can hope to find a quick road to better relations with the population by strategic dumping or glutting with goods, which to some extent the Malenkov group attempted, although perhaps more in promise than reality.*

Virtually all aspects of the Soviet regime's pattern of operation seem calculated to interfere with the satisfaction of the Russians' need for affiliation. The breakup of the old village community and its replacement by the more formal, bureaucratic, and impersonal collective farm is perhaps the most outstanding example, but it is only one of many. The disruption and subordination of the traditional family group, the church, the independent professional associations, and the trade unions are other cases in point. Additional effects of a marked kind are created by the strains which the regime has created on friendship relations between two or more individuals, by its persistent programs of political surveillance, its encouragement and elaboration of the process of denunciation, and its assumptions about mutual responsibility for the failings of particular individuals. The problem may be assumed to be further aggravated by the regime's insistence that its elite maintain a substantial social distance between itself and the rank and file.

The nonnurturant quality of the regime has already been mentioned. Here we add its quality of always "pushing" on the masses, of urging and insisting that individuals be responsible and carry on "on their own" with whatever resources are at hand, its

---

* Subsequent to this writing the early spurt of effort to improve the consumer-goods situation apparently slackened considerably, but there is no clear evidence of its outright rejection or abandonment.

insistence on will and self-determination, none of which is very congruent with the need felt for dependent relations. At the same time, the popular image of the regime as one with a strong sense of direction, and its emphasis on a massive formal program of extensive social-welfare measures — even if not too fully implemented — may be viewed as regime strengths relative to the need for dependence. This "directedness" relates as well to the problem of submission. Although the regime has the quality of a firm authority which is able to give needed direction, it does not gain as much as it might, because it is viewed as interested in the maximization of power per se. This appears to alienate the average Russian.

Everything we know about Soviet society, and most of what we learn from our interviews, makes it clear that it is difficult for a Soviet citizen to be at all sure about the good intentions of his national leaders and his local political bosses. They seem always to speak of support and yet to mete out harsh treatment. Because the behavior pattern of the leaders is split in this way, it very likely aggravates the apparent Russian tendency to see the intentions of others as problematical and the area of trust-mistrust as one posing a dilemma. On the basis of our interviews, one might describe this dilemma of whether or not to grant trust as very nearly *the* central problem in the relations of Soviet citizens to their regime. The dilemma of optimism versus pessimism, of whether outcomes will be favorable or unfavorable, presents a very similar situation.

The regime, as we well know, tries exceedingly hard to utilize public shame to force or cajole Soviet citizens into greater production and strict observance of established rules and regulations. Most available public documentary evidence indicates that the regime has not been very successful in this respect. Our clinical findings perhaps throw some light on the reason. The regime tries to focus shame on nonperformance and on failures to meet production obligations and to observe formal bureaucratic rules. To judge by the clinical sample, however, the Russian is little shamed by these kinds of performance failures and is more likely to feel shame for moral failures. Thus, the Soviet Russian might be expected to be fairly immune to the pressure of shame which the regime imposes on him. Indeed, the situation may well get turned around, and it is probable that the Russian feels that it is the regime which should be ashamed because it is the regime that has fallen down on these very moral qualities.

The general expansiveness of the Russian, his easily expressed feelings, his giving in to impulse, and the free expression of criticism can hope to meet only the coldest reception from the regime. It emphasizes and rewards control, formality, and lack of feeling in personal relations, along with discipline, orderliness, strict observance of rules, and the like. Thus, to begin with, the average Russian can hope for little official reward for his moral modes of expression; indeed, he can expect to run into trouble with the regime as a result of his proclivities. In particular, his expansiveness and his tendency freely to express his feelings, including those that are hostile, expose him to immediate retaliation from the punitive police organs of the state. And, insofar as he *does* exercise the necessary control and avoids open expression of hostile feelings, he may well be expected to experience a sense of uneasiness and resentment because this will seem to him an unwarranted imposition and will do much to color his attitude toward the regime.

In its effect on relations with others, perhaps more than almost any other point, the regime has created a system which runs counter to the basic propensities of the Russian character. The Russian's involvement in the group, his insistence on loyalty, sincerity, and general responsiveness from others, receives little opportunity for expression and gratification in the tightly controlled Soviet atmosphere where every small group is seen as a potential conspiracy against the regime or its policies. The people have striven hard to maintain their small group structures, and the regime persistently fights this trend through its war against "familyness" and associated evils. At the same time, it must be recognized that, to some degree, by its emphasis on broad group membership in the building of society and through its attempt to structure loyalties to the state by building certain local loyalties, the regime has probably, to some extent, captured and harnessed the propensities of the Russian to surrender himself wholly to group membership and group activity and goals. This may be most marked in the Komsomol and in sections of the Party.

The nonstriving quality of the Russian ties in with the characteristics of dependence and noninstrumentality previously mentioned. The regime, of course, is constantly pushing the citizen, urging him on, demanding greater effort, and insisting on a more instrumental approach to problems. Considering the average Russian as he is represented in our sample, it does not appear likely that the regime can hope to meet a positive response here, and indeed we may assume that it will instead encounter a substantial amount of rejection for its insistence on modes of behavior not particularly congenial to a large segment — probably a majority — of the population.

The preceding discussion strongly suggests that there is a fairly massive degree of incongruence between the central personality modes and dispositions of average Russians on the one hand, and the structure of Soviet society, particularly the behavior of the regime, on the other. This tends to be expressed, of course, mainly through complaints about specific policies, actions, and situations, and it would be a grievous error to ignore the factual bases for these complaints as such. The dissatisfactions appear to be intensified and given a more emotional tone because they are based *also* on the poor "fit" between the personality of the Soviet citizen and the matching personality and conduct of the leaders. To say that there is a poor "fit" between the personality of the Soviet citizen and many of the institutions of Soviet society and the behavior of leaders is, however, correct only in a limited sense. It might be equally correct to say that there is an excellent "negative fit" in the sense that these institutions and the behavior of the leaders are specific attempts — some conscious and some probably unconscious — of the Soviet leaders to offset such characteristics of the Soviet population.

16

Political Loyalty of Individuals

Political loyalty is in all instances the result of a multitude of affecting and disaffecting circumstances to which individuals react in a variety of ways with varying consequences to the society. This is always a complex problem. In the case of the USSR, it is particularly important to bear certain differentiations constantly in mind. Only Great Russians are necessarily loyal to "Mother *Russia*." But throughout at least most of European USSR there is genuine patriotism for "the homeland," for the Slavic nation-state, vaguely but nevertheless deeply conceived. This patriotism takes the practical form of psychological readiness on the part of the people to defend territorial integrity against attack by foreigners, who are in any case mistrusted.

The second level of loyalty is to Soviet institutions. This is not so clear-cut; yet, as already pointed out, some of these (the welfare state, the educational system, state control of heavy industry) do command the loyalty of a majority of Soviet citizens. Both patriotism and loyalty to institutions can, under various circumstances, be counteracted by other factors, e.g., hatred of the regime.

The third level, and the most complicated, is loyalty to the regime. Probably not more than 5 per cent of the total population are — for reasons of conviction or opportunism or both — *completely* committed to the present regime or even to this kind of regime. This group in the USSR would embrace most of the very highest Party, secret police, and bureaucratic elite, but perhaps an appreciably smaller proportion of the top military elite. It includes a smaller but sizable proportion of the lower elite groups in the Party and secret police. At the opposite end of the continuum is that small percentage of those who are honestly pro-Western or hate the police state *vehemently enough so that they would be willing, active collaborators* in any serious attempt to overthrow the regime. In between is the vast majority of people who have feelings that are mixed or who simply passively and unthinkingly accept but are not emotionally committed. In the members of this majority group who do think at all, there is an inner "I" which by no means agrees with everything and an outer "I" which for safety's sake must appear to agree with everything. "I pushed my doubts into the background" is a frequent remark of the *émigrés* who had a period of successful adaptation to Soviet society. The general formula is to express loyalty as frequently as possible.

Secret attitudes of mixed loyalty to the regime do not necessarily mean that the individual is not highly useful to the regime. Indeed, some people do an effective job precisely because they do *not* like the regime. Their work is their refuge *from* the regime because it brings them a reasonable measure of security and a chance to enjoy aspects of their personal lives through "the inner emigration." In general, the capacity of the Soviet system to absorb deviants must not be underestimated.

To say that criteria of political loyalty are employed in considering people for an exceptionally wide variety of posts in Soviet society does not mean that the regime is incapable of using deviant or potentially disloyal persons even in sensitive positions.* Spontaneous loyalty is seldom relied on by the Soviet leaders. Essentially, every person is regarded as potentially disloyal. The regime tries to control the life situation of each individual so as to insure the reliability of his behavior, regardless of his underlying political sentiments. In some instances — notably spying for the secret police — suspicion of disloyalty has been the very basis of recruitment. Individuals thus suspected were told that they would have to prove themselves by this type of work. Such jobs are ordinarily of a low order of sensitivity. However, there are known instances of the employment of persons of dubious loyalty on rather high-level assignment. The physicist Peter Kapitsa is said to have been prevented in this way

* Even as recently as 1955 official statements were made that the criterion of political reliability was of *primary* importance in the selection of responsible personnel.

from returning to Cambridge, England. Ilya Ehrenburg and Alexei Tolstoi, both noted Soviet authors, seem to have been "bought" by lavish material rewards and the opportunity to continue to live in their motherland. When paranoiac suspicion has been pushed to the extreme, there is no longer any real differentiation between the trusted and the mistrusted. Consequently, a totalitarian society such as the USSR has a surprising capacity to absorb and use potential deviants, though certainly it also loses the services of valuable people because of unwarranted political suspicions.

No society or ruling clique cherishes discontent and disaffection for its own sake. The persistence of such sentiments over a period of time implies an incapacity to relieve sources of dissatisfaction owing to the nature of the system and the priority of other goals. The Soviet regime's goals involve an expansion of heavy industry and armaments at the expense of the interests of the citizen. The regime's notion of how to effect social change is still based on a direct assault on goals with only a secondary consideration of how the people react to the regime. This statement must be tempered in view of the behavior of the leaders in the period since Stalin's death, but we continue to believe that popular feelings continue to be decidedly secondary to the broad developmental goals of the leaders. Disloyalty and incipient disloyalty are handled by isolation and by suppression of manifestations. Citizens have little chance to do other than conform. In any case, most of them are politically inert. However, some acts that are not politically disloyal in intent have the same consequences as deliberate sabotage (e.g., the stealing of state property when motivated only by immediate personal interest).

The Soviet leaders are aware that they have created much hatred for themselves among those large groups in the population who have suffered directly from regime policies and action. They know too that they have not satisfactorily met the needs of the "normal, loyal citizen" and until recently have refused to make substantial concessions in that direction. Accordingly, they realize that they cannot rely on the great mass of the population to support them on the basis of sentimental allegiance; therefore, they place primary reliance on external coercion. They see to it that the individual's life situation is structured in such a way that conditions under which his loyalty is put to a genuine test occur as seldom as possible.

Both the nature of Soviet society and the regime's handling of the loyalty problem tend to concentrate the issue sharply on the top leadership. Sentiments of disloyalty are apt to be directed against the *regime,* i.e., against the men who determine and execute policy and not against Communist institutions. However, the lower classes draw this distinction less consistently than do the upper classes.

During periods of social stability the regime can count on behavioral conformity on the part of the majority of the people. Under these conditions, there are only three kinds of deviation from complete conformity: withdrawal; deviant behavior of nonpolitical intent; short outbursts of hostile feelings. The psychology of these, their frequency, and their consequences to individuals vary with the degree to which the person is involved in or is distinctly peripheral to the core of the system. Withdrawal may indicate either covert opposition to the regime or simply a desire to avoid the tensions associated with involved positions. Withdrawal means that the regime cannot make use of the *full* capacities of these citizens. As we indicated in our discussion of the satisfactions and dissatisfactions associated with working conditions, the regime has been successful in preventing *mass* withdrawal from responsible, politically involved jobs because of the compensating attractions linked with these jobs, notably high pay. Deviant behavior, such as theft of state property or illegal practices, even when clearly nonpolitical in motivation, is ordinarily more dangerous to those centrally involved in the system, since they are under closer surveillance. Hostile outbursts much more often take the form of an open expression of feeling than of actual sabotage. Those who are latently hostile to the regime suffer from continual anxiety lest they make such slips. All Soviet citizens (with the possible exception of the 5 per cent or so who are totally committed) suffer corrosive effects upon their personalities because of the interminable succession of doubts, fears, and compromises they undergo. The psychology of this process varies with the personality of the individual concerned and with his position in society, but to some extent it is a source of strain for every citizen.[1]

Thus far we have been talking about loyalty predominantly on a subjective level, i.e., whether the citizen "likes" or "dislikes" the regime, his nation, and the type of society in which he lives. What is distinctive about the problem of political loyalty in the Soviet Union is the relatively low importance of this aspect of loyalty. The regime would *like* to have most citizens be subjectively loyal, but realizes that for effective social control it must rely ultimately on external sanctions. The citizen, being fully convinced of the effectiveness of these sanctions and seeing no alternative for himself except to live within the framework of existing institutions, gives little serious thought to converting his subjective disloyalty into active disloyalty. As a matter of fact, if he entertains disloyal thoughts, he will, in many cases, attempt to suppress them, since they are a potential source of danger for him: he may blurt them out or they may subtly suggest to him some behavior which will be called disloyal.

What is most striking about the question of political loyalty in the Soviet Union is that, because of the regime's predominant reliance on external controls as the assurance of loyal behavior, the problem of loyalty becomes indistinguishable from the problem of administrative control. It is, to a great extent, misleading to speak of loyalty and disloyalty, since the regime is less concerned with subversion in its Western connotation than with universal and day-to-day conformity to and consistent effort in behalf of its directives. Since all organized activity in the USSR is managed by the Party center, the work of all individuals becomes an expression of how they accept its leadership. From the regime's point of view, the loyal person is one who carries out its policies with complete "Party vigilance." Even the "subjectively loyal" citizen can easily be defined as "objectively disloyal" by the regime. This is particularly true of persons in positions of administrative responsibility whose notions of "how things should be done" or whose identification with the needs of a particular institution or organization prompt them to act contrary to official policy in greater or lesser detail. Such deviations from "Party vigilance" are labeled variously as "formalism," "organizational patriotism," or "local patriotism" by the regime. "Formalism" and "local patriotism" challenge the regime's effective control over strategic areas of Soviet life and are treated as symptoms of disloyalty, even though they may stem from "loyal" motives.

Such problems of control probably reach their peak in the military because of the high degree of professionalization of Soviet military leaders, the degree of organizational loyalty required by an effective military organization, the isolation of military life, and the commitment of military leaders to the defense of the nation. The relevance of control over the military, additionally, is important for the leadership because of its command over the weapons both of organization and of violence, and because, more than any other instrument of the regime, it has won the confidence and affection of the Soviet people. (For example, virtually none of our respondents thought the military would defend the regime in the event of a popular uprising or war of liberation. On the contrary, they suggested that the military was of the people and for the people.)

The regime itself acknowledges the extent to which considerations of administration and loyalty merge in the case of the military by its frequent attacks in the press of the armed forces on "formalism" and "organizational patriotism" in the military establishment. Officers who confine themselves to military specialties and neglect political activity are ridiculed. Members of the Party apparatus assigned to control the military are criticized for becoming too closely identified with their problems.

While these factors are exaggerated in the case of the military, they are different only in degree from those which are found in industry, agriculture, the government bureaucracy, and scientific and artistic work.

ALTERNATIVE LOYALTIES

It is characteristic of national loyalty in all states that loyalty to the nation is very much complicated by loyalties to family, business, region, religion, which are the effective bases for loyalty to the state in a liberal society. To the extent that the interests of these other groups are not in conflict with the interests of the state, the citizen's membership in and loyalty to such groups binds him to the state. It may well be argued that it is a central feature of a totalitarian state to tolerate no such alternative loyalties, that it stresses and attempts to create direct, unmediated ties of loyalty between individual and nation — a relation that is present but relatively rare in a liberal society. Considering the potentially reinforcing role which such alternative loyalties might play, the "ideal" totalitarian state would be one in which such loyalties would be rationally organized for the support of the state. The fact that this is not so, and that the heads of totalitarian states are generally opposed to all alternative loyalties, is the result of two circumstances: (1) the totalitarian state tends simply to disregard the interests of subgroups within the society; (2) it has at its disposal the resources with which to override the interests of these groups, and its leaders have the disposition to do so. It is the second of these circumstances which makes the first possible. However, it must be underscored that the violation of alternative loyalties can be effected in any state only at a very considerable price, and that even in a totalitarian society it is inherently desirable that these alternative loyalties reinforce the ties of the citizen to the state, provided, of course, that this can be brought about without the sacrifice of some other objective.

The Soviet regime, before many years had passed, succeeded in alienating almost every group and subgroup within Soviet society. Since such subgroups were loci (real or potential) for the mobilization of anti-Soviet sentiment, campaigns were carried out either to undermine alternative sources of loyalty or to destroy the very groups and institutions to which such alternative loyalties might attach themselves: the family, Russian nationalism, the church, the Tsarist army. In a few instances concessions were made to alternative loyalties and there were even a few attempts — somewhat half-hearted and aborted — to capitalize on them and weld them into the framework of loyalty to the new Bolshevik regime. Perhaps early policies toward national minorities would be a good example of such an attempt. It was recognized that the difficulties of overriding such loyalties were great, and that a considerable advantage might be gained by disassociating the Bolshevik regime from Tsarist nationality policies. Hence, there were, for a while, conspicuous attempts to exploit the sentiments of cultural nationalism among the minority peoples. During the thirties, however, the regime became more concerned with negative dimensions of loyalty to minority national groups and a campaign was waged against minority nationalism.

It continues today under the slogan of opposition to "bourgeois nationalism."

In the course of time, as the basis for old loyalties antagonistic to the Soviet regime atrophied somewhat and a crisis developed in the regime's reliance on direct loyalty of the citizen to the Soviet state, there has been a partial relaxation of the regime's antagonism toward alternative loyalties. During the mid-thirties, steps were taken to reintegrate the family into the framework of loyalties to the state. In the early years of the Second World War the regime acknowledged the powerful influence of Russian patriotism and religious loyalties and exploited them to bolster the strength of the Soviet state. In the years since the war, the regime has continued to stress Russian nationalism.

As of this day, the Soviet regime relies less exclusively on ties of direct loyalty than it did in very early days. *To some extent* it relies on and partially exploits a few alternative loyalties, such as those to family, Russian national culture, and religion. With perhaps the exception of Russian nationalism — and, to some extent, Pan-Slavism — however, these are uneasy liaisons. Inherently, the Soviet leaders are still suspicious and distrustful of alternative loyalties. This distrust is understandable because the leaders are aware of the high potential for disaffection in the life situation of the Soviet citizen and of the threat to the regime posed by alternative loyalties.

This situation is most clearly seen in the regime's constant campaign against "familyness" — which is an alternative loyalty for which the regime and its program are directly responsible. By placing excessive demands on its citizens, the regime creates a situation in which small groups become bound together by ties of mutual interest of the "you-scratch-my-back-and-I'll-scratch-yours" variety. These small, mutual protective societies grow up on the local level among people bound together by self-interest and ties of responsibility which set them off against "the Center." Thus, the seeds for the generation of alternative loyalties that are distasteful to the regime are inherent in the regime's policies and programs. It should, however, be noted that the "family groups" are not political in intent, and it is a moot point whether in the relatively long run they are favorable or detrimental to the interest of the regime.

There is also no question but that certain other sources of alternative loyalty remain a problem for the regime, as is evidenced by the postwar campaign against "cosmopolitanism," and by charges laid against various leaders and officials of "exploiting" nationalist feelings to their advantage. The basic target for the attack on "cosmopolitanism" was "absence of militancy" toward wartime allies and Western democracy, curiosity about Western culture, and resistance to the self-isolation of the Soviet system. In addition, it seems clear that for many persons, particularly intellectuals, there is a sufficient attraction to the values and norms of international groups with which they partially identify themselves to have aroused concern on the part of the regime in recent years. Similarly, no matter what assessment we may make of the over-all nationality problem in the Soviet Union, there is sufficient nationalist feeling in some members of the national minorities to create an active problem for the Soviet rulers.

It is probably true that no one of these alternative loyalties has, throughout the history of the Soviet Union, been consistently either creative or destructive of loyalty to the regime. Over the course of time, the centrifugal force of the alternative loyalties has been reduced. This course, however, has not been an entirely even one. During the early and mid-thirties, for example, there was something of a tendency for the negative effect of certain alternative loyalties — to minority nationalities, to professions — to increase sharply as such groups were attacked by the regime. It may be anticipated that if the regime enjoys relative peace and stability and eases its pressures on the population, most alternative loyalties will tend to reinforce national loyalty. Acting counter to this trend are: (1) the regime's distrust of and hostility toward alternative loyalties; (2) a reasonable probability that for the foreseeable future the regime will continue to have sufficient difficulties in maintaining the stability of the system and attaining its own goals and that it will (*a*) continue to violate the interests of established groups, and (*b*) generate local loyalties antagonistic to certain of its goals. Barring unforeseeable internal prosperity and success, therefore, the problem of alternative loyalties will continue to plague the regime. In the USSR alternative loyalties will continue to undermine, rather than reinforce, national loyalty. Russian nationalism — presumably as distasteful to members of the minorities as it is pleasing to the Great Russians — is the only alternative loyalty that the regime seems to have embraced clearly and unequivocally, although with the proviso that one must not admit too openly a policy of Russification of other nationalities.

Part IV

SOCIAL AND PSYCHOLOGICAL
CHARACTERISTICS OF SPECIFIC GROUPS

17

The Ruling Elite[1]

Knowledge of the composition and nature of the Soviet elite is indispensable to an understanding of the functioning of the Soviet system. As Franz Borkenau has pointed out:

It is the innermost meaning of Leninism-Stalinism to segregate a small elite from the masses. This elite alone knows the real meaning of the whole movement, and in consequence the real meaning of its tactical moves. It is only a logical development from this starting point that the elite, more and more, hides first its aims and then also its personnel.[2]

SIZE

1. *The ruling elite*. All of these are members of the Party and have a place in Party structure in addition to whatever roles they may carry out in the bureaucracy or in the military. Therefore, an estimate on the basis of Party organization will be only roughly valid. In 1937, Stalin said that there were "about 3,000 to 4,000 first-rank leaders whom I would call our Party's corps of generals." Making allowances for changes in numbers since 1937, and for certain other factors, an estimate of 10,000 would not be far wide of the mark for the total ruling elite of the USSR.

There are, of course, various hierarchies within this group. The Party Presidium is at the top; then comes the Central Committee, and there are perhaps another hundred top-ranking officers or bureaucrats who are not members of the Central Committee. It should be noted than even at this high level there are some individuals who appear to be largely ornamental, like Budenny, or who at least cannot make critical decisions affecting the lives of other people or the activities of major echelons of the Party and government apparatus. A still larger group which represents a distinguishable echelon of the ruling elite would include the 1,192 voting members of the Nineteenth Party Congress (1952) — or, rather, their equivalents today after the changes following the death of Stalin and the dismissal of Beria. The 1,359 individuals at this congress, plus a few hundred key individuals who, for one reason or another, were not there, suggest a still more extended echelon. Here again, there are individuals who are present largely to serve as ornaments or symbols, and at this level the comparable proportion of such figures, while still small, is larger than the comparable proportion in the Central Committee category.

In short, we get a pyramid something like this:

At the top are the five or six members of the collegial governing clique.*

The second layer of the pyramid consists of those 10–15 persons who are not firmly in the collegial clique but are in the Presidium or likely candidates for it in case of vacancy.

There are 250–300 next in line and moving up. Here would come most of the nonornamental Central Committee members, the non-Presidium members who man top central bureaus of the Party (and often of the government, the military, and industry), and the important leaders of the more than 100 republic, territorial, and regional (*oblast'*) Party committees.

Next come the 1200–1500 who are more important than the rank-and-file ruling elite but definitely below the highest and mightiest. Here we would place a large part of the 1,192 voting members of the Party Congress. This group therefore includes many people prominent in industry, the military, and civil administration, and significantly overlaps with second secretaries in the Central Party Bureaus, a few second in line at the republic and important regional levels, the secretaries for important rural and urban districts, and so on.

Last are the 5000–8000 rank-and-file ruling elite. Here we

* In the earlier version of this report (1954), a footnote to this line stated: "There are some slight recent indications that a duumvirate (Malenkov and Khrushchev) is in control. But the more conservative view is to assume the collegial group of five or six." The subsequent demotion of Malenkov strengthens our support of the "more conservative view" as the more accurate description of the situation as of August 1955.

would place people who are "section chiefs" at the top or central Party-government level, plus many second- and third-line officers of larger republic units, and first secretaries of major and some rural Party districts. In the non-Party apparatus, this would include many generals and heads of the largest factories.

These figures do *not* include perhaps an additional thousand individuals who are, in some sense, members of the Soviet Union's "top elite" — but not of the *ruling* elite. This group would be made up mainly of scientists, professional people, scholars, artists, and technicians who play roles of great importance in Soviet society, but who do not have much power in day-to-day or month-to-month political decisions.

2. *The middle elite.* Stalin spoke in 1937 of "30,000 to 40,000 middle-rank leaders who are our Party corps of officers." Perhaps today we could think of the Soviet middle elite as comprising about 100,000 persons.* This would include Party functionaries of middle rank, officers of the grade of colonel and above, important bureaucrats (judges, diplomats, many division chiefs in ministries, directors of important factories), and some scientists and technicians.

The middle elite includes almost no one who is not a member of the Party, but there is not the same correspondence between Party role and role within the total structure as is the case with the ruling elite. For example, more than 86 per cent of Soviet officers of the grade of captain and above are today Party or Komsomol members, and appointments as colonel and above must be approved by the Central Secretariat of the Party. But this does not mean that many colonels and generals (apart from the key *zampolits*, or political officers) occupy key places or otherwise exercise leadership in the Party organization.

3. *The lower elite.* Stalin spoke of "100,000 to 150,000 of the lower rank who are the Party's noncommissioned officers." However, the lower elite of the USSR undoubtedly includes hundreds of thousands of men and women who are not even NCO's in the Party's chain of command. A case can be made for saying that all of the 6,882,145 members of the Party constitute an elite

* There appear to be 100,000 to 150,000 persons in the USSR who receive incomes equivalent to $20,000 per year or more. Some of these are artists and technicians who are not strictly part of the governing elite.

group,* but this figure is too large to be meaningful, if we are thinking in terms of those persons who can immediately and directly influence the course of events, as long as the total organizational structure remains essentially unbroken. We place the size of this group in the order of 1,500,000 persons.

DEMOGRAPHIC COMPOSITION

1. *Age.* Of 1,192 voting members at the Nineteenth Congress, 61.1 per cent were between forty and fifty, 5.9 per cent were under thirty-five. At the Eighteenth Congress (1939), nearly half were under thirty-five.† The ruling elite is now a distinctly middle-aged group.‡ Even so, it is increasingly a group which has had little firsthand contact with the outside world except for limited military contacts during World War II and except for the small number who have served as diplomats abroad, or who, like Saburov, were among the limited number who studied engineering and production methods in the United States between 1931 and 1933.

2. *Sex.* Of the voting delegates at the 19th congress 12.3 per cent were women, but of the 125 full members of the Central Committee only two were women. For all practical purposes, the ruling elite must be regarded as male. As in other areas of Soviet life, it is clear that there is a gross disparity between the much idealized image of the role of women in Soviet society and the reality of their access to positions of power.

3. *Ethnic origin.* Great Russia had a markedly higher percentage of voting delegates at the Nineteenth Congress (in proportion to population) than did the Ukraine and other areas.[3] The composition of the Central Committee and of the Party Presidium

* Nicholas DeWitt "Professional and Scientific Personnel in the U.S.S.R.," *Science,* 120:1–4 (July 2, 1954), estimates that at the end of 1953 there were 5,940,000 individuals in the USSR who had completed higher professional and technical education. These also in some sense constitute an elite group (most of them are Party or Komsomol members) but they are by no means all "elite" in the power sense. However, there were only 2,500,000 persons having such training in the USSR in 1940.

† In large part because of the great purges which just preceded this congress.

‡ Of the 1,347 deputies at the 1954 Supreme Soviet only 27 per cent were under the age of forty.

also shows clearly that the ruling elite is predominantly Great Russian.

4. *Education.* Of 1,192 delegates, 709 had completed their higher education, and eighty-four more had received some higher education. In view of the fact that some of the delegates have really only local power, but are included as delegates for purposes of regional representation, we can assume that the educational level of the true ruling elite is high — at least in Soviet terms. They are mainly, today, trained technicians of one sort or another.*

ORGANIZATION

Bertram Wolfe provides a terse summary of the general structure of the elite:

> The real power levers in this struggle are three: the party machine; the secret police; the armed forces. Potentially other power groupings may be in process of formation: an *esprit de corps* among the state bureaucracy, for example, or among the industrialists and technicians. But these are only embryonic forces and not real power levers at present.[4]

As is well known, an outstanding feature of the structure is the system of interlocking wheels. The Party checks on the secret police and the secret police check on Party operations. There are recent indications that the military may, at least in some areas, have the capability of cross-checking on Party and secret police. Developments since Stalin's death suggest a trend toward greater independence of the various bureaucracies. However, insofar as there is still a set of threads that tie together the total system, these threads are to be found in the Party structure. The Party is the one organization to which virtually all members of the elite groups belong. General officers, members of the National Academy of Sciences, presidents of republics are all publicly rebuked by the Party hierarchy and are all subject, in a variety of ways, to Party discipline. Because Party membership

---

* In the USSR engineers have a position comparable to that of lawyers and business executives in the United States. DeWitt, *Science,* 120:1–4, estimates 467,000 engineers in the USSR at the end of 1952, as compared with 283,000 at the end of 1940.

tends to create homogeneity of interest and outlook, the segmentation of the Soviet elite has very definite limits. It is true that, in some contexts, the military elite as a group has a common point of view which may be at variance with that of the secret police, for example. Nevertheless, key individuals in both organizations have also a common frame of reference and one which often takes priority — that of the Party. The power of appointment, removal, and control of factory directors, commissioned officers of the secret police, and military personnel from the grade of colonel upward is actively exercised in the central locus of power, the Party Secretariat. This means, inevitably, a strong brake upon tendencies toward marked partisan loyalty to a single branch of the Soviet system as well as considerable power to contain any attempt of the army to destroy the secret police or of the secret police to dominate the army. Beria's downfall tends to confirm the picture of the supremacy of Party controls.

The system of cross-checks is a distinctive feature of the Soviet system. The fact that the Party cuts across all other organizations and, to a considerable extent, ties the whole system back together is a second crucial feature. The composition of the Central Committee as of October 1952 is instructive in this regard. While 46 members were full-time Party functionaries, there were also 37 government bureaucrats (excluding members of the Presidium who were ministers), 24 military men (not counting political commissars and military politicians like Voroshilov and Bulganin), and a sprinkling of scientists, artists, and the like. In other words, both symbolically and functionally, the Central Committee unites, at virtually the top of the pyramid, the various groups that make up Soviet society.

The third distinctive feature is, of course, the hierarchical nature of the system. The "Apparat" is carefully safeguarded against possible control by rank-and-file membership. Members of Party committees at county, city, district, provincial, regional, and Union Republic levels cannot be disciplined by the cells to which they belong but only by a two-thirds majority of the local Party committee.* Real power rests in the hierarchy of

---

* This is a formal provision, but nevertheless indicates the structure.

committees, and more specifically, in their secretaries — who are appointed by the central Secretariat in Moscow.

As Philip Mosely has recently written, "In effect, the Nineteenth Congress consolidated the fusion between Party and state." [5] On behalf of the ruling elite, the Party performs three principal functions: mass indoctrination, supervision of performance, and recruitment of personnel.

OPERATIONS

The authority of those at the very top is essentially personal rather than organizational. The division of functions among the various ruling bodies is so loose and the overlapping so great that the system can function only through the personal fusion of conflicting authorities.* Take the military situation as an example. The armed forces are controlled ideologically and politically by Party organizations and political workers who are under the control of the Central Committee. The armed forces are, at the same time, permeated with the Special Sections of the Ministry of Internal Affairs (MVD). Finally, they are subject to the strictly military chain of command. The situation would be impossible were it not for the fact that the top representatives of the three organizations have close personal relations.

At intermediate and lower levels, individuals are kept in line through far greater specialization of function and control. While the dictatorship fuses authority in a small group of persons at the top, it diffuses authority on the lower planes. Local Party leaders are forced to become specialists. They are so occupied with daily economic and administrative problems that they must leave "higher politics" to their rulers. Authority on policy is firmly held in the top hands. Responsibility for results is with equal firmness shoved downward. Even though the ruling elite operates on the assumption that nobody is fully trustworthy, nevertheless numerous individuals must be held responsible for what is demanded by the Center. Primarily, these are the Party secretaries of the republic, *oblast'*, and *raion* organizations. Secondarily, factory managers, military commanders, and the heads of various scientific, communications, and artistic enterprises are also, of course, held directly accountable.

* In the past via a single leader.

Though there is a strong tendency to concentrate policy decisions at the upper levels, the line between policy makers and administrators is not quite as clear-cut as may be suggested above. At middle (and even lower) levels there is limited participation in policy making in Party organizations, though little in the bureaucracy as such. In general, responsibility for policy decisions is a more dangerous job to have than is administration. The administrator who fails or who proves incompetent may be severely punished, but, unless there is evidence or strong suspicion of political deviation, he is seldom liquidated. Those, however, who are too often on the wrong side of the ideological fence disappear or, at any rate, sink into complete obscurity. If they have powerful friends at the top or in the echelon just above them, they may be permitted to repent repeatedly in public through "self-criticism" and may rise again to prominence. Also, the relative strength of factions changes — sometimes rapidly. Members of the middle elite sometimes reappear in considerable power after one of these shifts. Nevertheless, all sophisticated Soviet citizens realize that the risks of involvement in decision-making are more nearly all-or-none than those of simply carrying out orders. Administrators are punished more often, probably, but policy makers more severely — hence, they are in greater danger.

PSYCHOLOGICAL CHARACTERISTICS

The elite* constitutes a differentiated, privileged social class. They are the favored beneficiaries of the Soviet system. Hence, they have a vested interest in maintaining and perpetuating it. This disposition is, or may be under certain circumstances, counterbalanced by the following forces:

Patriotism: the conviction that the ruling clique is acting contrary to the interests of the nation-state. This takes the form most often of a fear that the regime is taking risks (either in pursuit of its personal power or through favoring international Communism at the expense of Russian national interest) which jeopardize national security and the hard-won gains of the last generation (industrialization, literacy).

* The Project had in its sample only a few members of the *upper* elite. Our picture of this group is derived largely from what our respondents said about the upper elite and from published and other sources of information.

"*Disillusion*": the conviction that the regime has betrayed or is betraying the Revolution and that the humane goals of Marxism are being sacrificed for power aggrandizement. The number of individuals among the elite whose attitudes and behavior are seriously influenced by considerations of this sort may be small today. However, an appreciable number of refugees fall into the category of "disillusioned idealists." It is probable that some of the ruling elite are "idealists" — not disillusioned — in the sense that they are not just playing the personal game but sincerely believe in Soviet policy and in world revolution. These individuals are, of course, both among the most dangerous antagonists of the non-Soviet powers — if they are also realistic — and, simultaneously, the most dangerous potential opponents of Soviet order if and when they become "disillusioned" because they turn sharply.

Personal insecurity: Many of these persons who have had access to positions of power have felt that their privileges in goods consumption, power, prestige, and special opportunities for family members have been bought at the too high price of constant strain and worry. They have been plagued by the knowledge that a single misstep can mean degradation, imprisonment, and death. Most of those affected importantly by this psychology engage in the so-called "inner emigration" or merely resort to what George Fischer[6] has called "inertness." Although our evidence is scant, we would judge, projecting from our subjects in the intelligentsia who were in the near elite, that while conditions are stable and their personal life is going smoothly few indeed overtly — or covertly — oppose official policy. Under conditions of crisis, an appreciable number might be expected to take some risks in opposing the regime, since our respondents seem often to have made the decision to break away at such times.

Nevertheless, the elite does have a distinctive "mentality," although care must be taken not to accept *in toto* the official Soviet mythology on this point. "The new Soviet man" is neither as new nor as completely unique as the regime would have its own people and the outside world believe. Nor has the regime been able to fashion its elite to a predesigned role nearly as completely as it would like. Some of their motives they share with all mankind, as they do some other characteristics that distinguish bureaucratic elites in all dictatorships. Nevertheless, when all these qualifications have been made — and they are important — the fact remains that the Soviet elite has special qualities which make it dangerous to project Western psychology onto this group, even to the extent that this was possible with the Nazi or Italian Fascist elite groups. The most important of these characteristics are:

1. *Suspicion of "foreigners" and their motives* — to the point of pathology. There is, on the one hand, a grudging recognition and even admiration of superior science and technology in the West. On the other hand, there is deep resentment of what is felt to be derogation or contempt on the Western side, and a stubborn conviction that Slavs in general and Russians in particular have a strength and a peasant kind of shrewdness which, in the long run, will triumph over "the decadent West." As Henry Dicks[7] has pointed out, this is well symbolized by the Russian folktale of the three brothers, in which the youngest brother — slow, stupid Ivan — finally wins out over the older, clever brothers.

In its contemporary phase, this whole trend is closely tied to a number of other psychological currents: pride in the fact that the USSR today does have a power in the world scene which Russia never had before; vague but powerful conceptions that the USSR represents "the wave of the future," and that Britain, Germany, the United States, and other countries have all had their day as top nations — now it is the turn of the USSR; Pan-Slavic movements reaching back into the last century and implemented at present by international Communism under Russian leadership and even by the Russian Orthodox Church.

Distrust of the outside world has been enormously reinforced by a number of factors. The most obvious, of course, is isolation of the past generation, especially during the Iron Curtain period. There are also some crucial historical events. It is true that, immediately after the Bolshevik Revolution, Western nations, during a period of economic and political confusion, tried their best to crush the newly formed Communist state. The older leaders will never forget the support given the White armies and the Allied expeditionary forces of thirty years ago, and the younger leaders have had these facts drummed into them. The theme of Allied intervention, muted during World War II, has since been revived with renewed vehemence. Now the United States is accused, in both popular and scholarly treatment, of having spearheaded the intervention of 1918–1920. There was also the experience with the Germans. There is evidence that many members of the cultural and technical elite (and not just in the Ukraine and Byelorussia) regarded the German invaders initially as liberators and also as bearers of a "higher" civilization. But the brutality of the Germans and their open doctrine that the Slavs were *Untermenschen* had the effect of convincing many that the regime's "propaganda" had been the truth. Hence — as interviews with defectors and other material show — even the most cynical and sophisticated members of the Soviet elite are not quite sure but that what the ruling elite says about the "imperialistic" and "predatory" purposes of American policy may not actually be true.

2. *Loyalty.* This is the positive side of the first characteristic of the ruling elite, their patriotism. There are, of course, in the Soviet elite — as in all elites — some individuals who are concerned only with their own safety and personal advancement. It is probable that *national* patriotism is a comparatively less powerful motivation in the ruling elite than in the middle and lower elites. Proportionately more of the top elite probably are genuinely committed to "the world revolution," meaning world hegemony of the Soviet Union over a world order of Communist states, as opposed to pure national interest in the traditional sense. Yet, in the elite as a whole (and by no means excluding the ruling elite and most especially its military members) we must reckon with a kind of fanatic (and somewhat defensive) devotion to "the Homeland."

From our work with the defectors, we judge that true hostility to the regime and indeed to Communism as a system generally does not erase the deepest kind of identification with the nation-state. Loyalty and hostility to the regime are quite separable from attitudes toward the nation-state. However disaffected, on whatever grounds, members of the Soviet elite may be with the regime or with Communist theory and practice, only a small minority will forget their patriotism. This does not, however, preclude the possibility that, under the same conditions, even members of the ruling elite might act *against* the regime in the name of patriotism.

3. *Communist ideology.* This is the most difficult of all the characteristics to phrase precisely. One must steer a very careful — and quite subtle — middle course between two extremes that are all too fashionable. It is nonsense, of course, to think that the Soviet elite is motivated entirely, or even mainly, by this "secular religion." Nationalism, patriotism, and self-interest — to varying degrees and in varying combinations — are probably as strong or even more powerful as motivations for the majority. But it is equally incorrect to dismiss ideological factors completely. There are undoubtedly some individuals, and some key individuals, who still believe in a quasi-religious way in "Marxist-Leninist-Stalinist" doctrine. Even those whose conscious point of view is that it is simply a useful tool with which to manipulate the Soviet masses and to subvert foreign populations are still affected by the "theology." They are the prisoners of their own special vocabulary. It is a commonplace of psychology that the outlook of any group upon the world and experience is determined and reflected to an important extent by the clichés they continually use, by the habitual premises which they accept. No group which over many years preaches a doctrine, however much with tongue in cheek, has its thinking uncolored. If a person says something often enough and consistently enough, he will come to believe or half believe it himself — whatever his initial motives of expediency or cynical manipulation.

Over and above the responses which have become automatic in spite of initial skepticism, there is a great deal in Soviet practice (in contrast to dogma) which the Soviet elite consciously and sincerely accept and value. Just as one cannot equate opposition to the regime with lack of Russian nationalism, so, equally, one cannot equate disaffection with anti-Communist tendencies. Most of the refugees who have proved their opposition to the regime (or the fact that they were in serious trouble with it) nevertheless — and they will frequently talk frankly on this topic — say they still believe in many of the political, economic, and social institutions of the USSR: national control of heavy industry; most aspects of the welfare program; machine agriculture with the machinery supplied by the state.

The goals of the majority of the ruling elite, however, go beyond the preservation of these "achievements" of the Soviet generation. World revolution, or at any rate world domination, is an unchanging objective of the top group.* Some probably hold to this because they genuinely believe in world revolution on ideological grounds; more share this goal because they are convinced that the Soviet state can be "safe" only in a world where the USSR is unquestionably dominant; still more are influenced by both of these motives in varying blends. For this reason, Leites[8] was right in insisting that genuine agreement with the West would be inconceivable to the Politburo. Indeed, it has been said that, if there were no "capitalist encirclement," the leaders would have to invent it, since they justify the hardships imposed on the population by asserting such sacrifices to be necessary to insure military preparedness against probable attacks by the ring of hostile and aggressive "encirclers."

It is almost certain that the same considerations apply to the present Party Presidium, though there may be differences in the time scale and in the extent of temporary concessions which might be made. "Agreements" are conceivable — and some might be greatly to our advantage — but, in terms of the mentality of the Soviet ruling elite, they would be regarded merely as tactical or strategic moves with ultimate objectives little changed. Such "agreements" could, however, effect fairly stable relations which might, in turn, gradually produce changes in the Soviet system compatible with long-run "peaceful coexistence." This might mean an eventual change in the leadership's present stereotyped way of looking at international relations.

Another point should be made explicitly. Though the names of Marx and Engels are still given ritual honor, Soviet ideology is more and more Moscow-centered and more and more given to identifying the cause of Communism with the Soviet State. Even the phrase which has been applied to Lenin's doctrine,

---

* It will be apparent from the continued reiteration of this point in this revised version of our earlier report that we do not feel the goal of world Communism to have been abandoned. The objective may, however, atrophy under conditions of prolonged "peaceful coexistence."

"Marxism a la Tartare," is hopelessly dated. The bridge to Western European nineteenth-century liberal and leftist doctrine* is progressively weakened. French and Italian Communists of the more "idealistic" variety feel less and less a common body of values going back not only to Marx and Engels but to Sorel and other figures of the Western European heritage. This fact can become of considerable importance.

Finally, it should be remarked that if, as is probable, a good deal of the ideological vitality of Soviet youth is gone, this is not necessarily a disadvantage to the stability of the system. The present leadership probably prefers a docile, unquestioning youth whose lack of "revolutionary ferment" will eliminate possible political embarrassment.

4. *"Conspiratorial mentality."* This is a feature of International Communism† generally, and may seem too obvious to mention. Yet it is very difficult for Americans — who are, on the whole, accustomed to open and direct dealing — to give full weight to this factor. Perhaps only those who have had fairly intimate and sustained contact with former members of the apparatus of international Communism have a picture that approaches imaginative reality. The deviousness of behavior, the disposition to "read between the lines" and to interpret the acts of others at several different levels, the whole system of wheels within wheels — all of this is so foreign to American experience and psychology that it is all too easy to laugh it off as "E. Phillips Oppenheim stuff."

It must be remembered, also, that the present Soviet elite not only inherits the older Communist tradition of scheming and conspiratorial technique, but now has behind it a generation of specifically Soviet experience. The members of the present elite of the USSR are the most successful pupils of Stalin and his generation; they draw upon a whole bag of tested tricks. Moreover, they represent those — and only those — who have been

---

* In some Western European doctrine from the Jacobins on (and including the earlier Marx) there were definitely antiliberal tendencies. Some of these writers exercised strong influence on Lenin and his Russian precursors.

† This also, of course, has a special phrasing from pre-Bolshevik Russian revolutionary groups. On the whole, Lenin turned this "mentality" into an asset also.

skilled enough in these maneuvers to survive in competition with others who were also trained in the same devices.

5. *Caution.* The Communist state has twice within the life-time of present leaders come close to extinction. These leaders have also witnessed the downfall of once powerful rival cliques and individuals and must often have murmured to themselves privately whatever is the Communist equivalent of "There, but for the grace of God, go I." The effect of such experiences has been to develop a mental climate which is characteristically cautious. You do not act by choice in vital matters unless you think you have a pretty sure thing. Of course, if the choice is, or appears to be, that of acting or being overwhelmed by foreign or internal forces who are definitely about ready to move, then you act of necessity. But the characteristic and preferred strategy is clearly that of very careful and detailed preparation before any major risk is taken. The cost of failure is seen as too great. You probe your enemy's defenses first, seeing if he has a soft spot here or there. You engage in diversionary tactics and note how they are met. Only when you think you have a clear pic-ture of your opponent's behavior and when you think his weak-nesses are well known and when all is ready on your side, do you attempt a decisive blow.*

This general tendency toward caution about undertaking major offensives which involve elements of real risk to one's own central power base is an understandable product of Soviet history and experience. In it there may also be elements which evolved from Stalin's realization of some of his own limitations. He perhaps knew that he had neither the intellectual stature nor the moral

* See Borkenau, *European Communism*, p. 551: "To the communist the traditional sharp division between war and peace appears as 'undialectic' and that is why we have the cold war. If anything is certain it is that the Politburo does not think in terms of the day when the generals will take over from the politicians and fight it out. For them physical war is quite a subordinate aspect of politics. Even the atom bomb matters more for them as a political threat than as an actual means of destruction. No doubt they intend to use it; but not as a gadget for the removal of all political difficulties. They mean to use it exactly as Hitler used his tanks in France; to clinch, by a few short rapid blows, a long phase of slow disintegrative action. The opposite policy, that of a sudden, violent and decisive blow without political preparation — no doubt condemned by the Politburo as 'undialectical' — was finally rejected when Zhdanov was liquidated."

authority within Communism that Lenin had had. Therefore, he devised his procedures of playing the game slowly and cautiously, substituting cunning for intellectual power and moral force. A good case can be made for the view that the same considerations apply to Khrushchev, Molotov, and others currently at the top.* The way the system operated under Stalin's long rule tended to eliminate those who were threats as potential rivals to one-man dictatorship and to favor, on the whole, those who were shrewd, cautious plotters who took few unnecessary risks but had good organizational ability. We must not underestimate the abilities of the present rulers, though they lack the human qualities which Western peoples value. Their abilities are not identical with those of Western leaders, but the ruling Soviet clique has gone through a selective process stressing administrative ability, productivity, drive, and the capacity for survival.

In addition, we must recur to an ideological factor. The seriousness with which the Varga controversy and similar matters were taken by the ruling elite is prima facie evidence that the ancient Marxist dogma of the "internal contradictions" of capitalist societies is by no means a dead letter. There is no doubt that many of the Communist elite believe that economic collapse or wars between capitalist countries[9] will render Western countries easy prey to capture without global war. If your country has recently lost millions of its manpower and had vital economic resources destroyed on a vast scale, why run the risk of additional enormous losses when the plum will fall from the tree of its own weight — if you just wait a little? There is probably an additional reason that makes many Communist leaders feel that time is on their side: the curve of industrial production increasingly favors the Soviet bloc.[10] Some Western experts are convinced that by 1965 Soviet-bloc industrial productivity will equal that of the Western bloc. Therefore, even if the Communist ruling elite postulate the necessity of an eventual all-out war, why not wait until the ratio of nuclear weapons and industrial achievement is more favorable to the USSR?

This attitude of caution applies, naturally, only under certain

---

* We have here substituted the name of Khrushchev for that of Malenkov in our earlier report, but the point, of course, is not thereby changed.

conditions. Most Western observers believe that the regime would fight on an all-out scale if, for example, the United States and its allies appeared about to seize Poland successfully. There is a possibility that severe internal dissension at the Party Presidium level would result in one faction's choosing global war as an alternative preferable to their own loss of power. This has been argued by some well-informed people. However, it seems more probable to us that the ruling elite will prefer to avoid war as long as there is serious division of opinion on any major issue within the Party Presidium. The great fear of any faction is that, in a war crisis, another faction might "make a deal" with the West. Therefore no ruling clique will choose war unless they have eliminated potential rivals and consolidated their power.

Soviet caution, under all circumstances, is directly proportional to the armed strength, economic might, and internal unity of the Western bloc. It is also more than possible that the posture of caution is directly proportional to the direct experience of leaders with the strength of the West and the vividness of their personal picture of how difficult was the struggle to establish an independent and strong Communist state. When, as, and if the current regime feels itself secure, this "cautionary" psychology may appreciably wane.

6. *"Puritanical discipline."* * This ideal of the regime is by no means completely achieved, and yet it is real enough for us to take account of it. The Party elite do love their work to an extent paralleled in Western history only by militant religious orders and certain missionary cadres. Family, recreation, outside interests — all these in theory (and to an appreciable degree in practice) are utterly subordinate to the demands of one's "mission." Many Party functionaries live an ascetic type of existence, putting prodigious energy and vigilance into their work, with

---

* Many will find it difficult to think of Khrushchev as puritanical on the basis of his behavior at Belgrade, and after. We speak here, of course, mainly of the discipline of work rather than of a general character type. In addition, it has been suggested (Dicks, *Human Relations*, 5:111–175) that much of the rigid behavior of the Soviet elite reflects an effort by the individual to control those "oral" impulses which show through in Khrushchev's behavior.

only a very occasional splurge with the luxuries and facilities at their disposal.* The "careerists-opportunists" may submit to this puritanical discipline most unwillingly and only for motives of expediency — yet most of the time they must give a credible performance along these lines or they will take a treacherous fall from the treadmill. The rulers are still far, however, from persuading the people that the elite is uniformly — or even generally — incorruptible, wise, just, and genuinely concerned about the individuals with whom they deal and about the general welfare of the masses. Nevertheless, our respondents seldom accused members of the upper elite of seeking *personal* gain — other than in power terms. Those of high position are ordinarily regarded as incorruptible in this sense. "You can't use *blat* on the MVD," was a statement we frequently heard.

7. *Emphasis upon analysis of opponent's psychology.* The game of politics, whether played against internal opponents or in the international scene, is conceived as a struggle in which the capabilities of a rival individual or group to make decisions are tested and strained to the limit. The past moves of one's opponents must be most carefully analyzed in order to determine their strengths and weaknesses and also to forecast their probable future moves so that preparation can be made to counter them. Initiative is of the essence for success, but it cannot be taken in a vacuum. Opponents are assumed to be psychologically or materially committed to a set strategy of attack or defense. This strategy must be properly diagnosed, and then one's own next moves can be correctly calculated. There are no abstract principles that provide infallible guides. Rather, the decision-making capacities that are pitted against each other are (on *both* sides) limited and vulnerable. The "new Soviet man" considers all life a world of conflict in which each actor or group of actors must seek to impose his will upon the situation. Initiative can be wrested from one's opponents, or fully exploited if already held, only to the extent that one has a realistic picture not only of the objective capabilities and vulnerabilities both of the opponent's

* Often these spurges have a rather planned nature, and are geared in with the purposes of the leaders, as in the series of lavish parties and public displays of good humor characteristic of Soviet leaders at home and abroad in the summer of 1955.

and of one's own side but also of psychological factors affecting the behavior of both sides. Even the best knowledge of the positions of the two sides is provisional and limited by the reactions each side can be expected to make to various combinations of pressures and of timing. Wresting or holding the initiative means fighting the battle on ground that is psychologically (as well as otherwise) familiar ground.

18

The Intelligentsia*

The preceding chapter was concerned with the political elite. The political elite is a segment, or better an extension, of a more inclusive elite group which is identified by the Russian term *intelligentsia.* The official Soviet conception of the intelligentsia was clarified by Molotov, speaking before the Eighteenth Party Congress in 1939. Apparently basing his statement on data drawn from the suppressed 1937 census, he cited a total of 9.5 million members of this stratum of Soviet society. His definition was, however, exceedingly broad, designed to give an impression of an imposingly large group of responsible administrators, specialists, and technicians. For example, he cited not merely doctors (132,000), but intermediate medical personnel, including attendants and midwives; not merely accountants, but ordinary bookkeepers as well; not only statisticians, but also statistical clerks; not only factory directors, but the managers of shoe-repair shops and restaurants. Allowing for increases resulting from expanded advanced training and further growth of the relevant occupational groups, we may accept a figure of at least 13 million for the current size of the group to which Molotov referred.

An alternative basis for defining the Soviet intelligentsia is by educational level. At the end of 1952, there were about 5.5

* A rough current estimate of the Soviet population (adjusting on the basis of the 1939 census) would be: intelligentsia plus white-collar employees, 20 per cent; workers, 35 per cent; peasants, 45 per cent. Soviet census data usually group the intelligentsia and ordinary white-collar workers in one category. As we have indicated, for many purposes of analysis this group must be further distinguished. This section, however, is concerned only with the intelligentsia as more narrowly defined above. For a full description, see Alex Inkeles, "Social Stratification and Social Mobility in the Soviet Union: 1940–1950," *American Sociological Review,* 15:465–479 (August 1950).

million persons working in the national economy who had completed either a higher education (approximately 1.85 million) or a technical secondary education (approximately 3.7 million). In addition, there was a large body of individuals with higher education not reckoned in this count, as well as a still larger group possessing an ordinary (as against a technical) secondary education. In 1940, those with all forms of higher and secondary education numbered about 13 million, and a conservative estimate for the early 1950's would be 16 million.

Throughout this report, our references to the intelligentsia are to roughly the group encompassed by the two definitions used above. We include in the intelligentsia people in the technical, responsible administrative, professional, and related activities, regardless of formal education, as well as the well educated, regardless of occupation. This is roughly the way in which Soviet citizens use the relevant term (*intelligent*), and roughly the way they classify themselves. It is to be noted that we *exclude* ordinary white-collar workers, clerks, typists, salesgirls, ordinary bookkeepers, bottle washers in laboratories, and place these people in a separate group called "employees." There are, of course, many similarities between the intelligentsia and the employees as broad social groups which distinguish them from both the manually engaged worker and the peasant. But the intelligentsia — especially the upper and middle segments — can be considered part of the elite, whereas the "employee" or ordinary white-collar worker clearly falls outside this charmed circle.

A high proportion of the intelligentsia are not members of the political elite, and are essentially apolitical; they consist of artists, teachers,* technicians, and administrators. These people are especially crucial for the functioning of the Soviet system in that they possess those high orders of skills that affect the operation of the society's essential institutions. At the same time, they present special problems to the system. Persons occupying these posts are, for example, required to take considerable initiative,

---

* DeWitt (*Science*, 120:1–4) estimates 90,000 full-time teachers and professors in Soviet higher educational establishments at the end of 1953. He calculated 748,000 educational professionals of all categories (but many of these would now be "intelligentsia" in the Soviet sense) and 68,000 research scientists. See also Nicholas DeWitt, *Soviet Professional Manpower* (Washington, D.C., 1955).

and they have in many instances a good deal of power. Therefore, the ramifications of their actions may be considerable. Accordingly, the regime, while encouraging them to take initiative, to be bold, is constantly concerned with keeping a close control over their actions. Certain members of the intelligentsia, artists and intellectuals, are by profession the generators of new ideas — an extremely risky activity for both the individual and the state in a totalitarian system. Furthermore, many members of the intelligentsia have subloyalties, to professions, to their artistic or intellectual activities, or to the particular institutions which they serve. Such loyalties may occasionally cross national boundaries and result in the "homeless cosmopolitanism" about which Soviet leaders have complained in the postwar period.

The member of the intelligentsia is subject to closer surveillance than is the rank-and-file citizen; he runs a greater risk of punishment; more extreme demands are put upon him. The regime finds it necessary to compensate him more fully with prestige and material rewards. Additionally, he finds himself identified by others as the representative and supporter of the regime. To varying degrees, members of the intelligentsia see themselves as supporters of the Soviet order, and to some extent as responsible for the plight of their fellow citizens. Our data indicate that the intelligentsia are psychologically more involved in internal conflict over their role in Soviet society than are the members of other social groups. All-in-all, the position of the intelligentsia in Soviet society is a favorable one, but it is one that is highly charged with both positive and negative factors. The testimony of Project respondents bears directly on these points.*

As indicated in the discussion of sources of satisfaction and dissatisfaction, the life situation of the Soviet intelligentsia is more satisfactory than that of any other group (except possibly the top elite) on virtually every level, although this by no means implies that they do not have a certain number of complaints. Their standard of living is generally satisfactory. Food, which is a problem for many other groups, is complained of by only a

---

* Since at this point and in the chapters which follow immediately we once again deal with conclusions based on the statistical findings of the Project, we refer the reader for guidance in evaluating them to the statement concerning the assumptions we make which is presented in Part III

minority. They are bothered by crowded housing and desire greater privacy in their dwelling units. Their biggest source of discontent is the inadequacy of clothing. However, only 25 per cent of the *émigré* intelligentsia feel that their material conditions were below those "of the majority" of the people, as compared to 80 per cent of the peasants.

By and large, they feel that their rate of pay is fair. They are three times as likely as the peasants to feel that their pay was adequate for the job they did, and nine times as likely as the peasants to feel that they got their fair share in comparison to what other persons got. However, they are almost unique in complaining that other persons were advanced over their heads for political reasons.

With their material needs essentially taken care of, the intelligentsia's primary concern is that they have interesting work. This aspect is the major criterion of the job, according to our intelligentsia informants. The fact that this requirement was met while they lived in the Soviet Union is indicated by approximately three-fourths of the intelligentsia respondents who said they were satisfied with their jobs. Since work is an important source of satisfaction for the intelligentsia, many of them flee into their jobs as an escape from other aspects of Soviet life.

Much more than any other group, the intelligentsia are bothered by the penetration of politics into every aspect of Soviet life. Frequent changes in Party line and reversals of ideological position affect this group most sharply. The purging of literature and the arts in general and attacks on former policies are almost certain to affect the intelligentsia directly and to violate their values.

The child born into the intelligentsia family is relatively fortunate. His material wants are taken care of. If he desires a college education and eventually a professional or administrative position, as he almost certainly will, the odds are strong that he will succeed. (Even during the early period of Soviet rule, when obstacles were set systematically against the older intelligentsia, their children were very successful in getting the schooling and jobs they wanted.) Not only will his family be able to help him financially, but its values are such that he can count on it for full support. (About three-fourths of the members of the intelli-

gentsia in our sample felt that their families gave them full support in getting an education.) Despite the stress of Soviet life,
his family will act in most cases as a solid unit, with each member
supporting and helping the others.

Even though the pay of the main breadwinner is comparatively
good in intelligentsia families, the size of the family will be
restricted so that the standard of living may be maintained. The
chief drawbacks to life in the intelligentsia family are the long
hours which members of the family work — only 29 per cent in
our sample reported that they worked under nine hours a day —
and the danger that some member of the family may be arrested.
Within the intelligentsia group, those who have administrative
responsibilities are twice as likely to be arrested as those who do
not.

Members of the intelligentsia, both absolutely and relative to
other groups, are active in their contact with other people, over
half reporting having three or more friends, and only about one
in ten saying he had no friends. These friends tend to be people
with whom they share common interests. Although they have
frequent access to cultural and recreational facilities, the intelligentsia are distinguished by the extent to which they rely on
their own sources of recreation — on their friends and on family
activities.

Members of the intelligentsia are highly involved in the Soviet
communications network. Nine out of ten read newspapers and
books frequently, and a majority report frequent exposure to
almost all other sources of information. Newspapers and word
of mouth are the most important sources of information for the
intelligentsia. They seem to have good informal sources of information, and as a result nearly all are convinced that rumors
and word of mouth are in general more reliable than are official
sources of information. This opinion is markedly more prevalent
among the intelligentsia than among the lower classes. The intelligentsia, having a better educational background and more
highly developed critical faculties, are more discriminating than
other groups in assessing the reliability of what they find in the
official media. They are not inclined, however, to reject completely what they read and hear, but only to judge each bit of
information critically.

In all their attitudes and relations with regard to the Soviet regime and the Soviet system, the intelligentsia are characterized by a relatively high degree of differentiation and discrimination. Even among the refugee intelligentsia, whose deep-seated hostility toward the regime can scarcely be questioned, we find that 78 per cent are willing to consider keeping some aspect of the Soviet system, such as the social-welfare provisions, the educational system, or the state ownership of basic industries and the means of transportation and communication. These choices they share with all other groups, and, like all other refugee groups, they are united in rejecting the system of collective farming. They are distinctive, however, in opposing, in the proportion of three to one, continued state ownership of light industry. That aspect of the Soviet system which the intelligentsia reject most vigorously is the system of police control — the "terror." Any improvement in this aspect of the Soviet system on the part of the post-Stalin leadership will strike a very responsive chord in the intelligentsia. Even so, the intelligentsia show less violence than other refugee groups in their rejection of the regime and the leadership. Furthermore, they are less likely in retrospect to deny to the Soviet regime and system certain of its factual accomplishments, such as the expansion of education and the increase in tractor production.

A combination of the facts that the intelligentsia are relatively free of anxiety over their basic material needs and have a long-standing cultural tradition of service to society makes them predisposed to accept a social order in which the interests of the individual are subordinate to those of the state. However, more than four out of five would favor a state which guaranteed personal freedom as opposed to security. The intelligentsia took this position more strongly than did any other social class. They would, therefore, favor a system in which service to the group was effected voluntarily.

In viewing the Soviet system, the intelligentsia are apt to be more optimistic in assessing chances for advancement in it for all its members than is the remainder of the population. They are also most likely to see personal ability as the basis on which one advances, although they are also those who complain most about the unwarranted advancement of others on political grounds rather than on the basis of competence.

Again, we must comment briefly on certain sex differences in this regard. Women occupy many professional jobs in the Soviet Union. In the medical profession, for example, they comprise a substantial majority. However, high-ranking technical and administratively responsible jobs, while certainly not closed to women, tend to go in an overwhelming majority of cases to men.

19

The Peasants

As he reports his own experience, the peasant is outstandingly the most oppressed, exploited, and disadvantaged man of the Soviet era. This is true not only when he compares his lot to that of the better-off groups such as the intelligentsia, but equally in terms of the absolute level of deprivation which he feels. For example, over 90 per cent of the refugee peasants felt that they had had no opportunity for a career, about 85 per cent were dissatisfied with their job situation on the *kolkhoz*, only about 15 per cent felt that their pay was commensurate with that of people doing other types of work, and only 10 per cent felt that by comparison with the average their material conditions of life placed them in the "better-off" category.

This was not limited, furthermore, to the peasant's *feeling* deprived, but was reflected in the objective conditions of his life. This is best illustrated by considering the life chances of boys born into a peasant family, and to keep the issue clear we will consider only those born or mainly raised under the Soviet regime. Only about 5 per cent succeeded in getting to college, and a mere 10 per cent got through advanced secondary school training. These young people are, furthermore, aware of their relative educational deprivation, because less than a third feel their educational opportunity to have been equal to or better than the average. No more than 20 per cent rose to white-collar or professional jobs; and, since many more aspire to such positions, the young peasant has the greatest relative chance to be frustrated in his occupational aspirations. The income available to be spent on each child in the peasant families of our sample was on the order of only a fifth of the income available for each child in an upper-class home. And because of the many basic changes which the whole pattern of rural life has undergone, the child who grew up in the peasant family was five times as likely as someone raised in an intelligentsia family *to feel* that his family grew apart rather than closer together under the impact of Soviet conditions. This does not necessarily mean that peasant families broke up more often, although the collectivization probably did create a high proportion of broken families in the countryside. But for the peasants the greater physical and economic mobility brought about by Soviet conditions was *perceived* as a growing apart of the old solidary family ties, whereas workers — and particularly the intelligentsia — took mobility more for granted and thus did not see it as a blow to family ties.

A further indication of the deprived status of the peasant is the fact that capable young men tend to get jobs in the towns or cities, or with the machine tractor stations. The younger generation of field hands on Soviet collective farms consists mostly of women.

Many of the depressed and deprived qualities of the peasant's life experience could perhaps be blamed on relatively impersonal forces, including the general process of industrialization in the USSR. The peasant, however, will have no such nonsense. He (or she) apparently prefers to *personalize* responsibility for his state of affairs, and he is a very angry man indeed. A fair amount of the peasant's hostility is projected onto other social groups in Soviet society. Indeed, in large measure, the peasant tends to see the difficulties of his group as being the fault of the intelligentsia, probably because in his mind the intelligentsia and the regime are linked. This is partly because so many of the people who do things to him, acting as agents of the regime, are members of the intelligentsia — officials, judges, and agricultural directors. This naturally leads to some blurring of the lines and a generalization of the image of members of the intelligentsia as government agents. This is not to say, however, that the peasants do not discriminate among the intelligentsia, and indeed hold in high regard those they feel to be of the old type who have high standards or who serve the people.

It is when dealing with the regime that the real intensity of the peasant's hostile sentiments becomes apparent. The peasant is outstanding in his punitive attitude toward the leadership;

about 75 per cent of his group advocate violent death for the top leaders, and about 80 per cent are willing to drop an atom bomb on Moscow, at least as a last resort. Interestingly enough, however, the peasants are outstandingly *low* among all social groups in claiming that the Bolsheviks were worse than the Nazis, probably because of all social groups they were most frustrated by the Nazi failure to break up the collective farms.

The collective-farm situation is, of course, the crux of the issue for the peasant. He sees it as *the* cause of his deprived status and as the reason for the loss of independence, autonomy, and integrity which he so keenly feels. In his mind the collective-farm system is a simple creation of the regime and the regime alone, for which he feels it must bear full responsibility. Apparently, he will be satisfied with nothing short of its dissolution. This is not to assert, of course, that there are no elements associated with the present collective-farm system which the peasant would not be willing to permit and even encourage if the *kolkhozy* were dissolved. For example, many peasants have no objection to agricultural coöperatives so long as they are voluntary. About one-fourth of our peasant respondents favored the system of machine pools so long as the machinery is owned and managed by the coöperatives of farmers and not by the government. Improvements in the supply of goods and in opportunities for social mobility would have an effect on his attitudes, but the result would be minor compared with the impact of such an improvement on working-class and middle-class individuals.

Of all the social groups the peasantry is least prone to acknowledge any accomplishments or achievements on the part of the regime and the Soviet system, which partly reflects the peasantry's general hostility toward the system and partly stems from the fact that, as far as they could see, there *was* little accomplished in their own immediate milieu. Although the peasant appears to be so determinedly at odds with the regime, he turns out to be rather disappointing as a political activist. He is less likely than a member of the intelligentsia to have left the Soviet Union voluntarily, his emigration more likely being a result of forcible evacuation by the Germans. Once outside Soviet territory he is more likely to give fear as a reason for not returning, and less likely to cite some essentially political or ideological basis for opposition to the regime. The peasant, in other words, gives the impression of someone who would just as soon stick close to his land and try to beat the regime at its own game, rather than go off on political and military campaigns to fight Bolshevism.

Like the other groups in our sample, the peasants find many of the general *institutional* features of the system quite acceptable. More than eight out of ten favor government ownership of heavy industry and of transport and communication, and indeed they are twice as likely as the intelligentsia to favor government ownership of light industry! Furthermore, they are among the weakest in their allegiance to principles of civil liberties, being most likely of all groups to remain indifferent or to reconcile themselves to government restrictions on freedom of assembly and speech. In general, like the rest of the population, they want the government to guarantee every man a job, and they favor security in their jobs over advancement.

How can one, then, formulate the distinctive political character of the Soviet peasantry? Centrally and overwhelmingly they want the collective-farm system done away with in its present form, because they see it as enslaving the peasant and making him a serf of the state. They would probably retain some co-operative farming on a voluntary basis and would almost certainly want some form of locally owned and controlled machine tractor stations to accompany a general return to private peasant holdings. Beyond this, they would like some kind of benevolent welfare-state government with health and other guaranteed benefits. It does not seem likely that this government would be objectionable simply because it was authoritarian so long as, in the eyes of the peasant, it was also just and nonexploitative and avoided the extremes of the secret-police type of control. For the rest, assuming decent educational and social opportunities for his children, the peasant would be quite content to leave the routine problems of state to the urban people. In brief, the peasant seems to aspire to a kind of New Economic Policy set-up.

Peasant morale in the USSR appears to be very bad at present. The peasantry is progressively less included in the *symbolic* top elite, the Supreme Soviet. The 1954 Supreme Soviet included only 40 per cent workers and peasants,* as contrasted with 52 per cent in the 1952 Supreme Soviet.

Just as the collective-farm system has been the economic institution most generally opposed by the Soviet populace, and the peasantry the most alienated segment of the populace, so has the collective-farm system been the least successful of Soviet productive institutions. The peasant's hatred of the collectives and the economic ineffectiveness of collectivized agriculture are related, but certainly not identical, phenomena. The failures of Soviet agriculture are at least partially due to insufficient capital investment in this sector of the economy and to defects of organization and administration as well as to the poor morale of the peasant. Furthermore, on the part of the peasant, we must distinguish between his alienation from the collective farm as an institutional form and his lack of incentive to work effectively as a member of the collective. It is quite possible that, if the peasant were to receive a greater reward for his efforts on the collective, he might devote more energy to making it work as a productive unit — in his interest to increase his own share of the income of the collective farm — even though he might at the same time continue to yearn for a return to private ownership of the land. All this is to say that we must not confuse the great unpopularity of the collective-farm system with its economic ineffectiveness. Admittedly, it would take a marked change of policy to bring about the necessary organizational improvements, the requisite investment of capital, and an adequate system of incentives for the collective farmer. However, it is at least conceivable under such conditions that the collective farm could be made effective and the collective farmer induced to work harder despite his antipathy to collectivized agriculture.

* These figures are generally given by *social origin*. In other words, it should not be assumed that the proportion of people among the delegates actually employed as peasants or workers was as high as these figures might indicate.

20

The Workers*

On most of the questions on which there was variation in attitude between different social groups, our data revealed a fairly smooth gradient of opinion, with the intelligentsia at one pole and the peasants at the other. The general pattern of response to questions dealing with life experiences and basic social attitudes has already been discussed (Chapter 12), along with a description of the more important aspects of the life experience and attitudes of the two polar groups in preceding chapters. To avoid repetition and excessive covering of the same ground, we shall omit here separate profiles of the other three major social groups to which the remainder of our respondents belonged — the employee (white-collar) group, the skilled workers, and the ordinary workers. The precise differences between the groups are taken up in detail in the various portions of the forthcoming book by Alex Inkeles and Raymond A. Bauer. It should suffice to note here that for most purposes an adequate, although rough, working distinction can be made between the manual and nonmanual groups in our sample, with the intelligentsia representing the nonmanual side quite well and the peasants the manual side. Nevertheless, the workers are quite clearly a significant group in Soviet society, and we will therefore give brief attention to two relevant points: how the workers are internally differentiated and how they differ from the other manual group, the peasants.

It is important to recognize that the Soviet policy of marked differentials in pay and other rewards according to skill and productivity has apparently succeeded in introducing marked

* Almost exclusively urban. The "urban" (excludes small towns) population of the USSR has increased from 11.5 per cent in 1897, 18.4 per cent in 1913, 32.8 per cent in 1939, to an estimated 36 per cent in 1954.

distinctions within the working class. These distinctions are so wide that for some purposes it is unwise to consider the workers as a single homogeneous class. The segment of the working class which separates itself under the self-designation "skilled worker" is much more satisfied with its job experience in general, and with its pay in particular, than is the rank-and-file worker group. In this greater occupational satisfaction the skilled workers are closer to the nonmanual groups than they are to their fellow workers.

The differences in occupational experience are reflected in other attitudes. Skilled workers, for example, are generally closer to the nonmanuals than they are to other workers in their early adolescent occupational aspirations, apparently having more hope and ambition to advance themselves in life. Furthermore, the skilled workers tend to take a view of the relations between classes in the USSR which is more typical of the nonmanual than of the manual group. They see much more harmony between classes, and especially between manual and nonmanual groups, than do their less fortunate unskilled worker friends. These are simply a few of the outstanding examples of differences in the life experiences and attitudes of subgroups nominally both within the working class.

Although the skilled worker is better rewarded, more satisfied, and more ambitious for himself and his children than the ordinary worker, he overwhelmingly identifies himself with the working class and not with the employee and intelligentsia groups. There seems, furthermore, to be little antagonism left between the two working-class groups, unless the skilled worker openly identifies with the regime and becomes its instrument in pushing up work norms.[1] Indeed, most of the ordinary workers seemed to look up to the more skilled workers, and strove to attain this more favored position for themselves wherever possible by improving their skills.

We turn now to differences between the peasants and the other half of the manually employed. In their attitudes toward and feelings about the Soviet regime, its institutions, and their functioning, the workers and the peasants are very much alike. This may be assumed to result in part from the fact that many of the workers have not been too long away from their rural background and still maintain connections with it, and in part from the fact that in many ways both workers and peasants are greatly deprived by the regime. At the same time, it is obvious that the situation of the man living in a city or town and working in a factory is fundamentally different from that of the man living in the countryside and working on a collective farm. It is important to note two apparent differences which distinguish the manually employed peasant from the manually engaged industrial worker.

The worker's feelings are much less intense and forcefully expressed than are those of the peasant. It will be recalled that we referred to the peasant as the "angry man" of the Soviet era. The urban worker's judgment of the regime lacks this intensity and violence; he seems less likely to defy authority if given the opportunity, and more likely to be easily placated if the regime can provide a few sops to drain off some of his hostility and restore his hopes for better things to come. He has much less sense of outrage and, to a substantial degree, lacks the feeling of complete loss of autonomy and the sense of having been dragooned which one sees in the peasant.

Closely linked with this difference in intensity of feeling is the difference in orientation to the immediate institutional setting in which the worker and peasant spend their working day. To the peasant, the collective farm is an excrescence, and he seeks its complete annihilation. In contrast, the Soviet worker appears to take the Soviet factory and its special form of organization for granted and as the natural way of doing things. He is unhappy about the low pay, he wants the harsh labor laws eased or eliminated,* he would like the pace eased and would be happy to have better materials to work with, but he questions hardly a single major aspect of the general organization of the Soviet factory system. This is graphically illustrated in the responses to the question on what should most certainly be changed in the Soviet system. Almost half of all peasants *spontaneously* cited the organization of agriculture as something they would be sure to change (when questioned directly, they were, of course, virtually unanimous on this issue) and, interestingly enough, almost the same proportion of workers cited the same need. In contrast, labor

* The post-Stalin leadership has made gestures toward meeting this wish.

conditions, presumably the basic problem for the worker, were spontaneously cited as certain to need change by only some 10 to 15 per cent of the workers. This clearly has important implications for the degree to which the work experience, which is for most men the most important in their daily lives, has a disaffecting impact on the peasant as against the worker.

In general, however, our data lead us to emphasize the similarities rather than the differences between the worker — at least the ordinary worker — and the peasant. This was to be expected, of course, on the basis of our knowledge of recent Soviet history as reflected in census data. The great industrialization of Soviet Russia during the period from 1928 to World War II was accompanied by extensive urbanization. The new city dwellers were overwhelmingly drawn from the countryside. Between 1926 and 1939, about 20 million persons moved or were moved from rural to urban areas, so that at the time of the 1939 census two of every five city residents were recent immigrants from the countryside.

It should be no great surprise, therefore, that among our respondents who were workers about 40 per cent came from peasant families, that is, their fathers were of peasant origin. These earlier ties with the countryside were, furthermore, frequently maintained. For example, a substantial proportion, perhaps as many as one-third, of the workers in our sample lived not in cities or towns but in villages and rural areas. Under the circumstances, it is certainly understandable that on most attitudinal questions not directly connected with their occupational experience workers and peasants constituted a kind of occupational "bloc" of manual workers as distinguished from the nonmanual intelligentsia and employees.

21

Generational Differences[1]

In any large population there are likely to be important differences in attitude among various age groups. Some of these differences will result primarily from the fact that the groups are at different points in their respective life cycles. For example, younger people may assume that they have substantial opportunities for advancement because they are indeed at the beginning of their occupational careers, whereas the older individuals, who are already more fixed in their ways of life and have perhaps also a more realistic picture of experience, are more likely to say that they do not have much opportunity for advancement. It is likely, however, that when the younger group has reached the average age of the older group it too will report that there is less opportunity for advancement. Such a difference is, therefore, essentially a life-cycle difference. Each group, as it reaches the appropriate age, may be expected to manifest certain attitudes characteristic of the given age level.

Other differences between young and old groups, however, may largely reflect differences in their average life-experience pattern, resulting from differences in the social milieu in which they grew up. Such differences are more likely to be lasting and will not even out when the younger group reaches the age which now characterizes the older group. As an example, we may choose an obvious demographic characteristic such as education. If we compare the educational level of those in our sample between the ages of twenty-one and thirty with the level of those between forty-one and fifty, we find that twice as many of the younger groups completed a full (ten-year) primary school education. The higher level of education attained by the younger generation may be expected to affect the *attitudes* the younger group will hold when *it* reaches the higher age bracket, particularly with regard to evaluations of the educational system, but also concerning other issues, since level of education appears to be strongly correlated with opinion.

Similarly, if the young and the old have lived through different social eras, especially in a society undergoing rapid change, not only their personal attributes, such as education, but also their life experience may show a significant difference that is unlikely to be evened out as the presently younger group reaches the age of the older group. For example, our older respondents, those over forty in 1950, had reached maturity or were well along in their adolescence when the forced collectivization of agriculture took place. In some significant sense they all actually lived through the collectivization, even if they were not in the countryside at the time. In contrast, those under thirty-five in 1950 were either in their early adolescence or mere children at the time of collectivization. They can "experience" the collectivization only as they are told about it or through the delayed effects it may have produced, such as the chronic food shortage. Time cannot eliminate this difference. When the currently younger people reach the present age of the older group, this difference may be expected to show in their personal image of their early life experience and in their attitudes and opinions.

Generational differences of the types described, in contrast to ordinary life-cycle differences, have major significance for any assessment of the future state of Soviet social structure. Insofar as there are major generational differences of this kind in the Soviet population, we may expect them to have significance as bases either for future change or for stability in the system. We may equally expect that the personal adjustment to the system of these differing generations will vary significantly.

There are many specific differences in experience and attitude between the older generation in our sample, those forty and over in 1950, and the younger generation, particularly those under thirty-five in 1950. Underlying and reflecting these specific differences, however, there is an important over-all difference between the generations. In general, we find that old people are oriented to values and express judgments largely with reference to a standard of past conditions. They seem always to remember or recall "how it was," and then make their judgments in the light of the memory or past standard. To the younger generation their whole life situation seems much less problematical. For them the Soviet world in which they lived was not only the real world but, in significant degree, it was the *only* world; one does not normally think of any other — least of all one that is past. Consequently, their judgments are made largely with reference to standards arising from the present situation, and in particular with reference to the instrumental or material adequacy of the present system. Once the young have found their place in the system, they are most likely to evaluate it by asking, "Does it give me what *I* want and need?" The old would phrase the question in comparative and moral terms: "Are things better or worse nowadays than in the old days?"

Closely related to the general response pattern of the generations is the greater acceptance of "Soviet reality" on the part of the young. "Acceptance" is not necessarily to be understood as approval. We mean that the younger generation appear to take "Soviet reality" for granted, without noticeable self-consciousness or awareness. For example, they are less likely than the older generation to discuss with their friends events which are taking place in the Soviet Union. They report less utilization of rumor as a source of information — which implies that they draw more of their information from the official sources — and they tend to grant less reliability to what they do get in rumors. This indicates that they look upon Soviet developments less as objects of wonder or amazement than as routine affairs to be accepted as natural.

This acceptance of things as they are is also evident in the lower awareness in the younger generation of some things which particularly attract the attention of the older people, who have the standard of the past as a guide and stimulant to perceiving the distinctive features of the system. Younger people, for example, see little difference between Party and non-Party people. They are, further, not overly sensitive to the politicization of education and work in the Soviet Union, whereas the older groups are acutely aware of this fact. In praising the school system, the older generation mainly selects such facts as the increase in educational *facilities*, something they would be likely to notice with reference to the past. The younger group appears to take the extensive facilities for granted, as if they had always been there, and selects for praise some particular area or subject which it knows to have been well taught. Finally, the younger generation is more apt than the older to state that if the leaders were better the Soviet Union could be made a better place to live in, which, of course, involves a fairly clear if implicit acceptance of the system as it exists and shifts the emphasis to making what exists better or at least not so bad.

On the whole, the younger group shows a markedly better adjustment to and assessment of occupational life in the USSR. There was probably no other general area in which the young and the old in our sample were so sharply differentiated as in the area of occupational aspirations and experiences. This is of special interest, because the occupational structure is of central importance in a large-scale industrial system such as that of the Soviet Union. At the same time, however, it must be recognized that there are few areas in which the differences found are more likely to reflect primarily life-cycle rather than generational differences. The younger group, on the whole, has not yet entered upon, or is still at an early stage in, its occupational career, and many of the disillusioning experiences which come through time have not yet had a chance to manifest themselves. Nevertheless, we feel that, in substantial measure, the differences encountered here also reflect changes in the life experience of the generations. The older group worked throughout the period of confusion and turmoil in which large-scale Soviet industry was being formed and developed, whereas the younger generation began work in a more stable scene. They started work with more familiarity with the system and, on the whole, were better trained and equipped to handle the demands of the situation.

In any event, the younger group is distinguished by its greater tendency to express the *desire* to have a career under the Soviets, in feeling that an opportunity for such a career exists, and, if they had already been launched on it, in feeling that their early desires for a career had actually been *fulfilled* under Soviet conditions. On the job, they see the working atmosphere as friendlier; and, despite their greater ambition, they are in general more satisfied with their jobs than is the older generation. Part of their positive view is reflected in the fact that they are more likely than older persons to assume that if a person possesses ability he will indeed succeed. Furthermore, when they complain about the difficulties of their work situation, they tend to blame aspects of the system, such as the poor quality or inadequate quantity of materials, rather than the system of production itself. This again illustrates the greater tendency of the younger generation to take for granted the institutional features of Soviet society and to concentrate on how the institutions work rather than to question the institutions as such.

The younger generation is not particularly distinguished from the older in the general political and social values which characterize the population as a whole. In support of the welfare state, in assigning extensive powers to the government, and in their attitudes toward civil liberties, young and old are much alike. This is congruent with our general finding that these attitudes represent a relatively undifferentiated cultural residue more or less common to the population at large.

Insofar as there are notable differences, they suggest that the younger generation goes even further than the older generation in accepting the welfare state and the role of the government in maintaining it. On the critical question of government control of light industry, for example, a question on which there was substantial class differentiation, the younger group in each class tended more strongly to support government control. The younger group was also noticeably more in favor of having the government intervene to eliminate economic inequalities among the various segments of the population. It should be mentioned, in this connection, that the degree of religious belief among the younger generation members is definitely less than among the older respondents in our sample.

On the whole, the younger generation is much like the older group in its overwhelming rejection of such features of Soviet society as political terror and the collective-farm system. The greater acceptance of Soviet reality among the younger generation is, however, reflected in a rather more positive attitude in their evaluation of some specifically Soviet institutions. For example, young people in the manual occupations are less insistent that *only* private farming be permitted, and they allow more room for some kind of coöperative. They are more willing than the older generation to acknowledge Soviet achievements in the realm of the theater and medical care and are more likely to approve the Soviet system of education, both directly as a system and indirectly in the aspects they single out for comment. It appears, in addition, that in acknowledging Soviet achievements the young are in *relatively less conflict about recognizing this positive side*. This indicates that the younger generation identifies more simply and directly with Communist institutions.

A striking picture of great importance is presented by the differences in the history of the relations to the regime of the older and younger generations.[2] Those of the older generation are much more likely to declare that they were always opposed to the Soviet regime, whereas in the younger generation having been once in favor of the regime is a rather common response. Furthermore, both among those who were always opposed and among those who once favored the regime but eventually turned against it, there are important differences between the generations in the reasons for continued opposition or for turning against the regime. Among the younger members of nonmanual groups, for example, lack of freedom is less often, and terror and brutality are relatively more often, stressed as reasons for *constant opposition* than among the older respondents in the same status. Although it accounts for fewer responses, there is a more striking difference — and a more consistent one in that it is true of all classes — in the greater tendency for the old to base their opposition on principle. This strongly suggests that members of the younger group are likely to accept the system unless they fail to receive the opportunities they hope for or expect.

Similar conclusions are suggested by the contrasting reasons of young and old for *turning against* the regime if they were once in favor of it. Older respondents lived through the collectivization and show a much greater propensity than the young to cite the agricultural policy of the regime as the reason for their change of heart, a trend manifested by older members in all social groups. In sharp contrast, the young tend to cite their exposure to the West as the precipitating factor in their defection from the regime. They cite this reason with striking frequency and markedly more often than the older generation does. Since this exposure was an event *external* to the Soviet system, one must reflect that but for this exposure many of the young people would not have been nearly so likely to turn against the regime. Furthermore, an arrest in the family is much more likely to stimulate members of the younger generation to flee the Soviet Union voluntarily. Again, the impression one gets is that these younger people are much less likely than their elders to become alienated from the system unless *they* are rejected by it.

Although there may have been every reason, prior to the completion of the Project, to expect that the younger generation would be more accepting of "Soviet reality" and the Soviet regime, it is nevertheless important to have this confirmed by our data and to learn the strength of the trend. It was not previously known, moreover, to what extent the younger generation differed from the older in the reasons for constant opposition to and turning against the regime. It is of great importance that the opposition of older people was more a matter of principle, whereas the opposition of the younger groups was more situational. Perhaps even more significant is the fact that the collectivization of agriculture, a nonrecurrent event,* was so important in turning the older group against the system; whereas exposure to the West, something outside the system, was more often required to disaffect the younger group.

Combined with evidence about occupational aspirations and experiences, and with our data on the general values of the younger generation, these factors give a very definite impression of greater potential and actual support of the whole Soviet system by the rising younger generations. This support is developed "naturally" through time, becomes taken for granted by those who give it, and is not likely to be shaken by forces within the system itself. To bring about its withdrawal seems to require the necessarily limited occurrence of contact with the outside.

---

* The collective-farm system is, of course, a continuing one, and as such generates anew in those living under it certain regular frustrations and hostilities. But the act of forced collectivization occurred only once, thus exposing directly only those who were more than children at the time.

This argues that the Soviet regime may expect to increase the breadth and stability of its social support with the passage of time, particularly as death claims the older generations who characteristically opposed the system on principle and could not easily be reconciled. This assumes of course, that the post-Stalin regime will not attempt — or be pushed into attempting — any new cataclysmic domestic programs like the collectivization of agriculture or the mass purges, which would probably have an effect on the younger generation very similar to the impact of earlier events on the older generation. The current leaders may be less likely to make this error, however, than was Stalin.

At the same time, our findings concerning the younger generation have important implications as a limiting factor on the regime's freedom of operation. The younger generation, being more deeply involved in the system, is also more demanding of it. Young people automatically expect it to produce occupational opportunity, social mobility, an expanding standard of living, and so on, to a degree which the older generation — and even that part of the older generation more committed to the Revolution and therefore more prepared for sacrifice — did not expect or demand. In short, to hold the allegiance of the younger generation the system must produce, it must work reasonably smoothly, it must provide "normalcy" and security. Failure to provide these will form a marked basis for rejection of the present leadership and a desire to find a new one, even though perhaps within the same general institutional framework. This puts the regime under strong pressure to limit its program of action, to avoid overcommitment at home and abroad, and to concentrate on making the Soviet system work more smoothly and produce more abundantly with less coercion. Much of the program of the present ruling clique appears to move essentially in this direction, and it may therefore expect to find a particularly favorable response in the younger generation, which will perhaps regard the current leaders as comprising a young, businesslike administration which will really improve conditions. On the other hand, should the program fail signally, the younger generation is likely to feel the need for a still newer administration, and may do so without feeling either emotional complications on grounds of loyalty or fear of having committed thereby an act of treason. Thus, a change in the top leadership could, to that degree, take place in a less revolutionary and total way than would have been true in the earlier years of the Soviet system.

22

Nationality Groups[1]

Along with the role of ideology, the nationalities question is an area where informed American opinion is particularly apt to be in error, veering to one extreme or the other. In fact, this is an exceedingly complicated and subtle problem, and overgeneralization and oversimplification of the issues can be dangerous to American action and policy.

HISTORICAL BACKGROUND

The amalgamation of various areas and peoples into the USSR under the hegemony of Great Russia was not accomplished without major difficulties.[2] From the Revolution on, the nationality question has been a headache to the regime: there were vacillations, reversals of policies, temporary concessions. Initially, official policy reflected elements of the "idealistic" and the "enlightened." Even in the early twenties, however, the regime did not hesitate to apply crushing military force, as in Georgia, to keep the national areas and their indigenous leaders in line with central Moscow policy. Gradually the line toughened, and there has been a general drift over the years toward Great Russian nationalism and toward the "Russification" of all areas of the USSR. There is, of course, no exact correspondence between national identification and nationality origin, nor between residence and nationality. For example, the phenomenon of the "Russified" member of a national minority is well known. Also, many of the cities of minority areas may actually be composed of a large percentage of Russians, and a high proportion of the natives in such areas may be "Russified." Nevertheless, the figures on the Party for 1922 and 1927 show clearly how inadequately minority groups were represented in its membership. During the

Great Purge of the 1930's, a substantial proportion of the top political and intellectual cadres of the national republics was liquidated.

During World War II, certain national republics proved themselves conspicuously less loyal than the inhabitants of the Great Russian heartland. The dissolution of the Volga-German Autonomous Republic early in the war and the deportation of its population to the East might be viewed as a preventive measure. But along with the Volga Republic, the Soviet government also dissolved the Kalmyck, the Chechen-Ingush, the Crimean, and the Kabardino-Balkarian Republics. In these instances, the regime frankly admitted later that the minority nationals had been disloyal.[3] The Kalmycks were disloyal in various ways (about 4500 served in the Vlassov army) and were punished by loss of civil rights and mass relocation. There were, of course, also large-scale defections of Ukrainians to the Germans.

World War II antagonized the regime, and perhaps large groups of Russian citizens, against minority nationalism. Suppression of autonomous elements, national and otherwise, has proceeded further since the war than ever before. Some of the more vigorously nationalistic groups have been exterminated or deported (from the border regions of the Baltic states, the Western Ukraine, Bessarabia, and other areas). As Merle Fainsod has pointed out, Stalin's toast to the Great Russian people at the war's end was followed by the campaign against "rootless cosmopolitanism," which had strong anti-Semitic overtones, and by a purge of nationality deviations in the national republics which is still raging and which has already been accompanied by shake-ups in the top Party command in the Azerbaidzhanian, Georgian, Kazakh, Turkmen, Uzbek, Moldavian, Karelo-Finnish, Estonian, Latvian, and Byelorussian Republics.[4] The regime's line toward Tsarist treatment of the nationalities has undergone a startling about-face. The Tsarist government and armies are now often painted as civilizing forces which brought the minor nationalities the benefits of association with the Great Russian people.

PRESENT POSITION BY IMPORTANT AREAS

The Ukraine probably presents a more sensitive problem than any other area, and in it the nationality problem has not been solved. The Eastern Ukraine is progressively more "Russified," whereas the Western Ukraine (containing about one-fourth of the Ukrainian population) presents really serious problems to the regime, particularly in its resistance to the collectivization of agriculture. At least as recently as 1947, the Ukrainian Insurrectionary Army fought Soviet and Polish troops in the Carpathian Mountains of Western Ukraine. Conditions in the Ukraine are therefore generally still far from satisfactory to the regime. Apparently there are even Party members in the regime whose loyalty is to the Ukraine rather than to the USSR or to Russian Communism. At the Sixteenth Congress of the Ukrainian Communist Party (1949) Khrushchev and others sounded off heavily against "bourgeois nationalist errors and distortions" and referred to nationality deviation as "the most harmful and one of the most living residues of capitalism."

On the other hand, the Russian language is making massive inroads among Ukrainians. Thus, of those who completed our Ukrainian nationality questionnaire — a group probably biased in the nationalist direction — 75 per cent could read and write Russian in addition to Ukrainian, almost 60 per cent read a *Russian*-language newspaper while in the Soviet Union, and almost 20 per cent spoke Russian at home. According to census figures, between 1927 and 1937 the proportion of marriages between members of different nationalities in the Ukraine more than doubled, reaching almost 20 per cent, and our data indicate these levels to be reasonable figures. There is other evidence that national consciousness in the eastern Ukraine is weakening. Even the refugee Ukrainians endorse much of the social legislation of the regime. And the real grievances of the Ukrainians are, for the most part, common to the whole Soviet population, although, in some instances, their interpretation of these grievances retains a distinctively Ukrainian cast. Specifically, they not infrequently see these grievances as manifestations of Russian aggression. Finally, one must not overvalue or misinterpret the fact that after the last war many Ukrainians resisted repatriation; so did many Russians. This was primarily to avoid returning to secret-police surveillance or misery and poverty, not defection primarily on national grounds. In fact, Ukrainians claimed that they escaped from Soviet control voluntarily no more often than did the Russians, despite the fact that they may have had greater legitimate fear of reprisals for collaboration with the Nazis, since a higher proportion of Ukrainians than Russians lived under German occupation, and for longer periods of time.

There is a reservoir of nationality feeling in Byelorussia,[5] but it appears to be waning. The nationality ideology has found refuge and articulate expression abroad, but in Byelorussia it appears to be dissolving. The Germans were surprised at the relatively low level of nationality feeling in the areas they occupied. Nevertheless, the regime's behavior shows that it is not completely satisfied. Defectors report that city people often avoid using the Byelorussian language in the street lest they be suspected of "bourgeois nationalism." There have been many recent official criticisms of literary works in the local language. In 1951 the top echelon of government in this republic included only nine Byelorussians as against twenty-two Great Russians.

The aftermath of the Beria episode indicates that the regime either fears nationality deviation in Georgia or uses it for an excuse to purge on strictly political grounds. There is little doubt that the Georgians continue to be a proud and independent people. Recent reports suggest that a strong admiration for Europe and America still prevails among many Georgian intellectuals. Once again, however, we must note the increased use of the Russian language, Russification of the Georgian language, and the fact that most of the grievances and dissatisfactions are those characteristic of the total Soviet population — although not always so perceived by the Georgians. Georgian nationalism is probably stronger than the rather defensive nationalism of the Armenians. Our alliance with the Turks does bolster Armenian allegiance to the USSR. Recent Armenian defectors agree, on the whole, that most Soviet Armenians accept affiliation with the USSR for at least the foreseeable future.

Perhaps more than any other large minority elements in the contemporary USSR, the Moslems feel deprived of their cultural heritage. Furthermore, the relative isolation from the center of many Moslem groups and the wide gulf between their culture and that of the European Russians probably facilitate the relative endurance of a Moslem subsociety in the villages which is both an actual and a potential source of *passive* resistance to

Soviet and Russian penetration. However, resistance groups within the USSR are atomized; outside the USSR, they lack organization and quarrel among themselves. Russification and diminishing of strong nationality feeling have proceeded rapidly during and since World War II, owing to movements of peoples, liquidation of dissident leaders, industrialization, and increased literacy in Russian. Nevertheless, there is evidence that the regime is concerned, for these people have recently been singled out for special attention, concessions, and some prestige symbols. State-supported pilgrimages to Mecca have been given much publicity. Orthodox Christians have been forbidden to proselytize in Moslem areas, and one Orthodox seminary in this region has been abolished. For the first time a Turkish leader is a candidate member of the Party Presidium.

The Jews, although not strictly speaking a nationality in the same sense as the others because they lack a distinctive territorial homeland within the USSR, have traditionally been defined by the regime as one of the major national minorities. During the early years of the regime, roughly up to the departure of Trotsky, the Jews were, next to the Russians, the most prominent group in Party councils. Although the disproportionate representation of Jews in the Party councils had been decreasing "naturally" as more and more Russians and others were brought into the broadened base of the Party structure, the process was given great impetus by Stalin's decimation of the ranks of the "old Bolsheviks," among whom Jews figured heavily. Since the middle and late thirties, their role in the top echelon has been radically cut, and there is much evidence of continuing official anti-Semitism of a covert kind — such as exclusion from special Party, diplomatic, and military schools — as well as open outbreaks such as the Zhdanov war on "homeless cosmopolitans" and the "doctors' plot" business. Nevertheless, there is one Jew still in the Presidium, and there is little reason to believe that he is there merely for show purposes.

The Jews as a group are not a potently organized sociopolitical force in the same sense as are the other major nationalities. They are highly assimilated to the Russians, and they appear to have no distinctive national aims other than the hope of not being molested or discriminated against. If not treated badly, they may be expected to be predominantly loyal to the regime. But their fear of anti-Semitism is such that, if the regime were to appear to be clearly persecuting them, this group would be a potential source of mass defection.

MAIN PROJECT FINDINGS

In recognition of the importance generally attached to the nationality problem, the Project gave special attention to data collection in this area.[6] On the written questionnaire 22 per cent of the respondents were non-Slavic, a proportion roughly equal to that in the total Soviet population; 35 per cent were Ukrainian and 5 per cent Byelorussian, in each case about twice their weight in the parent population. Almost one-fourth of the oral life-history interviews were with Ukrainians. In addition, a special questionnaire on the nationality problem per se was administered to 511 Ukrainians, and dozens of oral interviews were conducted with representatives of the Ukrainian national leadership and other members of the intelligentsia.

Our most important and striking findings on the nationality problem cast serious doubt upon the assertions most often made by *émigré* nationality leaders concerning the central role of nationality status in determining the attitudes of Soviet minorities. The basic social and political values of our respondents, their attitudes toward the Soviet regime, and their life experiences and life chances were on the whole strikingly little determined by their nationality as compared with their social origins or their class position in the Soviet system. On *most* questions a Ukrainian or Georgian lawyer's or doctor's responses are more like a Russian lawyer's or doctor's than like a Ukrainian or Georgian peasant's. And the same goes for the Russian member of the intelligentsia as against the Russian peasant. We found this to be true with monotonous regularity on hundreds and hundreds of questions from the written questionnaire and the life-history interviews. Thus, we may conclude that basically a man's nationality is not a good predictor of his *general* social and political attitudes in the Soviet system, but rather that these attitudes are better predicted by knowledge of his occupation or social class.

Nevertheless, our exploration revealed a substantial amount of strong identification with national groups and hostility on the part of the minority members toward the Great Russians. There is substantial national feeling near the surface and already evident or easily aroused if properly stimulated. We were able to study only one group in detail, namely, the Ukrainians. Although we do not assert that findings for this major group can be generalized to all nationalities, we regard this case as most instructive. About one-third of our Ukrainian informants showed a strong spontaneous interest in the nationality question and high identification with the Ukrainian cause. This was reflected in their spontaneous mention of the problem of separatism, their view of the Ukrainian people as "oppressed," their high identification with Ukrainian national symbols, and their strong prejudices against the Russians. Indeed, in substantial measure, their feeling with regard to the nationality problem must be described as nine-tenths pro-Ukrainian and anti-Russian rather than anti-Soviet per se.

At the opposite pole, there is a group of about one-third of the Ukrainian respondents who feel that the nationality question is really no great problem, who seem either uninterested in or unconcerned with it, and who show no visible anti-Russian feeling. Indeed, many rather strongly affirm that there is no discrimination on grounds of nationality in the USSR, that all nationalities are equal, alike, and compatible. In between there is another third which is more ambivalent, and which shows national consciousness on some issues but is not very deeply involved on others.

Strong nationality feeling appears to cut fairly evenly across class lines. The most nationalistic tend to be those who claim they learned their national identification at home and who are members of the Ukrainian Autocephalous rather than the Synodal Church.* On the whole, peasants, workers, and people with up to middle-level education express their national consciousness more in a folk way by identifying with and valuing things Ukrainian. The better-educated members of the intelligentsia

* Both churches are Orthodox, but the Synodal Church acknowledges the authority of the Patriarch in Moscow, whereas the Autocephalous does not. In addition, the latter inclines to use the Ukrainian language rather than Church Slavonic for its services and in other ways manifests the characteristics of a self-consciously "national" church. During the early years of the Soviet Union the regime rather encouraged the Autocephalous Church, hoping thereby to further weaken the power of the central Orthodox Church, which it regarded as the main force to be reckoned with. The Autocephalous Church was later dissolved, and its leaders tried, because of alleged nationalist, separatist, and anti-Soviet acts.

who are nationalistic express the feeling more through blaming the Russians for such things as the misdeeds of the regime or job discrimination on nationality grounds.

Particularly important is the relation of age to national consciousness. Contrary to the argument posed by some about young firebrand nationalists, our data indicate that it is primarily the older people who are knowledgeable about and identified with Ukrainian culture and folklore, which indicates some success for the regime's effort to suppress knowledge of certain historical figures and events. Even more important, however, is the fact that the younger, well-educated respondents are *least likely* to charge the regime with mistreatment of the Ukrainian people.

SOME CAUTIONS

One must discount the testimony on the nationality question of some of the refugees representing these nationalities. Most nationality *émigrés* give fairly balanced accounts. There are, however, some self-appointed "professional" nationalists who represent exile groups with intense in-group sentiments. These individuals tend to report not upon things as they *are*, but as they *were* or "ought to be." Moreover, many of these "national" *émigrés* represent primarily a small, though articulate, minority of intelligentsia who were not representative of the elite in their region, even at the time they left the USSR. In several important nationality groups, V-E Day found precisely the most active nationalists out of their native lands; indeed, many of the leaders of nationality movements were not part of the World War II escape group, but rather dated their exile from the Revolution or the early twenties.* Nationality feeling and hatred of the Great Russian regime on the part of the *émigré* population have usually been heightened in exile. In extreme cases, the *émigré* leaders have a personal power interest in playing up nationality trends. They make both their economic and their psychological livelihood this way. Often, when confronted by some fact they find unpalatable, such as our finding that only about half of our Ukrainian sample could correctly identify a series of the "culture

* Most of these statements about *émigré* national leaders also apply quite strictly to those who are Great Russian by nationality. We do not mean here to suggest an invidious comparison.

heroes" who nationalist propaganda would lead one to believe were dear to the hearts of *all* Ukrainians, they respond by claiming that those who conducted the research are really covert Russian nationalists. It goes without saying, of course, that most nationality spokesmen are not *fanatical* nationalists and many are clearly expressing the legitimate and widespread grievances and aspirations of their people.

Nationality feeling undoubtedly still exists and is of genuine importance in a number of groups within the USSR. However, while ethnic minorities represent half or more of the total population of the Soviet Union, their power is not proportionately great. The minorities do not, by any means, present a united front. On the contrary, they have their own frictions and jealousies. Second, individuals from the minor nationalities occupy a disproportionately small number of power positions in the total system. In general, nationality groups feel the same resentments toward the regime and the same dissatisfactions with the system as other citizens of the USSR, although they may feel them somewhat more intensely. The additional grievance on the nationality question adds to the more general hostility or ambivalence. What this means as far as behavior is concerned is that the chance — other things being at all equal — that a Ukrainian will flee or oppose the regime actively or passively is a bit better than the chance that a similarly placed Great Russian will act in this manner. Fainsod emphasized this point in stating:

The political cohesiveness of the USSR is still subject to severe nationality strains . . . One of the most serious points of tension in the Soviet policy involves the position of the Soviet-trained native intelligentsia. Once these persons have been educated for administrative and other responsibilities, they aspire to real as well as formal authority, and they become increasingly restive under the rigid control exerted by the plenipotentiaries whom Moscow dispatches to supervise their activities. When they express their restiveness, they are charged with bourgeois-nationalist deviations, removed from office, and drastically punished. [The decimation of the native intelligentsia during the Great Purge was often explained by our interviewees in these terms.] This phenomenon of incipient internal Titoism has been little noted, yet it would appear to be of considerable significance, and it constitutes an interesting counterpart to the difficulties encountered by Western imperial powers in dealing with the native intelligentsia in their colonies.[7]

On the other hand, neither *émigré* interviews nor published materials warrant the conclusion that the nationality policies of the Soviet regime have not had some success other than that achieved by force. Refugees from the less well-developed areas point to the positive achievements in the direction of racial equality, increased educational opportunities, and technological and industrial advance. The regime has claimed and received credit in the eyes of many non-Russians for improved medical facilities, the increased literacy rate, the growth of the theater and cinema, and other developments.

Time is mainly on the side of the regime as far as the nationality issue goes, particularly because of the trend among the youth noted above. Population transfers and purges of the national, political, and cultural leaderships, while increasing the resentments of articulate elements in the national populations, have even further reduced the possibility of their raising an effective opposition against the regime. Most of the various minority borderlands are increasingly dependent on Moscow because of more and more economic specialization. Local situations in some cases (e.g., Armenian fears of the Turks and jealousy of a strong Georgia) also reinforce ties to the center. Most of all, the drift through time is enhanced by larger processes which tend to destroy folkways and nationality feelings, such as urbanization, industrialization, and increasing Union-wide literacy *in Russian*. Project data show rather dramatically the extent to which, even a decade ago, attitudes had become homogenized along social class rather than nationality lines. However, the very process of minimizing national differences in the USSR produces resentments, especially in the trouble spots of the moment.

Even today we must not lose sight of the *potential* of nationality consciousness in various parts of the USSR. Although they have the same personal complaints as others, the minorities also complain "for their people." Further, much of the blame they put not merely on the Communist elite but upon this elite as the latest form of Russian-Moscow domination. Such groups have a genuine potentiality for special action when aroused along nationality lines.

Part V

CONCLUSIONS

23

Summary

To keep our summary brief and succinct we have elected to forego a running commentary on the interrelations of our findings and to present instead a series of short discrete paragraphs. This summary is, however, followed by an evaluative chapter in which we deal with some of the implications of our findings for an assessment of the strengths and weaknesses of the Soviet system. This leads, in turn, to some forecasts of future developments. Following the pattern of our study as already presented, the summary begins by listing some of the repetitive patterns or recurrent themes which may be defined as the operating characteristics of the system. This is followed by material on the attitudes, life experiences, and patterns of adjustment of the Soviet citizen, the realm in which we feel our Project makes its distinctive contribution. The paragraphs have been numbered largely to mark off major transitions rather than as a simple count of the points made, since in some cases several different, but related, points have been brought together in one summary paragraph. The sequence in which the paragraphs are presented is at some points necessarily arbitrary. On the whole, we have sought to group them to provide a logical internal development and a cumulative effect. Finally we are cognizant of the repetition in this summary of some points dealt with again in the subsequent evaluative section, but it was our intention to keep this summary a relatively complete, independent unit in itself.

1. Ideology plays a distinctive role in Soviet society. As an instrument of policy, it is carefully manipulated by the leaders to implement their program both at home and abroad. At the same time, it importantly influences the thinking and behavior of the leaders. This ideology cannot, of course, be simply read

out of a book. Rather, it is an amalgam of formal and openly expressed principles, informal and covertly held ideas which are nevertheless consciously shared by the elite, principles of action which are merely implicit and often not consciously formulated by the leadership, and lessons learned from experience in the hard school of Soviet politics. Correct interpretation of Soviet behavior, adequate assessment of their intentions, or accurate prediction of their probable behavior cannot be made without weighing the role of ideological factors together with "objective conditions" as an influence on the actions of the leaders.

2. The long-range goals of Soviet policy are importantly influenced by ideological considerations, and appear to be generally directed toward maintaining and substantially strengthening the present structure of Soviet society and toward creating a world predominantly, if not wholly, Communist under Soviet leadership or hegemony. Current policy is, of course, always considerably influenced or determined by the actions of the United States and other nations involved in the total international scene and by practical considerations arising from the resultant balance of forces. In addition, the regime's long-range policy appears subject to the important reservation that every precaution should be taken to avoid immediate and major risks to the security of the home base. Thus, ultimately, the domestic requirements of the system set an absolute limit on the degree of risk undertaken in foreign affairs. Nevertheless, many of the difficulties on the domestic front stem from the regime's ambitious foreign policy goals and the consequent commitments to offensive and defensive preparedness, which strain the resources of the system to the utmost.

3. While the long-range goals of the leadership are highly stable, there have been, from a shorter-term point of view, enough sudden alternations in both domestic and foreign policy, both between rigidity and flexibility and between two drastically contrasting courses of policy and action, to justify naming "cyclical behavior" one of the most distinctive operating characteristics of the Soviet system. This adds an important element of insecurity to the life situations of both the elite and the rank and file, which the regime may exploit to its advantage, but

which also makes it more difficult for the Soviet citizen to regard the system with equanimity.

4. In large measure, the internal problems of the regime stem from the leaders' persistent tendency to overcommit the system's resources. The system involves, in effect, permanent rationing and perpetual mobilization. Goals are invariably set too close to the theoretical capacity of the available resources in the effort to stimulate each unit to maximum output. Furthermore, effective expenditures of energy are usually characterized by mass assault on a single objective or a relatively narrow range of objectives, while other considerations are ignored until their sheer neglect causes sufficient problems so that they, in turn, rise to a high position on the scale of priorities and become the focus of mass assault. As a result, despite the extensive machinery of allocation, there are always localized scarcities of resources, resulting in hoarding and inevitable costs in the form of malcoördination of effort. Overcontrol and overcentralization are therefore chronic features of the system.

5. Both because of their addiction to rational planning and because of their conviction that "everyone who is not completely for us is against us," the ruling elite have made tremendous efforts to stamp out growing centers of independent power and communication. Their success, however, is not complete, particularly with regard to the military, who retain continuing capabilities for independent action and are possessed of notably increased relative power and prestige.

6. The needs of the citizen are relatively low in the priority scheme of the leaders. Nevertheless, the individual is recognized as the most flexible resource in the system. The regime is therefore necessarily concerned with the morale of the population — not as an objective in itself but as an unavoidable prerequisite to effective economic production and military preparedness. The regime's objective is to extract from the citizen a maximum of effort with a minimum of reward. The purge and the terror are the standard instruments for insuring unhesitating obedience to central command. But to maximize incentive the regime also relies heavily on sharply differentiated material and social rewards. Further, it may periodically relax the pressure and make a show

of concern for popular welfare when the results of increased pressure appear to have passed the point of diminishing returns.

7. Certain features of Soviet society win strong, widespread support and approval. These are notably the welfare-state aspects of the system, such as the health services, government support of the arts, and public educational facilities. In addition, the regime is credited with major achievements in the technological development of the country, in which Soviet citizens take obvious pride. The armed might and international prominence of the regime are recognized and held somewhat in awe. The depth of loyalty to "the motherland" is an outstanding sentiment in all classes of the population, irrespective of religion, political attitudes, and personality structure. This is coupled with a genuine fear of foreign aggression. These sentiments are strongest in the heartland of Great Russia, but they prevail generally.

8. Our data show that ignorance and distorted views of the outside world are deeper and more widespread — even among the intelligentsia — than heretofore had been realized by most students of the USSR. It is almost impossible to exaggerate the ignorance of the outside world prevalent among Soviet citizens. And, while feelings toward the American people and toward certain American achievements have distinctly positive elements, there is a general distrust of American intentions and a fear of "capitalist aggression." Most attitudes toward the West change after emigration, but not in a uniformly favorable direction.

9. The general features of Soviet life and the Soviet system that are most intensely resented are the low standard of living, the excessive pace of everyday life, the invasion of personal privacy, and the "terror," i.e., the threat of arbitrary political repression. We found little concern with "civil liberties" per se, and little pressure toward a democratic form of government. The specific institution most resented was the collective farm, which all groups, virtually without distinction and nearly unanimously, want eliminated. There was strikingly little complaint about the factory system other than dislike of harsh labor-discipline laws, which now are no longer being stringently enforced.

10. Hostility is directed mainly toward the regime — the actual people in power — rather than toward the idea of a welfare

state with high concentration of economic and social as well as political power in the hands of a few men. There is a strong tendency for the rank-and-file citizen to establish a "we-they" dichotomy, in which "they" are the people, regardless of rank, who are closely identified with the regime. In general, but not exclusively, this distinction tends to correspond to that between Party and non-Party personnel, although some members of the Party are accepted in the "we" category. In any event, wherever the line is drawn, "we" see "them" as having no regard for "our" feelings, depriving "us" of just rewards, terrorizing "us" without cause, and generally failing to show proper trust and respect for the citizenry. All classes appear to channel much of their hostility and aggression in this way. Indeed, many of the routine daily frustrations of life are charged to the regime because the immediate source of those frustrations is defined as a representative of "them."

11. The conflict over straightforward matters of policy, which creates a gulf between the leaders and the rank and file, is aggravated by the important psychological differences which separate the elite and the masses. The masses remain rather close to the traditional picture of Russian character. They are warm-hearted, impulsive, given to mood swings, and contradictory in behavior. The goal of the elite is the rather puritanical "new Soviet man": disciplined, working steadily and consistently, subordinating personal conduct and motivation to the requirements of Party discipline. It appears that the Soviet leaders have succeeded to a certain degree in developing among the elite a considerable proportion of people of an externally disciplined and driving character, and their patterns of behavior add to the sense of alienation felt by many of the rank and file toward the leaders.

12. Despite the high level of dissatisfaction and discontent, there seems to be only a relatively small amount of disaffection and disloyalty. The life histories of our respondents left little doubt of the extent to which most of them were unhappy about many aspects of their life situations. But these same life histories indicated that most of the citizens of the USSR feel helpless in the face of the power of the state and desire only to live peacefully. There is scant evidence for the view that more than a very

tiny part of the population would, except under conditions of extreme crisis, take appreciable risks to sabotage the regime or to aid Western democracy.

13. Certain traumatic experiences, such as being arrested, had less effect than we had anticipated. Being arrested has virtually no impact on a person's general social and political attitudes and values. The individual does not generalize his experience to the point of revising his judgment concerning the kind of society in which he lives, or would want to live. Arrest, however, does increase the *intensity* of his hostility *to the regime*. Furthermore, arrest — whether his own, or that of a family member — makes him anxious about his own future, and thereby increases the probability of his leaving the Soviet Union voluntarily if the opportunity arises.

14. Degree of dissatisfaction with, or even disaffection from, the system does not necessarily detract from the energy with which a person does the job assigned to him by "the system." The disaffected person often does his job well and may work with a little extra energy, either because he feels he has to prove himself or because he finds comfort in his work. Thus, the fact that the Soviet system tends to produce dissatisfaction in its citizens does not in itself mean that it gets less effective work from them. This applies, however, mainly in the professional and white-collar classes. In the working class and the peasantry there appears to be a fairly direct relation between the individual's level of satisfaction and the quality and quantity of his work.

15. The Soviet elite, a markedly privileged social class, inevitably has a vested interest in maintaining and perpetuating the system. This tendency, however, varies with different individuals and under various combinations of circumstances and is partly counterbalanced by one or more of the following factors: (*a*) the conviction that the ruling clique is acting contrary to the interests of the nation-state; (*b*) the conviction that the regime has betrayed the humane goals of Marxism; and (*c*) personal insecurity. On the other hand, even when these factors are operative, the conflicted members of the elite often fall into line of their own choice because of deep-rooted attitudes, such as suspicion of foreigners and their motives; belief that, after all, national patriotism and loyalty to the regime are inextricably

linked; acceptance of Communist ideology; a conspiratorial mentality; and the habit of disciplined obedience.

16. A Soviet citizen's social class and his occupation largely determine both his opportunities for advancement and his attitudes toward the Soviet system, as well as his general social and political values. The individual's social position is more important than such factors as nationality or arrest history in affecting his hostility toward, passive acceptance of, or positive identification with the regime. Members of the intelligentsia, being the more favored beneficiaries of the system, understandably show substantial satisfaction with the conditions of daily life and with opportunities for development and advancement. They are generally the persons most accepting of the broad outlines of Soviet society, with the exception of its political patterns which hit them especially hard owing to the greater surveillance to which the regime subjects them and their work. At the other pole, the peasant emerges as the "angry man" of the system, strongly rejecting most of its features, convinced of his exploitation, resentful of his deprivation of goods and opportunities, and outraged by the loss of his autonomy. The workers shared many attitudes and life experiences with the peasants, thus forming a broad manual group which can regularly be distinguished from the nonmanual. The workers are, on the whole, less intense and resentful than the peasants and generally accept the sociopolitical structure of the Soviet factory as natural and proper.

17. It has been asserted that the Soviet youth, although showing a strong early allegiance to the regime, have a high probability of becoming disaffected as they mature and experience the full dimensions of the regime. Our materials indicate that there is a period of crisis in the relation of youth to the regime as the individual reaches maturity, but that only a small minority actually turn against the system because of disillusionment. In most instances, they are able to reconcile their conflicts. Furthermore, the younger generation is coming to accept as natural many aspects of Soviet life and the Soviet system against which the older generation rebelled. The youth is relatively unlikely to turn against the regime, in spite of experiences that Americans would think would lead to disaffection.

18. The individual's nationality appears to play a lesser role

in determining his attitudes toward the regime than has often been supposed. Indeed, people in the same occupation or social group hold essentially the same attitudes and values regardless of nationality, and those in the national minorities feel the same resentments toward the regime and experience the same dissatisfactions with the system as do all other citizens of the USSR. Generally, therefore, nationality is only a secondary, contributing cause for disaffection. There is a distinctive nationality feeling in sections of many national groups, however, and this national identification is supported by a sense of oppression and resentment of Great Russians.

19. Certain scholars had advanced the plausible and provocative thesis that political domination within the Soviet system was threatened by a "managerial revolution." Our data, however, indicate that technical and managerial personnel, having a stake in the existing system, have developed an interest in maintaining it in predominantly its present form. They are concerned mainly with reducing interference and extreme pressure from the center and in improving the system and making it work more smoothly. They feel that they can obtain the rewards they deserve without the risks involved in ownership.

20. The Project findings yield strong evidence as to the importance of informal mechanisms in the operation of a society that, on the surface, appears and pretends to be highly centralized, controlled, and rationalized. The rank-and-file citizen learns to apply complicated techniques of accommodation and evasion in order to carry on his day-to-day affairs and to maintain himself in reasonably successful, or at least untroubled, adaptation to the regime. In this he is often aided by others — doctors, for example — who serve as buffers between him and the pressures of the system. In addition, "localism" or "familism," the tendency for local loyalties and informal mutual protective associations to develop on the local level as defense against the pressures of the center, plays a major role. In fact, Soviet society works as well as it does only because of the existence of a series of informal, extralegal practices which are tolerated, up to a point, by the regime, even though officially disapproved. Nevertheless, these informal adjustive mechanisms create problems for the leadership

as well as facilitating the functioning of the society in significant respects.

21. The life histories of our respondents indicate that the stability of the Soviet system involves a nice balance between the powers of coercion and the adjustive habits of the Soviet citizenry. The stability of the. system and of the citizen's loyalty depend to a high degree on the citizen's own belief in the stability of that system and on his having no alternative but to adjust to the system. For the average citizen, political loyalty to the regime is a strange compound of apathy, passive acceptance, and cynicism. Among the elite groups, some individuals are conforming loyalists to the system; some, the "careerists," are really loyal only to themselves; more than a few are loyal to Communist "ideals." Our pessimistic finding is that the new regime can gain much more solid popular support if it supplies more consumer goods and better housing, eases up on the terror, makes some concessions to the peasants, and relieves somewhat the frantic pace at which all the population has been driven. Such a change of policy would not only alleviate many of the day-to-day grievances of the citizen, but also change his basic image of the regime as a harsh and depriving force. These may be precisely the lines along which the current regime is proceeding.

24

Some Evaluations by the Authors

Any social order is a series of compromises, of decisions to do things one way rather than another in order to attain certain goals for which the society must pay certain prices. Each system, therefore, has characteristic strengths and vulnerabilities, which are, in most instances, opposite sides of the same coin. A precise assessment of what a strength or weakness is usually demands an explicit statement of the context within which the system is being evaluated. The dimension of time must be introduced, since what is a short-run strength may prove to be a long-run weakness, and vice versa. In this discussion, we shall generally have in view a short time span of roughly five years.

The Soviet order was established on the assumption that there was an economic and social advantage in state ownership and control of the means of production and distribution and in pushing the rationalization of the economy as far as possible through centralized planning and coördination. As a correlate of this centralized economic system, a centralized political system has been developed that makes it possible for a small group of men to maintain effective control over a complex society. One of the salient advantages of this system is that it permits a high order of tactical flexibility, particularly in external affairs, by freeing the leaders, to a great extent, from the constraint of public sentiment. A second major advantage for the leadership is that it can concentrate a maximum of resources on any given objective: for example, it can develop military strength at the expense of the welfare of the population. This is facilitated, despite the economic difficulties from which the system suffers, by over-all planning and control which make possible rapid and relatively efficient mobilization of resources. This was the case in earlier periods with industrialization, and, more recently, with crash armament programs.

The most patent weakness of the system is the fact that it generates so high a level of dissatisfaction and violates so many interests of its citizens that the regime cannot count on more than minimum productivity, rather unenthusiastic compliance with its directives, and support, often grudgingly given, which is no greater than required for personal security. In short, the regime is not really generally liked, let alone loved and warmly and spontaneously supported. This, however, is the deliberate price which the regime pays for the freedom of action derived from not being guided by public opinion. The regime relies on direct and indirect coercion, which produce further alienation of sentiment and, thus, still more dependence upon coercion. Hence, freedom of maneuver in one dimension is bought at the cost of freedom in another, since it would be exceedingly difficult for the regime to reverse its practices to the point where reliance on coercion could be dropped.

Because the basic assumptions of the Soviet system are so different from those of the West, Western thinkers and men of affairs have tended toward extremes in their evaluations of the strengths and weaknesses of the Soviet system: they have usually been either too optimistic or too pessimistic. We do not think there is the least likelihood that the Soviet dictatorship will crumble from its own faulty structure within the immediately foreseeable future, nor do we anticipate any internal revolution other than a possible change in the personnel of the ruling clique. On the other hand, we are convinced that there are limitations and vulnerabilities attached to any totalitarian government, including the Soviet.

Our treatment of Soviet strengths and weaknesses will necessarily be selective. We have not attempted to draw up a relatively complete or definitive balance sheet of the strengths and weaknesses of the Soviet social system. Such a task would be more appropriate to a systematic, general treatise on Soviet society than it is to this report on the findings of the refugee project. Consequently, numerous issues of genuine importance, particularly those involving economic and political structure, will not be examined. Here we concentrate mainly on psychological and sociological problems, specifically on those features of the system where our data and related research experience give either promise of important new evaluations of established features or enable us to add a point of strength or weakness not previously adequately recognized or appreciated. As between strengths and vulnerabilities, we have given rather fuller treatment to the former, since we feel that in that respect we have relatively more to say that is new or different.

We shall deal with both latent and activated strengths and weaknesses. A latent weakness, for example, is vulnerability to purges among the ruling elite. The Russian industrial growth curve is an activated strength. The relative strengths of East and West at any given time are obviously composite functions of numerous operative elements. For full rigor we would have to examine in great detail each strength and each weakness with reference to an assumed situation at a specified time. Obviously, to treat systematically every conceivable situation in reference to each generalized strength or weakness of the Soviet system would lead to a report of enormous length. We must, therefore, compromise and try to indicate frequently how our appraisal would differ if other conditions prevailed. We cannot, however, do this explicitly in every case and in respect to all possible, or even likely, alternatives. We must depend upon the reader to keep constantly in mind the necessity of qualification or of shift (and perhaps reversal) of emphases under a great variety of circumstances. Finally, we are aware that in speaking of strengths and weaknesses we are inevitably making judgments about the future as well as the present, and this chapter should, therefore, be considered in close conjunction with the one on "Forecasts" which follows it.

ELEMENTS OF STRENGTH

Many of the most important strengths of the Soviet system are built into its formal structure, and it does not require the aid of refugee testimony to locate them and analyze them. For example, the fact that the Soviet leadership has absolute control of the media of mass communication gives it an obvious enormous advantage in its efforts to mobilize the Soviet population. As we have already indicated, our presentation will not stress such relatively well-known, formal features of the system, but will concentrate on aspects which the refugee materials have brought to light or have helped us better to understand.

Low level of active disaffection. One of the things which the Project staff has found most striking and challenging is the relatively low rate of active disaffection from the underlying ideas of the Soviet system as a way of organizing a society or, in more positive terms, the rather widespread acceptance of the basic principles of the authoritarian welfare state. There is, as we have pointed out repeatedly, a very high level of dissatisfaction with an exceedingly wide range of Soviet institutions and practices. Some of these institutions are, indeed, rejected outright and are the focus of intense hostility. These include notably the secret police-terror-purge complex and the collective-farm system. These resentments often lead to strong feelings of hostility to the regime, the particular group of men which is in power. There is, however, no direct and simple line leading from dissatisfaction with the conditions of life and hostility toward the regime to active disaffection from the whole form and practice of the Soviet system. On the contrary, we are struck by the long and involved path which most people trod before they came to feel genuinely disaffected from the Soviet system as such. Indeed, most of our respondents never reached that point while in the Soviet Union, and many refugees have not reached it yet. Rather than disaffection from the Soviet system as such, fear of the consequences of having been abroad was the prime factor in the motivation of most refugees not to return to the USSR.

Most Soviet citizens appear to accept and approve the basic structure of the Soviet welfare state and do not seem profoundly troubled by the gross fact of extreme concentration of power in the USSR; indeed, they seem to regard it as inevitable if not downright proper. The regime, therefore, has a tremendous potential source of strength here. This strength is, however, more latent than activated, full activation being forestalled by the resentment against the terror, the collective-farm system, the low level of material rewards, and the regime's past history of arbitrary and harsh treatment of the population and its constant intervention in and disregard for the citizen's personal life. Nevertheless, the fact that dissatisfaction seems rather rarely to become converted into active disaffection, so long as the citizen remains within the borders of the Soviet Union, is in itself a strength on the regime's balance sheet of strengths and weaknesses. In addition, the apparent acceptance of and support for many aspects of the Soviet system suggest that, if the regime can significantly reduce the pervasiveness of purge and general terror, it may be able to capitalize on much latent support in the population not now being fully called upon.

Atomization of resistance. Perhaps the reason why disaffection does not more often become converted into active disaffection lies in the apparent ability of the system to atomize tendencies toward resistance. The regime's control of the media of mass communication, the widespread use of informers, and the ever-present threat of action by the secret police make most Soviet citizens exceedingly cautious about expressing to others even the slightest doubts concerning the system. This means, of course, that they have little chance to learn from others what *their* feelings are. It was striking how often refugees would point out that it was only when they were outside the Soviet Union that they came to realize how many others felt as they did. While still inside the system, it often seemed that they alone had these feelings, since others were so careful to keep true feelings hidden. Often people described their surprise at discovering in the emigration a former colleague whose loyalty to the system they would never have thought to question. Thus, the elimination of the facilitating effect of the free expression of grievances must be reckoned a strength of the system.

Ignorance of the outside world. Control over the media of mass communication, and particularly over the amount and type of information about the outside world, must, on the basis of our data, be reckoned one of the sources of strength of the regime. Many more Soviet citizens would undoubtedly turn against their government, if they had a fuller *and believable* account of how the rest of the world lives. Unfortunately, foreign broadcasts and the like are not readily accepted as truth. Exposure to conditions in the West was one of the prime factors in turning Soviet citizens, particularly the younger generation, against their regime, partly because, seeing with their own eyes, they realized how they had been duped by their government and partly because they were for the first time in possession of an objective measure whereby to judge their own former way of life. The regime, however, is not likely to permit other than highly trusted and not very ordinary citizens to visit the free world.

As for foreign affairs, it is difficult to be sanguine about any attempt to convince the rank-and-file Soviet citizen of America's peaceful intentions unless and until the Soviet leadership modifies its propaganda line. Of course, a large proportion of Soviet citizens habitually question the good faith of their own government. But even these disaffected persons, while questioning domestic propaganda, exhibit a considerable degree of acceptance of official propaganda as far as the foreign scene is concerned. Once the Soviet citizen accepts the premise that his own government wants to avoid war, then there is little chance of getting him to change his impression of American "aggression," even if the regime does not succeed completely in controlling access to foreign news. Foreign broadcasts and pamphlets will tend to be largely neutralized for the bulk of the population by the belief that they are more propaganda — except in those cases where our own statements of our intentions are vindicated by later events directly observable by the Soviet citizen. In any case, the assumption held by many Western propagandists that, once the Russians hear the truth that is being withheld from them, they will automatically undergo a complete change of heart is wholly untenable. Nor is it the case that once the Soviet citizen shares Western doubts and Western indignation about conditions in the USSR his attitude will approximate that of an American or Englishman.

Efforts to offset other elements in the image of the West may fall into a booby trap, since attempts to convince the Soviet population of our high standard of living and the solvency of our economy may further reinforce the idea that we are both "arrogant" and "materialistic." Stressing our technological superiority is a potential advantage, but it may have the appearance of "H-bomb rattling" and reinforce the idea of our aggressiveness. Much as we ourselves like the free-enterprise aspects of our society, they are a poor selling point in addressing the Soviet citizen if they are phrased to imply an indifference to social welfare. A more advantageous argument would be that our high standard of living is a reflection of the fact that only a small portion of

America's economic potential is devoted to military production — in contrast to the situation in the USSR. This argument can refute the Soviet contention that we are arming for war.

The Soviet citizen has a genuine and eager curiosity about foreigners. Although the "Hate America" campaign may have turned him against our government, it has not succeeded in destroying the feeling of good will that Soviet peoples in general seem to have for Americans. The Soviet people value the frankness and the genuineness of the American and his day-to-day democratic attitude, especially since these characteristics contrast with their own leaders' concern for protocol. They are afraid, however, that the outside world is against them and that they have no foreign friends.

Patriotism. Disaffection from the regime does not automatically go along with rejection of all the achievements of the Soviet system in the period since the Revolution. Indeed, we found that our respondents took pride in the technological achievements of the Soviet Union and, on many points, suggested in no uncertain terms that we in the West would do well to study their methods and learn from them. There can be no question that, beyond the identification of the individual with his nationality group, there is a widespread general Soviet patriotism in the population, which is particularly evident among the younger people. Indeed, with these younger people there is substantial evidence of the strength of the romantic appeal of the world-building and world-beating components in Soviet ideology and propaganda. In addition, we noticed that there was a great deal of pride and a sense of legitimacy felt in the fact that the Soviet Union emerged from the war thoroughly accepted as a really great power. Both of these developments rest on a rather broad base of deeper-lying sentiment, the traditional intense love for and devotion to the motherland which appears to be very strong, at least in the Great Russian and, in less marked form, in a surprising number of non-Russians. The regime seems to have succeeded fairly well in identifying itself with the tradition of the Russian past and in defining itself as the main hope of Russia's future, and it gains much strength thereby.

Increased accommodation of the younger generation. As has

been apparent at several points in this study, we are struck by the difference in the younger generation of Soviet refugees. The fact that they have never known any other system, and escaped the full impact of the worst years of Soviet life encompassed in the collectivization and the purges of the thirties, gives them a much higher potential for full acceptance of the Soviet system in its basic form. They seem to take even those continuing elements of the system which most make for disaffection, such as the politicization of daily life and the police surveillance, relatively more for granted than does the preceding generation. This means that there is a whole order of problems in the relations of the regime with the older generation which largely do not exist, or exist only in muted form, in relations with the younger generation. The younger people appear to question less, and to question less deeply when they do. Their concern is with making the system work rather than with examining its basic premises and its fundamental validity. This is not to say, of course, that any leader in the Kremlin can count on their support regardless of circumstances. On the contrary, they probably exert substantial pressure for an improvement in the standard of living and undoubtedly are less hesitant than their forebears in expressing those desires, since they are much less self-conscious about the possibility of thereby being defined as counterrevolutionary.

Managerial acceptance of the system. Many leading experts on Soviet affairs have insisted that the mainspring of effective pressure for basic change in the Soviet system would come from the ranks of the technical and managerial group which, under the control of the Party, runs the factories, the army, and other major institutions of Soviet society. This theory is currently extremely popular, and many have seen in the post-Stalin concessions mainly the pressures exerted by the new middle class of Soviet Russia. We are certainly impressed with the apparent competence and vigor of the Soviet industrial managers we have met, and we have dealt in detail with some of their problems and the mechanisms whereby they adjust to the system.[1] We find extremely little, however, which would justify a conclusion that the managerial group is outstandingly alienated from the regime or disaffected from the Soviet system at large. On the contrary, we are struck by the degree to which the managerial group accepts the main structure of Soviet society, particularly the organization of such realms as industry, and regards it as worthy of respect and indeed emulation. The leadership of the government with regard to basic lines of policy in economic and related management areas is accepted as legitimate and absolutely necessary. There is great satisfaction with the rewards and honors given to management, and pride in the accomplishments of the system. Rather than wishing for a revolutionary restructuring of the managerial world in Soviet society, the managers seem to desire mainly ameliorative measures which would make it function more smoothly and thus create a more pleasant world in which to operate. The managers resent the lack of trust and confidence and the direct interference of political personages in the day-to-day operations of the manager. They feel strongly that they are overextended and not allowed sufficient resources to accomplish the tasks assigned to them. But apart from wishing to see such particular bad features eliminated, the managerial group seem basically to accept and support the main outlines of the Soviet system as it affects their professional working lives. Otherwise, they seem to share the same complaints and to have the same ambitions as the rest of the Soviet intelligentsia. We see little evidence, and from the regime's point of view not much danger, of a managerial revolution in the USSR.

The desire to live peacefully. To us, one of our most important discoveries was the realization of what perhaps should have been a most obvious fact, namely, that most people want to avoid trouble, especially with the authorities, and seek mainly to go quietly about the business of daily living. In the last analysis, this desire is probably the most important insurance the regime has that the people will do their job, keep reasonably quiet, and avoid challenging authority. When viewing conditions in the Soviet Union from the comfortable and fortunate vantage point of life in a democratic society, it is quite easy to become indignant and full of romantic images of what *we* would do were we citizens of Soviet society. It is quite another matter to actually be a citizen of the Soviet Union, a little man faced by the massive, indeed the overwhelming, power of the totalitarian state.

Most people decide — as did so many of our respondents — to put their doubts behind them and to try to accommodate as best they can to the demands of the regime. They act not so much directly from fear, but from the desire to be left alone to love their wives, raise their children, and enjoy such recreation and other pleasures as life permits — or, as they so often put it, "to live peacefully."

SOURCES OF WEAKNESS

Just as the formal organizationally "in-built" strengths of the Soviet system are relatively well known, so are many of its more glaring weaknesses. In recent years, for example, political scientists have made much of the fact that the system has a basic and inherent element of instability, because it does not provide for any orderly process of succession. When there is clearly one man in absolute control, as was the case with Stalin, there is a tendency toward the overlapping allocation of function which prevents any single chain of command from making major decisions without confronting other arms of the state's bureaucracy and thus bringing the issues into the open at top level. This is an efficient device for central control, integrated planning, and some types of flexibility of action. But it creates a vulnerability to overload and delay if too many issues are sent to the top for resolution. The Soviet rulers realize, at least in part, the dangers of rigid bureaucracy.[2] Under the present regime, however, the vulnerability to overload and delay appears to be appreciably less. It may increase once again if a single unquestioned leader emerges, as appears probable after an interval of more or less collegial rule.

There are other unmistakable weak spots in the system, such as the entire pattern of agricultural organization. The whole rate of Soviet economic growth will be constrained unless the Soviet leaders solve this problem. Continued failure will have very bad effects upon popular morale and upon the prestige of the regime with the masses and with the lower and middle elite. There is a strong probability that, if failure continues, there will be feuding within the top echelons and attempts to find scapegoats — or to make scapegoats of those whom the elite desire to get rid of for strictly internal political reasons.

Purges constitute another basic vulnerability of the system. It is well known that the networks of a purge spread downward and penetrate upward through the hierarchy. The purge involves not just a question of real or alleged disloyalty or of being on the wrong side of the political fence at a particular time. New leaders must also take care to replace as many as possible of those who bear witness to the past mistakes of the new leaders. Usually, Soviet officials look up rather than down. But in periods of purges the Soviet man who aspires to survival and to greater power must look in both directions. He must take care of those who may be useful in the future and eliminate those — even of lower status — whose continued existence may threaten him.

As we have stressed, however, we hope to make our contribution not through a reassessment of such formal aspects of Soviet society but through a discussion of those elements of the system on which Project data cast the most light. Here we examine the side of the coin opposite to that we looked at when we spoke of the low level of active disaffection as a strength of the system. Despite its high potential of popular support, and allowing for the fact that dissatisfaction does not automatically become converted into disaffection, the main social problem the Soviet regime must face is the high level of popular dissatisfaction, frustration, and resentment which at best makes many in the population half-hearted, poorly motivated, unproductive workers and at worst corrodes loyalties and engenders active disaffection.

In the area of values and expectations, the popular frustration level is affected by three main types of stimuli which are sources of actual alienation.

Historic failures. The regime's high point in approximating expectation and acting in accord with popular values was reached during the period of the New Economic Policy in the mid-twenties. Subsequently, the way in which the collectivization violated popular values in the most grievous fashion, and the rift thus created, generated countermoves by the regime which intensified the degree of alienation. Not only in the survivors, many of whom are still alive, but in many of the younger people who make up the majority today, those actions remain salient and forceful in marking the regime as untrue to the values and legitimate expectations of the people. The great purges had a similar effect and left a similar breach, except insofar as the regime deflected the hostility toward the secret police and, through the "purge of the purgers," satisfied the population that even the secret police could also be degraded and punished.

Chronic failures. The prolonged depression of the standard of living, the unrelenting pace of industrialization, the continued unchanged operation of the despised collective-farm system, the ever-present threat of terror, constitute typical chronic failures to meet popular expectations and satisfy popular values. These feed the resentments of historic failures and keep them alive. They also induce alienation in those not affected by or not remembering the historic failures.

Newly generated failures. New failures, less massive or imposing than the great historic failures of the past, appear to continue to be manifested with sufficient regularity to maintain the vicious circle of interaction between regime and people. The latest series came with the end of World War II, in the form of harsh treatment given to those who became prisoners of war or were suspected of collaborating with the Germans in occupied parts of Russia. Then there is the resentment generated by the awareness that rather than "a new day dawning" the postwar period was to mean continued tightened belts, continued restrictions, and general continuance of the chronic failures despite great expectations, perhaps even encouraged by the regime itself during the war, that everything would be different *after* the war. An excellent example is the tightening up rather than relaxation of the collective-farm system through the consolidation of farms, the increase of Party cells in rural areas, and new restrictions on the peasant's private plot.

The actual level of popular support for the regime cannot be measured by a simple calculation which states the total potential support and then subtracts the negative sentiment from that total. The nature of the existing alienation from the regime prevents much of the potential from being realized. There is a "halo effect" which spreads from a specific area or item of alienation into a general characterization of the regime or system as "bad" and which, in turn, leads to giving it less credit than might otherwise be expected.

Maximizing the potential popular support depends on general regime policy, on its tone, and on concrete results in a series of specific areas. On the policy and tone side, it is necessary for the regime to convince the average citizen that:

1. The government now has more trust and confidence in the loyalty and devotion of the people;

2. The regime is genuinely willing to slow down the grueling tempo of development;

3. The regime has more real concern for popular welfare and needs;

4. The regime will keep promises and avoid arbitrary and violent shifts in internal policy.

For the regime to achieve concrete results, there would have to be a sharp and clearly visible decrease in the number of arrests and an unmistakable increase in the availability of consumer goods for non-elite groups. If the present regime moves successfully in these directions, the effect of historic grievances would be much tempered and indeed would probably disappear among the younger segments of the population. In addition, much would be accomplished in diminishing the effect of chronic sources of alienation, thus tending to break the pattern of the vicious circle. If the regime's internal support were to be greatly improved, the ruling elite might well intensify a vigorous foreign policy of expansion. However, sustained popular concessions would also lessen the regime's freedom of maneuver.

It is unlikely, however, that the present regime will, in the near future, gain the full existing potential of popular support. Central is the fact that the most significant chronic source of alienation lies in the collective-farm system. That system would generate much less, indeed perhaps critically less, alienation if the peasant were granted more genuine autonomy and, most important, an appreciably higher and fairer economic reward for his effort. However, as we have indicated previously, there is no present evidence of ability to solve the problems arising from the collectives, at least in the short run. Nor is there any indication of an intention to abandon or modify present policies enough to ease the tension. Urban dwellers also dislike the collective farms, and the continued failure of agricultural policy affects the cities directly by persistent shortages in food supplies.* If the regime fails to gain popular support and fears the loss of complete control, there is likely to be a reversion to the high frequency of arrests and general tightness that characterized most of the Stalin period. This would cause a new wave of dissatisfaction based on newly disappointed expectations and would tend to set in motion anew the vicious-circle pattern.

From the social and psychological point of view, the present Soviet situation might be summarized as follows:

1. The regime has had many successes abroad and some at home. These successes have given it prestige among the Soviet peoples and have increased the belief of these peoples in the strength of the system. The regime is deeply committed to further external expansion but with a long time-scale in mind, a willingness to wait, and a substantial vested interest in avoiding external action that would endanger internal security.†

2. Substantial internal opposition exists, but it is thoroughly disorganized and atomized. As far as surface behavior is concerned, it largely expresses itself in passive acceptance of the regime. By the block system and the other machinery of a police state, the Soviet regime has largely cut off most of the traditional underground institutions and made the few remaining ones too hazardous for all but a few heroes.

3. Secure power is an outstanding goal of the Soviet leaders, but this goal is appreciably deflected to the extent that the leaders must make some concessions to the needs of the population and take into account the day-to-day requirements of Soviet society. Even a police state feels the necessity of a certain minimum of public approval. That the ruling elite fears bad morale (and hence unsatisfactory economic production), but also active disloyalty

---

* The new program for bringing new lands in the steppe area under cultivation is, of course, a major gamble on the possibility of solving the food shortage *without* accepting the necessity of change in the collective farm system. It is an "out-of-field" solution, but one we assume has poor chance of success. Even if it is successful, however, this will give the regime more security with regard to the cities but will not reduce the frustration felt by those still working on the collective farms.

† We feel that the substantial evidence in 1955 of a Soviet *détente* rather strongly supports the correctness of this earlier assertion.

is shown by many kinds of evidence. The very fact of exposure of millions of Russians to the outside world, whether by German occupation or by the entry of the Red Army into eastern and central Europe, convinced the regime that it could maintain itself only by the reintroduction of the most rigorous controls and by reindoctrination. Some authorities believe that the relative tolerance of the Orthodox Church is caused by the regime's anxiety to avoid this potential source of active disloyalty in the event of a war with the West.

4. Throughout the structure of Soviet society, there is a conflict between political criteria and criteria of technical efficiency. On the whole, however, management appears to accept the legitimacy of political determination of general goals and policy and resents mainly the direct intervention into problems it feels are strictly managerial. Tension surrounding this problem must be expected to persist, but we are struck by the degree to which our respondents gave the regime credit for improvement over time in the handling of the problem.

5. As long as the basic premises of Bolshevism are maintained, terror and the purge will be required to carry out large-scale social change. The pattern is one of flexibility at the upper echelons bought at the price of inflexibility in executing orders at the lower echelons.

6. The rigidity of the control apparatus that results from centralized bureaucratic controls results in evasions and illicit methods of getting things done. Rather than being simply signs of weakness, these evasive methods actually serve the regime by offsetting the rigidity of centralized controls and the inflexibility which terror tends to impose.

In general, therefore, we conclude that the control system forged by Stalin and taken over by his successors is neither an impregnable monolith nor a social structure so swept by storms and full of fissures that it would be simple to rend apart. It should always be kept in mind that the political vulnerabilities of a totalitarian state are different from those of a democracy. The stability of a democratic country depends upon the loyalty of its citizens, and their loyalty depends largely on the extent to which they feel the state provides, or will provide, the basic satisfactions to which they are entitled. The proposition tends to be reversed in a Communist dictatorship. Here the loyalty of the citizen is dependent upon the stability of the system. So long as the citizen thinks the system is stable he must perforce give his loyalty, or at any rate a reasonable facsimile thereof.

25

Some Forecasts by the Authors

Here, even more than in the preceding chapter, we go beyond Project data and make some "educated guesses." In making these, however, we are greatly influenced by the Project picture of internal conditions in the USSR as constituting limiting and instigating factors. We have no illusions about making predictions in the strict scientific sense. True predictions would involve both a far more refined model of the Soviet system and of international affairs than social scientists have been able to develop for any complex set of societal events, and also a mathematical statement of the parameters with which we are concerned. Only then could rigorous propositions about future events be generated. But here we cannot hope to make more than plausible statements — forecasts in which we estimate some situations as well as we can on the basis of the information available to us. As things stand, these forecasts must take the form of a series of alternatives along which the Soviet system may travel, with a statement of the relative probability of each and some estimates of the consequences which would follow from each course.

Furthermore the alternative roads along which the Soviet system may travel will undoubtedly be affected by the context of hot or cold war. Since this Project did not have available to it the many classified sources which would be necessary background for prediction in the event of all-out war, this chapter is restricted to forecasting propositions about future events under the assumption of continuing cold-war conditions. Developments in Soviet policy in the last half of 1955 make this assumption all the more plausible. However, it should be stressed that this is an *assumption* rather than a prediction. If the assumption proves wrong, the relevance of our forecasts will be considerably reduced.

Under this assumption we would reject the two extreme possibilities for the development of the Soviet system in the near future, namely, breakdown or continuation without any change.[1] We think the relative stability of the Soviet system is assured for the next five years or more, except in the event of a profound crisis, such as atomic war, serious trouble between the USSR and Communist China, or loss of one of the major European satellites. Except in a severe crisis, the strains in the system will produce a series of accommodations and compromises. There may well be further purges of some dimensions. But we anticipate continuity of *substantially* the present system over the next five years, no matter what the names of the ruling elite may be. The system survived the crisis of the death of a dictator who had held sole power for many years (as forecast virtually unanimously, incidentally, by the Russian Research Center group), and there seems every reason to postulate this kind of continuity for at least another five years, regardless of palace revolutions. It takes more to destroy a system — quickly, at least — than its own internal contradictions. Actually, systems persist, as people do, despite glaring defects and "impossible" behavior. We in the West must be careful not to overestimate the weaknesses (real though they may be) of the Soviet system. Human beings have a strong tendency to overinterpret the behavior of those by whom they are menaced.

These statements, however, are not meant to exclude the likelihood of the growth of significant trends of change within the system. We equally reject the other extreme possibility: continuity *without change*. No major social system is static or can be held static by even the most totalitarian means during the present epoch in world history. We forecast that the change in the Soviet system in the immediately foreseeable future will be evolutionary rather than revolutionary.

This evolution could conceivably follow one of the following main directions[2] or some specific combination of them:

1. A tendency toward a gradual reversion to Stalinism;

2. Increased emphasis upon rational bureaucracy with control passing more and more into the hands of managerial technicians as opposed to the ideological zealots of the Party;

3. A tendency to revert to certain traditional (pre-Soviet)

Russian patterns with strong development of Russian or Pan-Slavic nationalism and imperialism;

4. Gradual movement in directions likely to change — eventually — the essential nature of the Soviet system and to make possible stable accommodations with the West.

Let us now comment upon each of these possible directions and some of their interrelations.

In the initial period of the new regime there appeared to be an implicit — sometimes almost explicit — repudiation of certain features of Stalinism. There were even thinly concealed attempts to place the blame upon Stalin as an individual for some of the practices most resented by the people. Some of the differences evident today, however, are more substantial. Present-day Soviet foreign policy is more subtle than Stalin's. The present regime seems to be more responsive to reality, both internal and foreign, and less given to rigid formulae. There are characteristic differences in propaganda phrasing. For example, before Stalin's death the main line against the West was the accusation of planning and plotting war. Now dominant emphasis has been given to accusing the United States of obstructing the settlement of outstanding international questions.*

We must, however, distinguish between "Stalinism" as a doctrine and Stalin as the political leader who originated that doctrine. Even though he as an individual may be repudiated, elements of his doctrine may be employed. It is even possible that "Stalinist methods" may be used in the guise of "anti-Stalinism," say in the form of a purge of persons identified with Stalin. If this is so, it may be due to the automatic reassertion of old habits, or it may be influenced by a conscious decision on the part of the ruling elite that their experience with limited concessions to the people indicates that they can maintain themselves in power and pursue their goals of external expansion with safety only if they resort anew to Stalin's methods (possibly after having already reaped considerable public-relations benefits from their initial partial repudiation of them).

If and when a single leader attains to unquestioned supremacy,

* There may have been a further change in line, leading to a grudging acknowledgment as a result of the summit meeting, that the United States is also interested in peace. It is, however, too early to tell whether this line will actually develop.

still more reversion to Stalinism may be anticipated, because one-man dictatorship in the Soviet system seems in the nature of the case to require such tactics. And it may also be expected that there will be continued struggle for power within the governing clique. This is almost inevitable in the Soviet state unless a genuine change in the nature of the system occurs. The present situation may be one in which there is an insecure "first among equals" — all of whom are determined to protect their own power prerogatives, and indeed their lives, by withholding from him or any other single individual the full range of command that Stalin exercised. Or it may be an uneasy duumvirate or triumvirate with one man carefully but slowly taking steps to seize complete rule for himself.*

It is conceivable that collegial dictatorship may have a greater capability of stability in the USSR than Westerners are likely to forecast.† This would be because of the trend toward managerial bureaucracy. It is interesting that on the death of Stalin, the major secondary figures clung to the *administrative* instruments from which their power derived.[3] Some have even speculated that the real meaning of Malenkov's relinquishing the Party secretariat was that it was no longer of indispensable importance. We are not convinced by this interpretation.‡ Nevertheless, it is certainly true that there has been some crucial crystallization of Soviet society. A new kind of bourgeoisie has become accustomed to relative luxury. Social stratification is apparently more rigid. The decrease in social mobility has lessened a certain kind of vital dynamism which characterized Soviet society for a long period. An intrenched group has strong vested interests in the status quo. There is a conflict between two conceptions: the old ideal of Party asceticism and that of "the rich new life." The younger elite appear to be less emotional, colder, more interested in per-

* In our earlier report we cited Malenkov as the first among equals. Today Khrushchev would generally be assigned this position by Western observers.

† A year since this was written the evidence of the actual operation of a collegial rule has become quite substantial.

‡ Subsequent developments provided a further basis for rejecting this interpretation. It is obvious that the post of Party secretary remains a crucial base of power, as evidenced by Khrushchev's status in the hierarchy.

sonal security and advancement and in technical proficiency as such. "Business as usual" is an effective solvent for ideological fervor, particularly because of its own ordinarily unideological pragmatic character,

The central bureaucratic structure appears less sharply segmented than formerly. In April 1954 the MVD was deprived of control over state security, which was entrusted to a committee attached to the Council of Ministers (although the chairman is an MVD colonel general). With the practical elimination, for the time being at least, of the police as a major independent political force, the military represents the only concentration of power which may not be firmly in the grasp of the central bureaucracy (which may or may not be still essentially coterminous with the core of the Party structure).

All of these developments merit very careful watching, and there is unquestionably some tendency in the direction of managerial bureaucracy. We must, however, be extremely hesitant in interpreting such a trend in a manner that would be justified in thinking about a Western country. The history of the Soviet state is too distinctive. The ideological element in Communism weighs against a very rapid bureaucratic dominance in the USSR.

The third trend — that of nationalism or Pan-Slavism — undoubtedly has developed since 1941, and is present in incipient form in many aspects of Soviet life. But its overt development and official approval is severely limited by the hegemony of Russian Communism in International Communism and by the role the Soviet has elected to play in "colonial" areas, as the alleged defender of oppressed and underprivileged peoples regardless of their language, race, or historical background. Most crucial of all at the moment is the fact that the Russian bear now has the Chinese dragon by the tail. The USSR can hardly hope to maintain a solid alliance with the Communist nations of East Asia if it allows Pan-Slavic or Russian nationalistic tendencies to become too open and too evident.

The fourth possible trend, the evolutionary — together with some closely related aspects of the second, increased emphasis on rational bureaucracy — constitutes the only real long-term hope in the international situation. It also contains some elements of real danger for the West. This trend must be discussed with some care, not only because of its heartening possibilities but also because of the danger of basing too optimistic estimates upon its elements of hope. First, as a necessary background, we must survey some other recent trends and the central elements in what appears fairly clearly to be the regime's policy for the near future.

It is remotely possible that we are presently witnessing a profound change in the operating code of the Soviet elite. A long-standing controversy was waged in Bolsehevik history over the relative emphasis to be placed on "spontaneous" forces in society and on "consciously directed" forces. Lenin, and particularly Stalin, advocated direct action and intervention into the historical process. Of course, this is entirely a matter of emphasis. To some extent, both Stalin and Lenin always relied on "spontaneous" processes in that they were alert to capitalize on existing sentiment and to capture existing movements and organizations. Yet, in the period from 1928 to 1936, there was absolutely no question but that the emphasis shifted strongly toward reliance on "consciously directed" forces. In the past several years, even before Stalin's death, one gets the feeling that perhaps this tendency was reversing. It may turn out, in the perspective of history, that the first steps in the reversal were taken by Stalin himself in the mid-thirties, when he moved to restore the status of the family as a stable social institution and began to elevate the status of law as a device for regulating behavior in the socialist state.

Since the war, there have been increasing symptoms of such a trend. The theory of "socialism in one country" appears to be a dead issue — officially and ideologically, as well as actually. Stalin announced in his last major work that the USSR, like all other societies, operated under universal laws which cannot be altered or evaded by any state. A similar development was the reintroduction of the compulsory teaching of formal logic in the Soviet educational system and the broader acceptance of "Western" science, albeit with the reservation that "bourgeois" scientists were often perverted by a false ideology into misinterpretations of perfectly good scientific facts and theories. Stalin's famous statements in the Marr linguistic controversy are along the same lines. Both Communist and capitalist countries, he said, are dependent upon universal laws of human behavior and of history.

The symptoms of a reversal of policy on this basic issue of reliance on "spontaneous" versus "consciously directed" forces in history — a matter which in the past has had great practical implications, particularly for Soviet tactics — ought to be: (1) a tendency to set up and rely on automatic instruments of social control internally (such as the family and the law); (2) an emphasis on general laws of society which cannot be overridden; and (3) a reliance on "spontaneous" processes in international politics. As indicated above, there is evidence that the first two orders of symptoms exist in sufficient quantity to make us at least raise the question of their potential import. The symptoms on the international scene are perhaps even more pronounced (although possibly subject to alternative interpretation).

Since approximately 1951, the Soviet Union has been somewhat less blatantly and overtly aggressive in world politics and more inclined to capitalize on and foster "spontaneous" divisive forces in the non-Soviet world.* It is true that this change of tactics may be simply a result of the feeling of the Soviet leaders that Western strength had reached such proportions that they had no alternative except to alter their policy. Regardless of the motivational interpretation we put on this change, the fact remains that, on the whole, this new policy means that Soviet leaders invest less of their own resources and concentrate proportionately more attention on exerting their influence at strategic spots and times in order to accelerate certain trends (nationalism in the colonial areas, French dissatisfaction with EDC, China's disposition to expand) and inhibit others. In one way or another, they seem persuaded that the formula of "direct action," often laid to Zhdanov, will not pay off, except possibly in cases of local nuisance actions. To a significant degree, the foreign policy of the USSR is now two-pronged.

One prong, ironically enough, involves "containment" of the revived strength of the West by obstructing French ratification of EDC, stirring up old hostilities between Germany and France, and dividing the United States and Great Britain on China policy. Increasing emphasis is placed on "intra-imperialist" conflicts and upon the allegedly disastrous eventual consequences of "internal

---

* The Soviet "peace offensive" of 1955 is the outstanding expression of this trend.

contradictions" in Western economies. There seems to be a
rather definite decision — at least for the immediate future — to
let our Western system fall to pieces through its own internal
dynamics, with a certain minimum amount of nonmilitary facilitation on the part of the Soviets. The other prong, of course, is
a continued policy of nibbling away at the choicest of the over-
ripe colonial morsels; Indo-China is the latest victim, but others
in Asia and Africa are presumably on the list.

The present over-all strategy of the Soviet leadership can be
described as one of consolidating their internal position and exploiting the weakness of the non-Soviet world by propaganda,
diplomacy, fifth-column movements, and local rebellion, while
waiting for the processes of history to produce the predicted
decay of capitalism. The immediate precipitant of this policy
seems to be a combination of the increased strength of the West
and the accentuation of internal difficulties in the USSR. However, this "new" way of operating (it is, of course, in no sense
completely new, but does constitute a significant shift of emphasis in the postwar period) may fit in with evolving trends in
the operating code of the leadership and eventually find some
element of ideological support.

While this sounds as though the leadership is becoming less
aggressive, it should give us little reason for complacency. The
success of the new policy in Europe is already demonstrated and
seems to be one with which we are less able to deal effectively
than we were with a direct Soviet military threat. The Soviet
attitude toward "coexistence" is that it is tolerable as a temporary
state of affairs. It can be a dynamic equilibrium in which there
is a continuing struggle by both sides to improve their relative
positions. The Communists probably do not expect to win by a
knockout, but rather on points. They are convinced that capitalism is historically doomed, but they do not expect "world revolution" to progress in one straightforward line. They reckon on
a spiral: "one step back and two steps forward." The tide will
rise and ebb, but "the correct solution" will insure that each
high-water mark is a little higher than the last.

The tactics of this strategy are multifarious and well known.
The Soviets support the World Peace Council to fan popular
hysteria over the hydrogen bomb. They build up — for the time

being — the international position of China. While the West is strong, the Communist leaders are prepared to "negotiate." They will accept a proposal "in principle" but then will argue at length on the agenda and use the conference table as a sounding board to make propaganda throughout the whole world. They stand on protocol and haggle endlessly about irrelevancies. It is clear that the present leadership intends to "coöperate" with the free world only to the extent that, in their judgment, this will advance the eventual prospect of a completely Communist world. For this and lesser reasons, "negotiation" with the Communists is inherently difficult and frustrating both to the negotiators and to public opinion in the West.* Soviet negotiators, from motives of self-protection at home, doubtless often act as blockers and distorters of Western communications rather than as transmitting instruments — lest they be accused of "capitalist sympathies." Western negotiators have much to learn about Soviet patterns and the necessary techniques for meeting them. Probably — in the short run, at least — Western negotiators would get further if they talked less about principles in which the Soviet negotiators do not believe and more about the hard facts of Western self-interest.

While these maneuvers go on abroad, the regime is committed at home to a policy of "relaxation of internal tension." In many ways, the most interesting and important question in the whole world at present is how far the Soviet regime will go with this policy and what the consequences will be if they go some distance. Will even a slight removal of external restraints permit suppressed resentments to come quickly and powerfully to the surface? Will present and possible future concessions generate within the system demands for freer communication with the West (including travel, interchange of scientific, scholarly, and technical personnel and knowledge) which the present regime can neither countenance nor perhaps easily resist?

The rulers clearly want better internal morale and various improvements. At the 1954 Supreme Soviet, Malenkov and Khrush-

---

* When we say that negotiation with the Communists is difficult, we do not mean that dealing with them under all circumstances is beset with such problems. When there is concurrence of interests, Westerners may be surprised at the speed with which matters may proceed, since under such circumstances the Communists may dispense with ordinary protocol.

chev complained about the standard of labor discipline, the quality of output, and the rate of increase in productivity. The combination of the regime's endemic concern with the problem of labor productivity and the closely related problem of developing a modern technology will be a continuing source of pressure for the modification of many aspects of the Soviet attitude toward the individual citizen. Especially during the first few five-year Plans, Soviet industry lagged behind the best countries of the West by decades in its technology. Under such circumstances, and with a vast reservoir of manpower still not absorbed into the industrial system, it was economically feasible to regard a good portion of the labor force as expendable and to rely on a system of incentives that involved a minimum of spontaneous identification with and interest in the functioning of the factory. The implications of a modern technology for Soviet manpower policy can be seen quickly if we think for a moment of the "automatic factory" of the future — a technological development which would fit well into the Soviet idealized image of the socialist society that is to be. The amount of training required of the personnel operating such a plant and its necessary service facilities would be such that each worker would represent a capital investment considerably greater than the worker of the thirties or even the fifties. Furthermore, optimal work performance would be more dependent on a high state of morale and voluntary participation than is true of the unskilled and semiskilled workers who compose the bulk of today's labor force. In particular, the worker of tomorrow will have to be given more autonomy in carrying out his job. The Soviet technology of today is somewhere midway between the electronic age of tomorrow and the iron-age, essentially nineteenth-century, technology of two decades ago. But the increasing modernization of Soviet industry will force the leadership to take more and more seriously into consideration the morale of the average worker and to regard him as less expendable than in the past.

The Soviet leaders are indeed facing a dilemma, but we must not be guilty of easy optimism as to the outcome. In the first place, we must remember that a small bribe can go a long way in the Soviet system. Expectations are low, and there is still sufficient belief in the reality of "capitalist aggression" to make the people satisfied with small concessions. A slight increase in food supplies, for example, would psychologically and practically make much more difference to them than it would in the United States.

Let us explore a bit further the potential impact of any even mild increase of concessions on the part of the regime. Probably a slackening in the tempo of existence would produce the most profound results, since it would affect many of the characteristics of overcommitment. This, coupled with an improvement of material conditions, would probably effect a sizable improvement in Soviet morale. Hence, it is very arguable whether American national policy should or should not endeavor to encourage the regime to relax. If the process went on long enough, the betting odds are that this — and only this — might make an eventual peaceful and stable reconciliation possible. On the other hand, if the present leadership or a similar one stays in power, the improved morale might be seized upon for an all-out war at a time when the West was relatively weak or internally split and when Soviet industrial production had approached equality to that of the West.

To continue our speculation, we estimate that anxiety over the secret police would be reduced markedly, and more or less automatically, if the tempo were relaxed and the standard of living improved, since many of the motives that force people into quasi-legal acts would thus be removed. An excellent basis for this forecast is provided by two items of evidence from our Project interviews. The first relates to the managerial personnel. Anxiety about the secret police was apparently lower among managers and engineers working on military production, because in those plants supplies were adequate, materials of excellent quality, and reserves normal. The second item refers to the entire *émigré* group. Their testimony indicates very clearly that there was a widespread easing of tension during a period of about a year overlapping parts of 1938 and 1939, at which time noticeable improvements in the conditions of life occurred. Some substantial contribution for this sense of well-being must, of course, also have come mainly from the easing of the unrestrained terror that preceded this period.

It can be predicted that an improvement in standard of living and a decrease in tempo, particularly if combined with some withdrawal of the government's intrusion into all aspects of private life, would certainly result in a marked increase in morale in the Soviet Union. There is no guarantee that this would have to be accompanied by any substantial change in government. The regime's main problem would be the extent to which it would be able to control increased appetites for economic improvement which would develop as a result of the increase in the people's level of expectation. If they were not able or willing to control this demand within fairly narrow limits, they might find themselves involved in an economic commitment which would reduce their capacity for maneuver in the international field. Our forecast for the immediate future, however, is that the regime can effect an appreciable increase in consumer goods without a *substantial* reduction in foreign commitments beyond what already has apparently been done.

On the other hand, there are forceful arguments for the view that, if concessions are further increased and are continued for some time,* the main result would not of necessity be only an improved morale which the regime could utilize for its purposes of aggrandizement when it felt the right time had come. For one thing, there is no reason to believe that an increase in standard of living would reduce appreciably the peasants' desire to return to a system of private farming. Furthermore, if pressure from the top slackens, informal mechanisms can be a source of the slow transformation of the regime. Demands and expectations are likely to mount and widen, and even a police state cannot, without great cost in loss of personnel and deflection of energies from other aims, abruptly reverse such policies once they have gone a certain distance. Already there is a good deal in the present regime's policies that, to a degree unknown since the NEP, encourages individual citizens (particularly of the elite groups) to question their environment. It may be doubted whether such a trend is altogether reversible at the regime's will. The younger

---

* The amount of time is the crucial variable here and one that is almost impossible to estimate with even rough reliability. An extremely crude guess would be this: five years would only begin a transformation of the Soviet system in directions favorable to American policy, but fifteen years of relative stability and relaxation of pressure could bring about some irreversible changes.

generation, precisely because it *is* more accepting of the system and the regime, is likely to demand more from it. Should the present regime's program (e.g., on the agricultural issue) fail signally, the younger generation may well feel strongly the need for a still newer administration. Under present conditions, a change, even a fairly radical one, in the top leadership could take place in a less revolutionary and total way than would have been the case in the earlier years of the Soviet system when Lenin and later Stalin were in sole command.

The social and psychological aspects of this involved problem can be summarized with some plausibility in the following series of propositions:

1. Unless Soviet leaders are able to persuade the population that the West is behaving extremely aggressively, renewed or tightened repression of workers, intelligentsia, technicians, and peasants will substantially increase present cleavages between the ruling elite and other groups and reduce economic productivity. Our estimate of the current ruling group is that they will go to some lengths to avoid a noticeable tightening of repressive measures. They may, however, slide or be precipitated into such action if there is a series of crises with associated unrest. Such unrest might occur if there were a decided food shortage following an unsuccessful agricultural campaign.

2. A rise in the standard of living, if accompanied by a return or increase of more extreme repressive political, economic, and security controls, will produce increased dissatisfaction — and even disaffection and resistance. Nevertheless, experience from the late thirties as described by our respondents and our general assessment of the propensities of this population oblige us to emphasize that the regime can apparently acquire large increments of good will and secure substantially improved morale by relatively modest improvements in the flow of food and hard goods, if these are *steady* and appear to be harbingers of more to come.

3. An increase in the degree to which administrative regulations are literally enforced (at the expense of tacit tolerance of informal adjustive mechanisms) will reduce economic productivity and tend to instigate a regime of the present type to return to a heightened terror.

4. The increased psychological and emotional isolation of the individual under these conditions will reduce his productivity and tend to make underlying antiregime attitudes stronger but necessarily more covert.

5. Alternating increases and decreases of repressive measures will produce greater adverse reactions to the regime than will the steady application of strong repression, unless this is imposed *after* many more concessions have been made than is the case at present.

6. Further increases in production of consumer goods will lead to even greater demands for higher standards of living and will increase the resistance to repressive controls. Increased standards of living, once in existence, will be difficult to take away. Nevertheless, although we reckon the current leaders as much less rigid than Stalin, we do not feel they are lacking in nerve. We assume that if, in their opinion, sufficiently urgent reasons of international policy required taking back the benefits given the people, they would not falter and would push through the program of retrenchment.

7. An improvement in the standard of living and a slackening of the tempo of development, accompanied by an easing of rigid administration and intense terror, could effect a substantial and perhaps profound reorientation of the population toward the regime. This might well induce the regime to relax still further with regard to tempo and living standards. The result might be a much more positive popular attitude toward the regime, including greater coöperativeness and general support.

The present leaders, in our opinion, are unlikely to embark on a full-scale reversion to Stalinism unless they begin to feel that the present situation is getting entirely out of control. Even in that event, however, we cannot safely predict the breakup of the system. Stalin managed it for many years, and there may well be another Stalin among the present collegial leadership. It would be a system operating far below its potential, but one which was nevertheless very powerful indeed, as recent history has demonstrated.

Our own best estimate, however, is that measures and approaches which are less Stalinist, even if not really non-Stalinist, will be favored by the present leaders. We anticipate that, if these plans succeed, even a modest improvement in the standard of living and a small decrease in the tempo would yield significant improvements in morale. Further, we feel it not unlikely that the regime might respond by relaxing somewhat more and granting further small benefits. The result would probably be general improvements in efficiency, morale, and productivity. Such strengthening of their rear would, in one sense, yield the leaders increased freedom of maneuver. This would, however, also be restrictive, since they could not easily take back these newly granted benefits. In addition, we anticipate that, as time goes on, the role of national technical bureaucracy in managing affairs, within the limits of set policy, will increase, and that such technical considerations may come to have more effect on the actual direction of policy.

We do not, however, share the view of some analysts that this would almost certainly become an irreversible process which would lead, *in fairly short order*, to marked changes in Soviet society — and those mostly in the direction of development of alternate loci of power, consequent democratization, and subsequent "pacification" of the Soviet regime. For one thing, we are convinced that the regime will not give up the collective-farm system, and this will remain a source of friction and tension and lowered production, despite an improvement of morale and a relative *rapprochement* between people and government. In the second place, although the regime may ease up on control and may "mothball" some instruments of repression, it is most unlikely to *scrap* them. We expect the weapons of terror to remain in reserve, *and* we expect that it will be some time before the present leadership becomes so flabby from long lack of exercise as to be unable or unwilling to use those weapons. In the third place, we do not expect the present leaders, even though they rely more on technical advisers, willingly to surrender their autonomy of decision-making to those advisers or to any other group, such as the military. Control will remain firmly in predominately political hands, and the politicians will be even more technically competent, or at least informed.* At various points in our report we commented that fragmentary but fairly consistant evidence indicated an increase in the influence of the mili-

* The remainder of this paragraph was added in the summer of 1955.

tary since Stalin's death. Subsequent events have, on the whole, suggested that this process has gone somewhat further during the past year. However, in view of the amount of discussion and interpretation of this trend in the press, we think it worth while to state explicitly that no information at our disposal would cause us to modify the forecast that power will remain "predominantly" in the political arm. The most that can be argued at present is that professional officers (as opposed to "political generals") may have gained some share in the decision-making process at the Presidium level. It is likewise true that greater symbolic recognition has been given to the military profession. For example, Zhukov is the first cadre officer since Tukhachevsky to be Minister of Defense. On the other hand, it would be naïve not to give weight to the possibility that the Presidium has found it convenient to manipulate American opinion by playing up Zhukov's personal relation to the President of the United States. Zhukov's well-publicized "personal" letters were certainly scrutinized, if not drafted by, the Presidium.

In brief, our best prediction for the short run is that at "worst" the present regime may revert to Stalinism and at "best" it may become a more popular, or at least less resented, but no less totalitarian government.

EPILOGUE

The proofs of this book were received by the authors shortly after the Twentieth Party Congress, at which Stalin's position in Soviet history was reëvaluated, and the domestic and foreign policies of the new leaders were further specified. These developments represent a surprisingly explicit manifestation of the tendency, discussed in our forecasts, to move in an anti-Stalinist direction.

Appendix

Reports and Publications of the Harvard Project on the Soviet Social System*

Unpublished Manuscripts†

I. *Summary Report*

Alex Inkeles and Raymond A. Bauer, *Patterns of Life Experience and Attitudes Under the Soviet System* (*Composite Survey*), 302 pages plus appendices.

II. *Topical Reports*

A. *Political Institutions*

1. "Political Activism and Social Cleavage in the USSR," consisting of the following parts: (*a*) David B. Gleicher, "Political Cleavage in the Soviet Union: Popular Images of the Party, the NKVD, and the Regime as Such," 42 pages; (*b*) Elisha Greifer, "Some Social Characteristics, Life Experiences, Attitudes and Opinions of Party-Komsomol Members, Compared with Non-Members: A Quantitative Survey Based on PPQ Materials," Appendix A, 27 pages; (*c*) Arthur E. Adams, "The Soviet Citizen and the NKVD," Appendix B, 208 pages; (*d*) David B. Gleicher and Anna Weintraub, "Party

---

* The Project was completed at the end of September 1954. We have listed only those publications printed or in press on November 1, 1955. Any system for grouping the Project reports by subject must necessarily be fairly arbitrary, since many of the reports touch on a variety of topics and problems. This list should, therefore, be taken only as a rough guide to the contents of the various reports.

† A file copy of each of these manuscripts is available at the Russian Research Center and may be consulted by qualified scholars. Copies are not available in sufficient quantity for distribution.

Member Types as Discussed by Former Party Members," Appendix C, 26 pages.

2. "Patterns of Ideological Orientation among Former Soviet Citizens," and consisting of the following parts: (a) David B. Gleicher, "Ideological Patterns and Their Value Sources," 36 pages; (b) David B. Gleicher, "The Meaning of the Keep Nothing Response: An Inquiry into the Extent of Opposition toward the Major Features of the Soviet Socio-Economic System," 25 pages; (c) David B. Gleicher, "The Meaning of Distortion: A Note on the Causes and Correlates of Hostility toward the Soviet Regime," 57 pages; (d) Isabel Caro, "Value Patterns of Former Soviet Citizens," 48 pages.

3. Raymond A. Bauer, "The Social Psychology of Loyalty to and Disaffection from the Soviet Regime," 65 pages plus appendices.

4. Sidney Harcave, "Structure and Functioning of the Lower Party Organizations in the Soviet Union," 148 pages.

5. Vera Dunham, "The Party Secretary in Post-War Soviet Literature," 166 pages.

6. Raymond A. Bauer, "Arrest in the Soviet Union," 35 pages plus appendices.

7. Raymond A. Bauer, "The Developmental History of the Political Attitudes of Individuals toward the Soviet Regime," 71 pages.

8. Barrington Moore, Jr., "The Strengths and Weaknesses of the Soviet System," 69 pages.

B. *The Nationality Problem*

1. "The Nationality Problem in the Soviet Union," consisting of the following parts: (a) Frederick Wyle, "The Nationality Problem in the USSR," 37 pages; (b) Sylvia Gilliam, "The Nationality Questionnaire," 187 pages; (c) Irving Rosow, "The Relation of Nationality to Experience and Attitude in the USSR," 82 pages; (d) John S. Reshetar, "The Nationality Problem in the Soviet Union," 48 pages.

2. John Reshetar and Michael Luther, "Aspects of the Nationality Problem in the USSR," interim report, 157 pages.

3. John Reshetar, "The Problem of National Deviation in the Soviet Union with Special Reference to the Ukrainian Republic," interim report, 19 pages.

C. *Social Institutions and Patterns*

1. Irving Rosow, "Education Patterns in the Soviet Union," 110 pages.

2. Alex Inkeles, "Social Change in Soviet Russia," 30 pages.

3. Edith Bennett, "The Time Budget: The Typical 1940 Working Day of Soviet Citizens," 95 pages.

4. Harvey Fireside, "Soviet Friendship Patterns," 18 pages.

5. Kent Geiger, "The Urban Slavic Family," 173 pages.

6. Kent Geiger, "The Solidarity of the Urban Slavic Family Under the Soviet System," interim report, 17 pages.

7. Alice S. Rossi, "Family Characteristics of the PPQ Sample: Marital Status and Size of Family of Procreation," interim report, 169 pages.

8. Alice S. Rossi, "Generational Differences in the Soviet Union," 546 pages.

9. "Stratification and Mobility in the Soviet Union: A Study of Social Class Cleavages in the USSR," consisting of the following parts: (a) Allen Kassof, "Social Class Cleavages in Soviet Society," 22 pages; (b) Alex Inkeles, "Images of Class Relations among Former Soviet Citizens," 46 pages; (c) Robert Feldmesser, "Observations on Trends in Social Mobility in the Soviet Union and Their Implications," 39 pages; (d) Gabriel Grasberg, "Problems of Stratification," 45 pages.

D. *Economic Institutions*

1. Joseph Berliner, "The Soviet Industrial Enterprise" (3 vols.), 881 pages.

2. Joseph Berliner, "The Soviet Business Enterprise," interim report, 486 pages.

3. Joseph Berliner, "Aspects of the Informal Soviet Organization of Soviet Industry (The Soviet Firm)," interim report, 286 pages.

4. Joseph Berliner, "Recollected Budgets of Soviet Households in 1940," 121 pages.

5. Alex Peskin, "Sociological Aspects of Soviet Industrial Management," 163 pages.

6. Jerzy Gliksman, "Conditions of Industrial Labor in the USSR: A Study of the Incentive System in Soviet Industry," 324 pages.

7. Carolyn Recht, "The Quantity and Adequacy of Soviet Urban Housing as Viewed by Former Soviet Citizens," 35 pages.

8. David Heer, "Differences between Men and Women in Occupational Placement and in Attitudes toward Occupation," 63 pages.

9. Babette Whipple, "Relationship of Sex to Other Demographic Characteristics of the PPQ Sample According to Occupation," interim report, 33 pages.

10. Babette Whipple, "Sex Differences in Attitudes Related to Occupation," interim report, 199 pages.

11. Babette Whipple, "Reports on the PPQ Questions that Relate to Occupation with Primary Emphasis on Sex Differences," interim report, 39 pages plus appendices.

12. Peter Rossi, "Positional Determinants of Occupational Ratings," 19 pages.

13. Peter Rossi, "Ratings of Selected Occupations in the USSR," 22 pages.

14. Frederick Wyle, "The Soviet Lawyer: A Memorandum with Appended Case Notes," 25 pages plus case notes.

E. *Medicine*

Mark G. Field, "Medical Care in the Soviet Union," Part I, "The Soviet Doctor — A Case Study of the Professional in Soviet Society," 65 pages; Part II, "Organization of Medical Services in the Soviet Union — A Study of the Professions under Soviet Conditions," 184 pages; Part III, "The Soviet Patient," 119 pages.

F. *German Occupation of the USSR*

1. "Aspects of the German Occupation of the Soviet Union," consisting of the following parts: (*a*) Alexander Dallin, "Some Implications of Vulnerabilities of Soviet Society as Revealed under German Occupation in World War II" (Part One), 35 pages; (*b*) Sylvia Gilliam, "Experiences and Attitudes under the German Occupation of the USSR" (Part Two), 254 pages plus appendices.

2. Alexander Dallin, "Reactions to the German Occupation of Soviet Russia," interim report, 47 pages.

3. Alexander Dallin, "The Kaminsky Brigade: 1941–1944 — A Case Study of German Military Exploitation of Soviet Disaffection," interim report, 96 pages.

G. *Clinical Psychology*

1. Eugenia Hanfmann and Helen Beier, "Psychological Patterns of Soviet Citizens: A Summary of Clinical Psychological Aspects of the Soviet Defection," 210 pages.

2. Helen Beier and John Orton, "The Responses of Former Soviet Citizens to the 'Projective Questions' Test," interim report, 129 pages.

3. Helen Beier, "The Responses to the Rorschach Test of Former Soviet Citizens," interim report, 59 pages.

4. Daniel Rosenblatt, Mortimer Slaiman, and Eugenia Hanfmann, "Responses of Former Soviet Citizens to the Thematic Apperception Test (TAT): An Analysis Based upon Comparison with an American Control Group," interim report, 112 pages.

5. Eugenia Hanfmann and Jacob W. Getzels with the assistance of Mortimer Slaiman and Philip Nogy, "Responses of Former Soviet Citizens to the 'Episodes' Test," interim report, 104 pages.

6. Marc Fried, "Some Systematic Patterns of Relationship between Personality and Attitudes among Soviet Displaced Persons," 133 pages.

7. Marc Fried and Doris Held, "Relationships between Personality and Attitudes among Soviet Displaced Persons: A Technical Memorandum on the Derivation of Personality Variables from a Sentence Completion Test," interim report, 125 pages.

H. *Methodological and Control Studies*

1. Allen Kassof, "A Comparison of the Attitudes and Experiences of Wartime (Displaced Persons) and Postwar (Recent Defectors) Respondents," 21 pages.
2. Daniel Rosenblatt, "Technical Report on Coding and Reliability Studies," 30 pages.
3. Edward Wasiolek, "Responses by Former Soviet Citizens to a Questionnaire vs Life History Interview," 17 pages.
4. Babette Whipple, "Munich-New York Comparisons as Validity Tests of the PPQ," 115 pages.
5. Peter Rossi, "A Latent Distance Scale for Attitudes toward Personal Freedom," 5 pages.
6. Frederick Wyle, "A Memorandum on Statistical Data on Soviet Displaced Persons," 17 pages.

I. *Miscellaneous*

"Glossary of Selected Transliterated Terms."

Note: In addition to the authors of manuscripts listed above, the following persons prepared major memoranda for the Project for circulation limited to internal staff use: Scott Anderson, Norman Birnbaum, Jean Briggs, Anthony Davids, P. W. Friedrich, Clifford Geertz, Mildred Geiger, Gardiner Lindzey, Herbert Phillips, John Rimberg, H. E. Roseborough, and John Zawadsky.

Publications of the Project

A. *Articles*

1. Raymond A. Bauer, "The Implications of the Succession Crisis in the Soviet Union for East-Western Relations," *Social Problems*, 1:38–43 (October 1953).
2. Raymond A. Bauer, "The Psychology of the Soviet Middle Elite," in Clyde Kluckhohn, H. A. Murray, and D. M. Schneider, eds., *Personality in Nature, Society and Culture* (New York, 1953).
3. Raymond A. Bauer and David B. Gleicher, "Word-of-Mouth Communication in the Soviet Union," *Public Opinion Quarterly*, 17:297–310 (July 1953).
4. Raymond A. Bauer, "The Bolshevik Attitude toward Science," in Carl J. Friedrich, ed., *Totalitarianism* (Cambridge, 1954), pp. 141–156.
5. Helen Beier and Raymond A. Bauer, "Oleg: A Member of the Soviet 'Golden Youth,'" *The Journal of Abnormal and Social Psychology*, 51:139–145 (July 1955).
6. Joseph Berliner, "The Informal Organization of the Soviet Firm," *Quarterly Journal of Economics*, 66:342–365 (August 1952).
7. Joseph Berliner, "Soviet Economic Policy Since Stalin's Death,"

accepted for publication by the American Academy of Arts and Sciences.

8. Henry V. Dicks, "Observations on Contemporary Russian Behavior," *Human Relations*, 5:111–175 (No. 2, 1952).

9. Robert Feldmesser, "The Persistence of Status Advantages in Soviet Russia," *American Journal of Sociology*, 59:19–27 (July 1953).

10. Mark G. Field, "Structured Strain in the Role of the Soviet Physician," *American Journal of Sociology*, 58:493–502 (March 1953).

11. Mark G. Field, "Some Problems of Soviet Medical Practice: A Sociological Approach," *The New England Journal of Medicine*, 248:919–926 (May 28, 1953).

12. Mark G. Field, "Social Services for the Family in the Soviet Union," *Marriage and Family Living*, 17:244–249 (August 1955).

13. Mark G. Field, "Former Soviet Citizens' Attitudes toward the Soviet, the German, and the American Medical Systems," accepted for publication by the *American Sociological Review*.

14. Mark G. Field, "Alcoholism, Crime, and Delinquency in Soviet Society," *Social Problems*, 3:100–109 (October 1955).

15. Mark G. Field, "The Professional in Bureaucracy: The Case of the Soviet Physician," accepted for publication in *Hospital Management*.

16. Maurice Friedberg, "Russian Writers and Soviet Readers," *The American Slavic and East European Review*, February 1955, pp. 108–121.

17. Kent Geiger, "Deprivation and Solidarity in the Soviet Urban Family," *American Sociological Review*, 20:57–68 (January 1955).

18. Kent Geiger, "Soviet Society Today," accepted for publication in *Current History*.

19. Kent Geiger and Alex Inkeles, "The Family in the U.S.S.R.," *Marriage and Family Living*, 16:397–404 (November 1954).

20. David B. Gleicher, "The Professional Soviet Officer," accepted for publication in *World Politics*.

21. Eugenia Hanfmann and Jacob W. Getzels, "Interpersonal Attitudes of Former Soviet Citizens as Studied by a Semi-Projective Method," *Psychological Monographs*, 69:No. 389 (No. 4, 1955).

22. Alex Inkeles, "Social Change and Social Character: The Role of Parental Mediation," *The Journal of Social Issues*, 11:12–23 (November 2, 1955).

23. Alex Inkeles, "The Totalitarian Mystique: Some Impressions of the Dynamics of Totalitarian Society," in Carl J. Friedrich, ed., *Totalitarianism* (Cambridge, 1954), pp. 87–108.

24. Alex Inkeles, "Social Change in Soviet Russia," in Morroe Berger, Theodore Abel, and Charles Page, eds., *Freedom and Control in Modern Society* (New York, 1954).

25. Alex Inkeles and Raymond A. Bauer, "Portrait of Soviet Russia by Russians," *The New York Times Magazine*, November 25, 1951.

26. Clyde Kluckhohn, "Recent Studies of the National Character of Great Russians," *Human Development Bulletin*, University of Chicago (February 5, 1955), pp. 39–60.

27. Ivan London, "Therapy in Soviet Psychiatric Hospitals," *The American Psychologist*, 8:79–82 (February 1953).

28. Ivan London, "The Scientific Council on Problems of the Psychological Theory of Academician: I. P. Pavlov: A Study in Control," *Science*, 116:23–27 (July 1952).

29. Ivan London, "Soviet Psychology and Psychiatry," *Bulletin of the Atomic Scientists*, 8: part iv (March 1952).

30. Ivan London, "Psychology in the USSR," *The American Journal of Psychology*, 64:422–428 (July 1951).

31. Ivan London, "Contemporary Psychology in the Soviet Union," *Science*, 114:227–233 (August 31, 1951).

32. Ivan London, "Research on Sensory Interaction in the Soviet Union," *Psychological Bulletin*, 51:531–568 (November 1954).

33. John S. Reshetar, "National Deviation in the Soviet Union," *The American Slavic and East European Review*, 12:162–174 (April 1953).

34. Peter Rossi and Raymond A. Bauer, "Some Patterns of Soviet Communications Behavior," *Public Opinion Quarterly*, 16:653–670 (Winter 1952–53).

35. Frederick Wyle, articles in *The Harvard Law Review*, March 12 and March 19, 1955.

B. *Books*

1. Raymond A. Bauer, *Nine Soviet Portraits* (Cambridge, 1955).

2. Joseph Berliner, "The Soviet Industrial Enterprise," in preparation.

3. George Fischer, *Soviet Opposition to Stalin: A Case Study in World War II* (Cambridge, 1952).

References

Chapter 1. The Harvard Project

1. The contract, which extended from June 1950 to November 1954, was monitored by the HRRI until its deactivization in February 1954; subsequent monitorship was by the Officer Education Research Laboratory of the Air Force Personnel and Training Research Center (under Air Research and Development Command) at Maxwell Air Force Base, Alabama.

2. A major piece of analysis was specifically focused on generational differences: Alice Rossi, "Generational Differences in the Soviet Union" (unpubl. report, Project on the Soviet Social System, Russian Research Center, Harvard University, 1954), hereafter referred to as Rossi, "Generational Differences," and Raymond A. Bauer, "Some Trends in Sources of Alienation from the Soviet System," *Public Opinion Quarterly* (Autumn, 1955).

3. An extended discussion of the history of the Harvard Project, its data, and the methodological questions connected with the use of these data will be found in Alex Inkeles and Raymond A. Bauer, "Patterns of Life Experience and Attitudes Under the Soviet System (Composite Survey)" (unpubl. report, Project on the Soviet Social System, Russian Research Center, Harvard University, 1954), chapters 1–3, hereafter referred to as Inkeles and Bauer, "Patterns of Life Experience and Attitudes."

4. Raymond A. Bauer, "The Social Psychology of Loyalty to and Disaffection from the Soviet Regime" (unpubl. report, Project on the Soviet Social System, Russian Research Center, Harvard University, 1954), hereafter referred to as Bauer, "Loyalty and Disaffection"; and Helen Beier and Raymond A. Bauer, "Oleg: A Member of the Soviet 'Golden Youth,'" *Journal of Abnormal and Social Psychology*, 51:139–145 (July 1955); and Eugenia Hanfmann and Helen Beier, "Psychological Patterns of Soviet Citizens: A Summary of Clinical Psychological Aspects of the Soviet Defection" (unpubl. report, Project on the Soviet Social System, Russian Research Center, Harvard University, 1954), hereafter referred to as Hanfmann and Beier, "Psychological Patterns."

5. Inkeles and Bauer, "Patterns of Life Experience and Attitudes," chapters 1–3.

6. Robert A. Feldmesser, "The Persistence of Status Advantages in Soviet Russia," *The American Journal of Sociology*, 59:19–27

(July 1953), and HRRI Technical Research Report No. 10, December 1952. HRRI reports may be requested as follows: by agencies of the Department of Defense or their contractors, for retention or loan, from the Armed Services Technical Information Agency, Document Service Center, Knott Building, Dayton, Ohio; by other agencies or individuals from the Office of Technical Services, United States Department of Commerce, Washington 25, D.C.

7. Allen Kassof, "A Comparison of the Attitudes and Experiences of Wartime (Displaced Persons) and Postwar (Recent Defectors) Respondents" (unpubl. report, Project on the Soviet Social System, Russian Research Center, Harvard University, 1954).

8. Hanfmann and Beier, "Psychological Patterns."

9. Babette Whipple, "Munich-New York Comparisons as Validity Tests of the PPQ" (unpubl. report, Project on the Soviet Social System, Russian Research Center, Harvard University, 1954).

10. Inkeles and Bauer, "Patterns of Life Experience and Attitudes," chapter 3.

Chapter 2. Formal Characteristics

1. General emphasis of the same order occurred in *Pravda*, January 1954.

Chapter 3. Creating and Maintaining Myths

1. Gabriel Almond, *The Appeals of Communism* (Princeton, 1954), p. 5.

2. Nathan Leites, *A Study of Bolshevism* (Glencoe, Illinois, 1953).

3. Alex Inkeles, *Public Opinion in Soviet Russia* (Cambridge, 1950), pp. 21–25, hereafter referred to as Inkeles, *Public Opinion.*

4. George Katkov, "The Political Opinions of the Soviet Citizen" (mimeographed, Saint Anthony's College, Oxford, October 1953).

5. See Chapter 13.

6. Drawn largely from a research memorandum by John Zawadsky, "The Impact of Marxism on Former Soviet Citizens" (unpublished, Project on the Soviet System, Russian Research Center, Harvard University, 1954).

7. This paragraph is largely taken from Sidney Harcave, "Structure and Functioning of the Lower Party Organizations in the Soviet Union," Harvard Project Report, published as HRRI Technical Research Report No. 23 (January 1954), pp. 47–48, hereafter referred to as Harcave, *Structure and Functioning of Lower Party Organizations.*

Chapter 4. Planning and Controlling

1. On the composition and organization of the ruling group, see Chapter 17. For full details, see Merle Fainsod, *How Russia Is Ruled* (Cambridge, 1953).

2. For detail see Joseph Berliner, "The Soviet Industrial Enterprise" (3 vols., unpubl. report, Project on the Soviet Social System, Russian Research Center, Harvard University, 1954) and Joseph Berliner, "The Soviet Industrial Enterprise" (in preparation). We wish to express our appreciation to Dr. Berliner for assistance in drafting this section.

3. Raymond A. Bauer, *The New Man in Soviet Psychology* (Cambridge, 1952), pp. 110–111, 169.

4. For details see Inkeles, *Public Opinion*, pp. 67–71; Peter H. Rossi and Raymond A. Bauer, "Some Patterns of Soviet Communications Behavior," *Public Opinion Quarterly*, 16:653–670 (Winter 1952–53) and HRRI Technical Research Report No. 9 (December 1952): Raymond A. Bauer and David B. Gleicher, "Word-of-Mouth Communication in the Soviet Union," *Public Opinion Quarterly*, 17:297–310 (Fall 1953) and HRRI Research Memorandum No. 15 (September 1953).

Chapter 6. Refusal to Allow Power

1. The major portion of this section on the army is taken directly from an unpublished Project memorandum on the military prepared by David Gleicher. This memorandum will be published as an article entitled "The Loyalty of the Soviet Professional Officer" in a forthcoming issue of *World Politics*.

2. Margaret Mead, *Soviet Attitudes Toward Authority* (New York, 1951), pp. 105–107.

3. Leo Gruliow, ed., *Current Soviet Policies, The Documentary Record of the Nineteenth Communist Party Congress and the Reorganization after Stalin's Death* (New York, 1953), p. 173.

4. Bertram D. Wolfe, "The Struggle for the Soviet Succession," *Foreign Affairs*, 31:548–565 (July 1953), p. 564.

5. Merle Fainsod, "The Soviet Union Since Stalin," *Problems of Communism*, 3:3 (March–April 1954).

6. See Kent Geiger, "The Urban Slavic Family and the Soviet System" (unpubl. dissertation, Project on the Soviet Social System, Russian Research Center, Harvard University, 1954), hereafter referred to as Geiger, "The Urban Slavic Family," and *The Solidarity of the Urban Slavic Family Under the Soviet System,* Harvard Project interim report, published as HRRI Research Memorandum No. 22 (January 1954).

7. Decree of September 8, 1945.

8. Rossi, "Generational Differences." Professor Nicholas S. Timasheff (Russian Research Center Seminar, April 16, 1954) estimates that in 1914, 90 per cent of the population of Russia over the age of sixteen had religious convictions; in 1936, 57 per cent; in 1954, 35 per cent.

9. Mark G. Field, *The Soviet Doctor: A Case Study of the Professional in Soviet Society (Part I),* Harvard Project report, published

as HRRI Technical Research Report No. 8 (December 1952), hereafter referred to as Field, *The Soviet Doctor;* and *Organization of Medical Services in the Soviet Union (Part II)*, Harvard Project report, published as HRRI Technical Research Report No. 26 (January 1954).

Chapter 7. Terror and Forced Labor

1. This topic has been widely and variously handled by a considerable number of Soviet specialists. The present discussion relies especially on Jerzy Gliksman's thesis on the prophylactic use of terror, "Social Prophylaxis as a Form of Terror," in Carl J. Friedrich, ed., *Totalitarianism* (Cambridge, 1954) and on work on forced labor recently done by Alexander Korol of the Center for International Studies of the Massachusetts Institute of Technology.
2. This material was communicated by Mr. Alexander Korol.
3. For documentation and elaboration see Bauer, "Loyalty and Disaffection"; Bauer, *Public Opinion Quarterly* (Autumn, 1955), David B. Gleicher and Isabel Caro, "Patterns of Ideological and Value Orientation Among Former Soviet Citizens" (unpubl. report, Project on the Soviet Social System, Russian Research Center, Harvard University, 1954), hereafter referred to as Gleicher and Caro, "Patterns of Ideological and Value Orientation."

Chapter 8. Adjustive Mechanisms

1. For a detailed exposition of the operation of these mechanisms in a single institutional set-up, see Berliner, "The Soviet Industrial Enterprise" (unpubl. report, Harvard University, 1954) and "The Soviet Industrial Enterprise" (in preparation).
2. For further detail see Berliner, "The Soviet Industrial Enterprise" (unpubl. report).
3. Field, *The Soviet Doctor.*
4. Bauer and Gleicher, *Public Opinion Quarterly*, 17:297–310 (Fall 1953) and HRRI Research Memorandum No. 15 (September 1953).
5. This point is developed at some length in Mead, *Soviet Attitudes toward Authority*, pp. 35–36, 52–59.

Chapter 9. Rigidity–Flexibility

1. See Gustav Hilger and A. G. Meyer, *The Incompatible Allies: A Memoir-History of German-Soviet Relations, 1918–1941* (New York, 1953).
2. Unpublished studies by Dr. Leopold Haimson of the Russian Research Center, Harvard University.

3. Most of this paragraph is taken from Harcave, *Structure and Functioning of Lower Party Organizations*, p. 41.

Chapter 11. Soviet Policy

1. For a detailed discussion of this relationship of the individual to the state in Soviet society, see Bauer, *The New Man in Soviet Psychology*.

Chapter 12. Sources of Satisfaction

1. The most recent extensive review of the question was made by Janet Chapman in "Real Wages in the Soviet Union, 1928–1952," *Review of Economics and Statistics*, 36:134–156 (May 1954).

2. In our treatment of the role of the family in the Soviet system, we are largely indebted to Geiger, "The Urban Slavic Family," and to Alice S. Rossi, "Family Characteristics of the PPQ Sample: Marital Status and the Size of Family of Procreation" (unpublished report, Project on the Soviet Social System, Russian Research Center, Harvard University, 1953).

Chapter 13. Attitudes Toward the System

1. The evidence for the propositions in this chapter will be found in David B. Gleicher, "The Meaning of Distortion: A Note on the Causes and Correlates of Hostility Toward the Soviet Regime" appearing in Gleicher and Caro, "Patterns of Ideological and Value Orientation"; Inkeles and Bauer, "Patterns of Life Experience and Attitudes," pp. 284–301; Bauer, *Public Opinion Quarterly* (Autumn, 1955).

2. This point in particular is documented in Bauer, *Public Opinion Quarterly* (Autumn, 1955).

3. Bauer, *Public Opinion Quarterly* (Autumn, 1955).

Chapter 14. Attitudes Toward the West

1. Frederick C. Barghoorn, *The Soviet Image of the United States* (New York, 1950); Leslie C. Stevens, *Russian Assignment* (Boston, 1953); Frank W. Rounds, *A Window on Red Square* (Boston, 1953); Marshall MacDuffie, "Russia Uncensored," *Colliers*, 133:90–101 (March 5, 1954), 25–31 (March 19, 1954), 96–101 (April 2, 1954), 58–61 (April 16, 1954).

2. MacDuffie, *Colliers*, 133:58 (April 16, 1954).

3. Raymond L. Garthaff, *Soviet Military Doctrine* (Glencoe, 1953).

4. Mark G. Field, "Former Soviet Citizens' Attitudes to the Soviet,

German and American Medical Systems: A Study in the Persistence of Expectations" (unpubl. report to the Far Eastern Sociological Society Meeting, April 1955).

Chapter 15. Russian National Character

1. Hanfmann and Beier, "Psychological Patterns." All quotations in this chapter that are not footnoted come from this source.

2. Eugenia Hanfmann and J. W. Getzels, "Interpersonal Attitudes of Former Soviet Citizens, as Studied by a Semi-Projective Method," *Psychological Monographs*, 69:1–37 (No. 389, 1955); Beier and Bauer, *Journal of Abnormal and Social Psychology*, 51:139–145 (July 1955).

3. The following four paragraphs are drawn from a previously published summary of these findings. See Clyde Kluckhohn, "Recent Studies of the 'National Character' of Great Russians," *Human Development Bulletin: Sixth Annual Symposium* (Committee on Human Development, University of Chicago, 1955), pp. 52–54.

4. Henry Dicks, "Observations on Contemporary Russian Behavior," *Human Relations*, 5:111–175 (No. 2, 1952).

5. In this paragraph we are closely paraphrasing, and at several points directly quoting, Dicks, *Human Relations*, 5:111–175 (1952), especially pp. 169–170.

Chapter 16. Political Loyalty

1. See Bauer, "Loyalty and Disaffection," pp. 43–53 for a description of varying types of accommodation to the Soviet system.

Chapter 17. The Ruling Elite

1. For an understanding of the elite group we rely for the most part on non-Project sources, although, as will be seen, Project data do contribute both directly and indirectly.

2. Franz Borkenau, *European Communism* (New York, 1953), p. 549.

3. For details see Fainsod, *How Russia Is Ruled*, Table 8.

4. Wolfe, *Foreign Affairs*, 31:565, p. 558.

5. Philip E. Mosely, "The Nineteenth Party Congress," *Foreign Affairs*, 31:238–256 (January 1953), p. 243.

6. See George Fischer, *Soviet Opposition to Stalin: A Case Study in World War II* (Cambridge, 1952).

7. Dicks, *Human Relations*, 5:111–175.

8. Nathan Leites, *Operational Code of the Politburo* (New York, 1951) and Leites, *A Study of Bolshevism*.

9. Stalin's speech of October, 1952.

10. Peter Wiles, *Foreign Affairs*, 31:566–580 (July 1953).

Chapter 20. The Workers

1. See Jerzy Gliksman, "Conditions of Industrial Labor in the USSR: A Study of the Incentive System in Soviet Industry" (unpublished report, Project on the Soviet Social System, Russian Research Center, Harvard University, September 1954).

Chapter 21. Generational Differences

1. For a detailed discussion, see Rossi, "Generational Differences."
2. In addition to the discussion of this issue in Rossi, "Generational Differences," documentation will be found in Bauer, *Publc Opinion Quarterly* (Autumn, 1955).

Chapter 22. Nationality Groups

1. See Sylvia Gilliam, Irving Rosow, and John Reshetar (with a summary and introduction by Frederick Wyle), "The Nationality Problem in the Soviet Union: The Ukrainian Case" (unpublished report, Project on the Soviet Social System, Russian Research Center, Harvard University, 1954), hereafter referred to as Gilliam, Rosow, and Reshetar, "The Nationality Problem."
2. See Richard Pipes, *The Formation of the Soviet Union* (Cambridge, 1954), pp. 241–282, and John Reshetar and Michael Luther, *Aspects of the Nationality Problem in the USSR*, Harvard Project report, published as HRRI Technical Research Report No. 3, December 1952.
3. See *Pravda*, June 28, 1946.
4. Fainsod, *How Russia Is Ruled*, p. 495.
5. See Nicholas Vakar, *Belorussia: The Making of a Nation* (Cambridge, 1956).
6. See Gilliam, Rosow, and Reshetar, "The Nationality Problem."
7. Fainsod, *How Russia Is Ruled*, p. 495–496.

Chapter 24. Some Evaluations

1. For a full statement, see Berliner, "The Soviet Industrial Enterprise" (unpubl. report; Harvard University, 1954).
2. See S. Kovalyev, "Intelligentsia v sovetskom gosudarstve," *Bol'shevik*, January 1946, No. 2.

Chapter 25. Some Forecasts

1. See Barrington Moore, Jr., *Terror and Progress USSR* (Cambridge, 1954), Chapter 7.
2. Moore, *Terror and Progress USSR*, Chapter 7.
3. Cf. *Pravda* editorial, April 16, 1953.

Index

Agriculture, 24–25; crisis in, 38, 40–41; inequities in system, 39–40; postwar policy, 85. *See also* Collective farm

Alienation, sources of: historic failures, 230–231; chronic failures, 231; newly generated failures, 231; alienation of subgroups, 149

Amnesty Decree, 56

Anti-Semitism, 85, 200, 203, 204. *See also* Jews

Armenian nationalism, 202

Army: Party control, 54–59; power and prestige, 56–59; representation in Central Committee and Supreme Soviet, 57; potentiality for independent action, 57–59; popular attitude toward, 58; and other elite groups, 58. *See also* Military

Arrest: family reaction to, 60; "prophylactic," 68–69; prevalence among refugees (Harvard Project), 70; political motives for, 72; as most important political danger, 101–102; and hostility, 216

Attitudes, of regime: subordination of individual, 27; toward discontent, 52; toward deviant behavior, 79–81

popular: pride in industrialization, 27; toward army, 58; toward system, 114; toward Lenin, 118; toward NEP, 118–119; toward collective farm, 119; toward ideal government, 119–120; toward governmental control, 121–122; toward civil liberties, 121–122; toward America and West, 125–132; toward capitalism, 126–127; toward social welfare, 132–133, 214; of youth, 217; role of nationality in determining, 217–218

Azerbaidzhan Republic, 200

Barghoorn, Frederick, 124, 125, 126

Beier, Helen, 134, 135, 138

Behavior: "cyclical," 84, 85, 212; deviant, 49, 74–76, 79–81, 146; of leadership, 139–140

Beria, Lavrenti, 23, 56, 65, 67, 156, 160, 202

Bessarabia, 200

Bias. *See* Harvard Project on the Soviet Social System

Blat (personal influence), 80, 172; definition, 76; use and success, 76–77

"Bolshevik mentality," 46

Bolshevism, 30, 48. *See also* Ideology

Borkenau, Franz, 155, 169n

Budenny, Marshal Semyon, 155

Bukharin, Nikolai, 50

Bulganin, Nikolai, 160

Byelorussia, 200, 202

"Capitalist aggression," 214

"Capitalist encirclement," 167

Census (1937), 174

Central Committee (Party), 40, 44, 75, 155, 156, 157, 158; military membership, 57; composition (1952), 160

Central Secretariat (Party), 42

Chechen-Ingush Republic, 200

China, 237, 244
Church, 139, 149. *See also* Orthodox Church, Religion
Civil liberties, 174, 184, 214; popular attitude toward, 121–122
Civil War (Russian), 86
Class, social. *See* Social class
Coercion, reliance of regime on, 145–146, 221
Cold War, 123, 133
Collective farm, 106, 113, 114, 119, 139, 182, 183, 184–185, 188, 194, 196, 196n, 231; postwar consolidation, 24; organization, 39; "labor days," 39, 40; "piecework," 39; attitude of peasantry toward, 106, 183; hostility toward, 116, 214; attitude of intelligentsia toward, 179; lack of success, 185; predictions concerning, 250. *See also* Agriculture
Collective Farm Statutes (1935), 38–39
Collectivization, 84, 94; purpose, 25
"Collegial" rule, 21, 34, 81, 156, 156n, 229, 239, 239n. *See also* Government, Soviet
Communication: control, 25–26, 41–44; access to technical, 43–44; "downward flow," 41; "upward flow," 41–43, 78, 82
Communism, international, 164, 165, 168, 240
Communist Party, 38, 114, 115, 118; membership among refugees (Harvard Project), 11; role in government, 21–22; organization, 22; as instrument of top elite, 22; function of elections, 34, 35; military membership, 56; structure, 75, 155–157; "cyclical" behavior, 85; deviations from "Party vigilance," 147, 148; size of ruling elite, 155–157; size and composition of middle elite, 157; size and composition of lower elite, 157–158; functions on behalf of ruling elite, 161
Communist Party Congresses: Eighteenth Congress, 34, 158, 174; Nineteenth Congress, 34, 56, 156,

158–159; Twentieth Congress, 251
Control, political, 23, 42, 46; Communist Party as instrument of, 22; of schools, 27; in industry, 36, 44–45; of communication, 41; of family, 59–60; of religion, 61–64; of science, 64–65; of nationality groups, 65; of professions, 65; of trade unions, 65–66; of informal groups, 66–67; reliance of regime on, 66; use of forced labor, 68, 71; use of terror, 68–70; of life situation, 144; of military, 54–59, 148, 161; crosscheck system of, 159, 160; as distinctive feature of system, 160; "managerial revolution," 218; rigidity, 234; probable continuance, 250
"Cosmopolitanism," campaign against, 151
Council of Ministers, 37, 240
Crimean Republic, 200

DeWitt, Nicholas, 158n, 159n, 175n
Dicks, Henry, 137, 164, 171n
Distortion Index, 14. *See also* Harvard Project on the Soviet Social System
Disloyalty: to regime, 146; subjective, 146, 147; active, 147; prevalence of, 215. *See also* Loyalty
Dissatisfaction, 27, 99–102; primary grievances, 28, 214; of peasants, 38, 39; shortages and, 46, 52, 139; with Soviet life reported by refugees (Harvard Project), 97; with politicization of life, 100–101; with material conditions, 102–104; with "tempo" of life, 111–112; among subgroups, 112; in relation to job performance, 179–180, 216
"Doctors' plot," 85, 203
Domestic policy: rigidity, 83; importance, 86, 87

EDC (European Defense Community), 242
Education: state control, 27; func-

tion, 47; as source of satisfaction, 106–107; expanding access to, 107; importance, 108–109; use to create "new Soviet man," 134; of intelligentsia, 174–175; generational differences, 189; effect on attitudes, 190

Ehrenburg, Ilya, 145

Elite, 26, 31, 45, 48, 49, 50, 58, 67, 84, 135, 137, 138, 139, 143, 145, 208, 212, 213, 215, 233, 237, 238, 239, 241; importance of ideology to, 32; attitudes toward war, 88–89, 170–171; attitudes toward rank and file, 138; general structure, 159; military, 160; operations, 161–162; psychological characteristics, 162–173; patriotism and loyalty, 162, 165–166; "disillusion," 163; personal insecurity, 163–164; "new Soviet man" as goal, 163, 215; qualities peculiar to, 164–172; work satisfaction, 171–172; attitudes, 216–217; "careerists," 219

    ruling: monopoly of power, 22; size and composition, 155–157; "top," 157; demographic characteristics, 158–159; Party functions on behalf of, 161; operations, 161–162; suspicion of "foreigners," 164; loyalty, 165–166; Communist ideology, 166–168; "conspiratorial mentality," 168–169; caution, 169–171; "puritanical discipline," 171–172; emphasis upon opponent's psychology, 172–173; policy-making, 161–162

    middle, size and composition, 157
    lower, size and composition, 157–158

Engels, Friedrich, 32, 167, 168

Estonian Republic, 200

Evangelical Christians, 61

Fainsod, Merle, 55, 58, 200

Family, 139, 149, 150, 171, 241; importance, 26–27; as independent unit, 59; and regime, 59–60, 108–109; reaction to arrest, 60; and religion, 63; strains on, 107–108;

cohesiveness among peasants, 182

"Familyness," 77, 80, 81, 141; concern of regime over, 66; as alternative loyalty, 150

Finnish War (1940), 87

Fischer, George, 163

Five Year Plans, 65; First Five Year Plan, 40, 126

Flattery Index, 14. See also Harvard Project on the Soviet Social System

Foreign policy, flexibility, 83–84; caution, 86–87; expansion as goal, 86–87, 233

Freedom (personal), desire of intelligentsia for, 179

Generational differences: in education, 190, 195; in life experiences, 191; general, 191–192; in acceptance of "Soviet reality," 193; comparison of old and young, 192; in attitudes, 192–195; in relation to regime, 195–198, 227; youth's demands on system, 197–198; attitudes of youth, 217

Georgia, 200, 208; nationalism, 202; Russian language, 202

Gliksman, Jerzy, 69

Goals, of leadership: 31, 88, 94, 145, 233; as basis of economic decisions, 22; long-range, 82, 89; flexibility in short-run, 83; short-term, 212–213; security of power, 233; world domination, 167
    of Soviet society, 46, 47
    of foreign policy, 86–87
    of production, 24

Government, Tsarist, 200
    Soviet: described as "total statism," 21; federal in form, 22; role of Communist Party, 21–22; main features, 21–23; role of top elite, 22; in ideal society, 119–120; popular attitude toward, 121–122. See also "Collegial" rule

Hanfmann, Eugenia, 134, 135, 138

Harvard Project on the Soviet Social System: origin, 3; publications, 4, Appendix; 1940 as baseline for data, 5, 98; distinctive aspects, 9–10; characteristics of sample, 10–15; comparison of wartime and postwar refugees, 13; problem of bias in sample, 8, 10–11, 12, 13, 14; "distortion" and "flattery" indexes as controls for bias, 14; American control sample, 134–138; nationality of respondents, 204

interviews and questionnaires: types, 5, 8; number, 8, 9; life-history interview, 8, 11, 122, 134, 204, 215, 219; written questionnaire, 8, 204; nationality questionnaire, 204; sentence-completion test, 134

findings: sources of dissatisfaction, 101–113; attitudes toward system, 115–118; attitudes about ideal society, 118–122; attitudes toward West, 126–133; image of system, 139; life situation and attitudes of intelligentsia, 176–180; life situation and attitudes of peasantry, 181–184; life situation and attitudes of workers, 187–189; generational differences in attitudes, 190–198; nationality groups, 204–208; importance of informal adjustive mechanisms, 218–219

Harvard University, 7

Hostility, to regime, 101–102, 118, 146, 179, 182–183, 214–215, 223; to system, 114–115, 118, 183; to "absolutist terror," 115; to collective farm, 116; as a result of arrest, 216

Human Resources Research Institute (Maxwell Air Force Base, Alabama), 3

Ideology, 47, 48–49, 60; basic Communist, 29–30; importance, 29–35; continuity and consistency, 29–35; profession of belief, 33; importance among émigrés, 33–34; and elite, 32; elite acceptance, 166–168; Moscow-centered, 167; role in Soviet society, 211–212; influence on goals, 212. See also Bolshevism, Marxism, Marx-ist-Leninist-Stalinist doctrine, Stalinism

Industrialization, 94, 108, 189

Industry, 245; expansion, 24–25; state control, 36–38; piecework system, 37; priority system, 38; use of "safety factor," 77; popular attitude toward ideal system, 119

"Inner emigration," 65, 105, 144, 163; of scientists, 65

Intelligentsia, 34; size and composition, 174–176; education, 174; as elite group, 174, 175; surveillance, 176; life situation, 176–178; politicization of life, 177; and family, 177–178; and arrest, 178; and friendship, 178; and recreation, 178; and communications, 178; and chances for advancement, 179; and desire for personal freedom, 179; and police control, 179; attitudes toward social welfare, 179; attitudes toward regime and system, 179–180; as group most accepting of regime, 217

Interviews. See Harvard Project on the Soviet Social System

Iron Curtain, 164

Jews, 61; importance of in government, 203; assimilation of, 203–204. See also Anti-Semitism

Journal of the Moscow Patriarchate, 61–62

Kabardino-Balkarian Republic, 200
Kalmyck Republic, 200
Kapitsa, Peter, 144
Karelo-Finnish Republic, 200
Kazakh Republic, 200
Kazakhstan, 40
Khrushchev, N. S., 21, 25n, 39 (Speech to Supreme Soviet, April 1954), 40, 44, 51n, 83n, 103, 156n, 170, 170n, 171n, 201, 239n, 244–245
"Kolkhozy," 24. See Collective farm
Komsomol, 141–142
Konev, Marshal, 56

Labor, forced, as instrument of Soviet system, 23, 68, 71; reasons for, 71, 72; number of people in, 72–73

Labor discipline, 111–112; laws, 214

Latvian Republic, 200

Law, "Soviet socialist legality," 23, 71; labor discipline, 214; extra-legal practices, 218

Leites, Nathan, 30, 31, 167

Lend-lease, 127

Lenin, V. I., 21, 32, 39, 41, 118, 167, 168, 168n, 170, 241, 248

Lithuania, 61

Loyalty, political: 234, 235; to regime, 81, 143–144; and administrative control, 147–148; to Slavic nation-state, 143; to welfare state, 143; and job, 144, 145; regime definition, 147; of elite, 165–166

alternative: 53, 148–152; definition, 148; and totalitarianism, 148, 149; regime's exploitation, 150; "cosmopolitanism," 151; trends concerning, 151–152.

group. See "Familyness"

Lysenko, T. D., 40; Lysenko-Michurin theory of genetics, 25

McCarran Act, 33n

MacDuffie, Marshall, 124, 125

Malenkov, G. M., 21, 85, 105, 139, 156n, 170n, 239, 239n, 244

Managerial bureaucracy, 240

"Managerial revolution," 218

Marr linguistic controversy, 241

Marx, Karl, 32, 47, 126, 167, 168, 168n

Marxism, 32, 33, 34, 50, 163, 170. See also Ideology

Marxist-Leninist-Stalinist doctrine, 30, 32, 47, 48, 166. See also Ideology

Mecca, 61, 203

Michigan, University of (Survey Research Center), 7

Military, 213, 240; control of, 161; membership in Party, 157. See also Army

Ministry of Agriculture (USSR), composition of, 39

Ministry of Defense (USSR), 75; and control of military, 55

Ministry of Finance (USSR), 38

Ministry of Internal Affairs. See MVD

Ministry of State Control (USSR), 38

Mobility, 182, 239; prevalence of, 26; aspirations for, 108

Moldavian Republic, 200

Molotov, V. M., 83, 170, 174

Morale (popular), 27, 42, 44, 70, 87, 94, 213, 233, 244–245, 246, 248, 250; peasant, 184–185

Mosely, Philip, 161

Moslems, 61; resistance to Soviet Union, 202–203

MVD (Ministry of Internal Affairs), 42, 58, 118, 172, 240; control of military, 55–56, 161. See also Police, secret

National Academy of Sciences, 159

National character, general characteristics of sample (Harvard Project), 135–138; basic characteristics of Great Russian males, 134–138; contrast between Americans and Great Russians, 135–138

Nationalism, Russian, 149; possible trends, 240

minority, 151; campaign against, 149–150; power and cohesiveness, 207

Nationality groups, historical background, 199–200

Nationality policy (USSR): of 1936 constitution, 65; of regime and its success, 208

"New Soviet man," 134, 163, 172; characteristics, 138; as goal of elite, 215. See also Elite

New Economic Policy (NEP), 85, 118, 127, 184, 230–231, 247; popular approval of, 118–119

Occupation: importance, 26, 108–109; sex differences, 180

Operating characteristics (Soviet system), 19, 20–21, 46, 82, 84, 85, 212

Oppenheim, E. Phillips, 168

Orthodox Church, 48, 61–62, 164, 203, 234; strength, 61; and Communism, 61–62. *See also* Religion

Pan-Slavism, 164. *See also* Nationalism, Russian

Patriotism, 117, 143, 214; of elite, 162; as strength of system, 226. *See also* Loyalty

"Peaceful coexistence," 167, 243

Peasants, 88; "dekulakized," 12, 13; and Bolshevik rise to power, 38; dissatisfaction, 38, 39; desire for economic autonomy, 106; attitude toward collective farm, 106, 183; deprivation, 181; life chances, 181; income available for children, 181; antagonism toward intelligentsia, 182; cohesiveness of family, 182; hostility to regime, 182; hostility to system, 183; as "political activists," 183–184; approval of welfare state, 184; political character, 184; morale, 184–185; as "angry man" of Soviet system, 217

Personality: traditional Russian, 134–138; "new Soviet man," 138; expansiveness of Russian, 141

Physician, role as stabilizer, 78

Planning (rational), 67, 213; as feature of Soviet system, 36

Poland, 171; invasion of 1920, 86

Police, secret, 44, 57, 68, 69–71, 115, 143, 159, 160, 231; reduction of anxiety toward, 246–247

Police power, 23, 46, 184; abusive use, 115

Police state, 233

Police system, 114

Politburo, 30, 84, 167

Politicization: of job, 179–180; as source of dissatisfaction, 100–101

Pravda, 36, 56, 119n, 124

Predictions concerning: stability of Soviet dictatorship, 221; stability of Soviet system, 237; change within system, 237; reversion to Stalinism, 237–239, 249, 251; collegial dictatorship, 239; managerial bureaucracy, 240; Russian nationalism, 240; emphasis on rational bureaucracy, 240–241; relaxation of internal tension, 244–247; increase in consumer goods, 247; change in top leadership, 248; standard of living, 248, 250; "terror," 248, 250; the individual, 249; popular attitude toward regime, 249; collective farm system, 250; political control, 250; military, 250–251

Presidium (Party), 37, 75, 155, 156, 158, 160, 167, 171, 203, 251

Press, Soviet, 40, 44, 79, 89n, 111, 124, 125

Production, goals, 24; resource allocation system, 24; agricultural, 24; morale, 27; problems of management, 76–77

Professions, 119; control, 65; professional associations, 139

Propaganda, 30–31, 41, 51; indoctrination as factor in promotion, 30; regime reliance on, 41; dissemination, 44; effect on children, 60; populace irritated by, 100–101; image of America and West, 125–131; success, 123, 124, 125, 133; attempts to create "new Soviet man," 134; "Hate America" campaign, 226

Protestantism, 61

Purges, 84, 100, 200, 213, 234, 238; Yezhovshchina, 68; "Doctors' plot," 85, 203; future, 237

Questionnaires. *See* Harvard Project on the Soviet Social System

Recreation, 171; interference with opportunity for, 111

Regime, Soviet: demands on individual, 93–95; identification of youth with, 99–100; accomplishments, 117, 214; interferes with satisfactions, 139; and masses, 139–140; use of shame, 140–141; reliance on coercion, 145–146, 221; efforts to stamp out independent power, 213; popular support, 231–232; stability, 234–235. *See also* System, Soviet

Religion, 27; strength of Orthodox Church, 61; strength of minority religions, 61; as independent locus of power, 61–62; attitude of regime toward, 61–64; "Conference of All Churches and Religious Associations in the USSR for the Defense of Peace," 62; indications of trends ' in strength, 62–63; in family, 63
Roman Catholicism, 61
Roosevelt, Franklin D., 125
Rounds, Frank W., 124
Russian language: in Ukraine, 201; in Byelorussia, 202; in Georgia, 202; increased literacy in, 208
Russian Research Center (Harvard University), 3, 7, 237
Russification, 199; of Moslems, 203

Saburov, M. Z., 158
Satisfaction: work, 104–106; school experience, 106–107; family, 107–109; friendship, 110; interference of regime in, 139
Science: regime control of, 64, 65; "inner emigration" of scientists, 65
Social change, 6–7, 250; use of totalitarian methods to effect, 51–52, 145, 234
Social class: importance, 26; stratification, 48, 239; determinant of advancement and attitudes, 217. *See also* Society
Social welfare: stress on, 140; attitudes of intelligentsia toward, 179
Society, Soviet: stratification, 26–27; as rationed economy, 139
Sorel, Georges, 168
"Soviet socialist legality," 23, 71
"Sovkhozy" (state farms), 24
Stalin, Joseph, 6, 21, 23, 25, 29, 31, 32, 34, 36, 41, 46, 51, 58, 62, 64, 81, 100, 112, 119n, 145, 155, 156, 157, 159, 168, 169–170, 197, 200, 203, 229, 234, 238, 239, 241, 248, 249, 251
Stalinism: as a doctrine, 238; possible reversion to, 237–239, 249, 251. *See also* Ideology

Stevens, Leslie C., 124
Strains, 4, 46; on family life, 107–108; caused by regime, 139; psychological, 146
Strategy of Soviet leadership, 243
Strengths of system, 3, 4; popular approval of social-welfare measures, 140, 184, 214, 223; definition of activated strengths, 222; control of mass communication, 222–223; atomization of resistance, 224; ignorance of outside world, 224–226; patriotism, 226; increased accommodations of younger generation, 226–227; managerial acceptance of system, 227–228; desire for peace, 228–229
Supreme Soviet, 21, 29, 39, 57, 57n, 184, 185, 244
Survey Research Center (University of Michigan), 7
Synodal Church, 205, 205n
System, Soviet: stability, 6, 219; definition, 20; "tempo," 23; economic policy state controlled, 23–25; communication policy, 25–26; social organization, 26–27; rational planning, 36; overcontrol, 44–45, 74, 213; as rationed society, 46; as mobilized society, 46, 52; overcommitment of resources, 46, 52, 74, 93, 213, 246; overcentralization, 74, 213; overcaution, 85; "worst features," 115–116; "best features," 116–117; popular approval of welfare aspects, 116; popular approval of state ownership of basic economy, 116–117; popular approval of general accomplishments, 117; cross-checks system in, 159–160; hierarchical nature, 160–161; youth's demands, 197–198; basic assumptions, 220–221; citizen as most flexible resource, 213. *See also* Strengths of system, Weaknesses of system

"Tempo," as instrument of Soviet system, 23; as source of dissatisfaction, 111–112, 214

"Terror," 112, 213, 234; and family solidarity, 60; as instrument of the state, 68; as result of arrest, 69; cited by refugees (Harvard Project), 69, 70; strength, 69–70; attitude of intelligentsia toward, 179; resentment toward, 214; possible relaxation, 246–247
Tito, 30, 86
Tolstoi, Alexei, 145
Totalitarianism, 65; definition of, 20; use of methods in Soviet Union, 51–52; alternative loyalties and, 53, 148, 149
Trade unions, 139; control over, 65–66
Trotsky, Leon, 203
Tukachevsky, Mikhail, 251
Turkmen Republic, 200

Ukraine, 61, 200; Russification, 200–202; grievances, 201; cross national marriage, 201; Russian language, 201; nationalism, 204–206
Ukrainian Autocephalous Church, 205, 205n
Ukrainian Communist Party, Sixteenth Party Congress (1949), 201
Ukrainian Insurrectionary Army, 201
Uniate Church, 61
United States Air Force, research contract No. 33 (083)–12909, 3, 7; Human Resources Research Institute, 3; Maxwell Air Force Base (Alabama), 3

Uzbek Republic, 200

Vasilevsky, A. M., 56
Varga, Eugene, 170
Vlassov movement, 62, 200
Volga-German Autonomous Republic, 200
Voroshilov, K. E., 160

Weaknesses of system, 3, 4; dissatisfaction, 221, 230; definition of latent weakness, 222; agricultural organization, 229; rigid bureaucracy, 229; process of succession, 229; purge, 230
Wolfe, Bertram, 159
Workers: distinctions among, 186–187; characteristics of skilled, 187; attitudes, 188; labor conditions, 188–189; similarity with peasant, 189; position in system, 217
World Peace Council, 243
World revolution, 165, 167, 243
World War II, 7, 13, 86, 98, 112, 113, 123, 158, 165, 189, 200, 203, 206, 231

Yezhov, N. I., 68
Yezhovshchina, 68. See also Purge
Youth, attitudes toward system and regime, 217

Zhdanov, A. A., 64, 85, 203, 242
Zhukov, G. D., 55n, 56, 56n, 251

RUSSIAN RESEARCH CENTER STUDIES

1. *Public Opinion in Soviet Russia: A Study in Mass Persuasion*, by Alex Inkeles
2. *Soviet Politics — The Dilemma of Power: The Role of Ideas in Social Change*, by Barrington Moore, Jr.
3. *Justice in the U.S.S.R.*, by Harold J. Berman. Revised Edition.
4. *Chinese Communism and the Rise of Mao*, by Benjamin I. Schwartz
5. *Titoism and the Cominform*, by Adam B. Ulam
6. *A Documentary History of Chinese Communism*, by Conrad Brandt, Benjamin Schwartz, and John K. Fairbank
7. *The New Man in Soviet Psychology*, by Raymond A. Bauer
8. *Soviet Opposition to Stalin: A Case Study in World War II*, by George Fischer
9. *Minerals: A Key to Soviet Power*, by Demitri B. Shimkin
10. *Soviet Law in Action: The Recollected Cases of a Soviet Lawyer*, by Harold J. Berman and Boris A. Konstantinovsky
11. *How Russia is Ruled*, by Merle Fainsod. Revised Edition.
12. *Terror and Progress USSR: Some Sources of Change and Stability in the Soviet Dictatorship*, by Barrington Moore, Jr.
13. *The Formation of the Soviet Union: Communism and Nationalism, 1917–1923*, by Richard Pipes. Revised Edition.
14. *Marxism: The Unity of Theory and Practice*, by Alfred G. Meyer
15. *Soviet Industrial Production, 1928–1951*, by Donald R. Hodgman
16. *Soviet Taxation: The Fiscal and Monetary Problems of a Planned Economy*, by Franklyn D. Holzman
17. *Soviet Military Law and Administration*, by Harold J. Berman and Miroslav Kerner
18. *Documents on Soviet Military Law and Administration*, edited and translated by Harold J. Berman and Miroslav Kerner
19. *The Russian Marxists and the Origins of Bolshevism*, by Leopold H. Haimson
20. *The Permanent Purge: Politics in Soviet Totalitarianism*, by Zbigniew K. Brzezinski
21. *Belorussia: The Making of a Nation*, by Nicholas P. Vakar
22. *A Bibliographical Guide to Belorussia*, by Nicholas P. Vakar
23. *The Balkans in Our Time*, by Robert Lee Wolff
24. *How the Soviet System Works: Cultural, Psychological, and Social Themes*, by Raymond A. Bauer, Alex Inkeles, and Clyde Kluckhohn *
25. *The Economics of Soviet Steel*, by M. Gardner Clark
26. *Leninism*, by Alfred G. Meyer
27. *Factory and Manager in the USSR*, by Joseph S. Berliner *
28. *Soviet Transportation Policy*, by Holland Hunter
29. *Doctor and Patient in Soviet Russia*, by Mark G. Field *
30. *Russian Liberalism*, by George Fischer
31. *Stalin's Failure in China, 1924–1927*, by Conrad Brandt
32. *The Communist Party of Poland*, by M. K. Dziewanowski
33. *Karamzin's Memoir on Ancient and Modern Russia, A Translation and Analysis*, by Richard Pipes
34. *A Memoir on Ancient and Modern Russia*, by N. M. Karamzin, the Russian text edited by Richard Pipes

RUSSIAN RESEARCH CENTER STUDIES

35. *The Soviet Citizen: Daily Life in a Totalitarian Society*, by Alex Inkeles and Raymond A. Bauer *
36. *Pan-Turkism and Islam in Russia*, by Serge A. Zenkovsky
37. *The Soviet Bloc: Unity and Conflict*, by Zbigniew K. Brzezinski †
38. *National Consciousness in Eighteenth-Century Russia*, by Hans Rogger
39. *Alexander Herzen and the Birth of Russian Socialism, 1812–1855*, by Martin Malia
40. *The Conscience of the Revolution: Communist Opposition in Soviet Russia*, by Robert V. Daniels
41. *The Soviet Industrialization Debate, 1924–1928*, by Alexander Erlich
42. *The Third Section: Police and Society in Russia under Nicholas I*, by Sidney Monas
43. *Dilemmas of Progress in Tsarist Russia: Legal Marxism and Legal Populism*, by Arthur P. Mendel
44. *Political Control of Literature in the USSR, 1946–1959*, by Harold Swayze
45. *Accounting in Soviet Planning and Management*, by Robert W. Campbell
46. *Social Democracy and the St. Petersburg Labor Movement, 1885–1897*, by Richard Pipes
47. *The New Face of Soviet Totalitarianism*, by Adam B. Ulam
48. *Stalin's Foreign Policy Reappraised*, by Marshall D. Shulman

* Publications of the Harvard Project on the Soviet Social System.
† Published jointly with the Center for International Affairs, Harvard University.
‡ Out of print.